Political Leadership in Morphogenetic Perspective

STUDIES IN POLITICS, SECURITY AND SOCIETY

Edited by Stanisław Sulowski
Institute of Political Science of the University of Warsaw

VOLUME 10

Filip Pierzchalski

Political Leadership in Morphogenetic Perspective
Translated by Maciej Adamski

Bibliographic Information published by the Deutsche Nationalbibliothek
The Deutsche Nationalbibliothek lists this publication in
the Deutsche Nationalbibliografie; detailed bibliographic
data is available in the internet at http://dnb.d-nb.de.

The work has been financed from the statutory research grant from the
Faculty of Humanities, Kazimierz Wielki University in Bydgoszcz.

Library of Congress Cataloging-in-Publication Data
Names: Pierzchalski, Filip, author.
Title: Political leadership in morphogenetic perspective / Filip Pierzchalski.
Other titles: Morfogeneza przywodztwa politycznego. English
Description: Frankfurt am Main ; New York : Peter Lang, Internationaler
    Verlag der Wissenschaften, [2017] | Series: Studies in politics, security and society, ISSN ISSN 2199-028X ; vol. 10 | Translated from Polish. |
Includes bibliographical references.
Identifiers: LCCN 2016052576| ISBN 9783631676929 | ISBN 9783653071818 (E-PDF) | ISBN 9783631710920 (EPUB) | ISBN 9783631710937 (MOBI)
Subjects: LCSH: Political leadership. | Morphogenesis.
Classification: LCC JC330.3 .P54 2017 | DDC 303.3/4--dc23
LC record available at https://lccn.loc.gov/2016052576

ISSN 2199-028X
ISBN 978-3-631-67692-9 (Print)
E-ISBN 978-3-653-07181-8 (E-PDF)
E-ISBN 978-3-631-71092-0 (EPUB)
E-ISBN 978-3-631-71093-7 (MOBI)
DOI 10.3726/b10740

© Peter Lang GmbH
Internationaler Verlag der Wissenschaften
Frankfurt am Main 2017
All rights reserved.
Peter Lang Edition is an Imprint of Peter Lang GmbH.

Peter Lang – Frankfurt am Main · Bern · Bruxelles · New York ·
Oxford · Warszawa · Wien

All parts of this publication are protected by copyright. Any
utilisation outside the strict limits of the copyright law, without
the permission of the publisher, is forbidden and liable to
prosecution. This applies in particular to reproductions,
translations, microfilming, and storage and processing in
electronic retrieval systems.

This publication has been peer reviewed.

www.peterlang.com

Acknowledgements

As Sándor Márai wrote *"big passion – in love or in art – is always joyful. Pseudo desire is gloomy, pompous and exhaustd"*[1]. These words best reflect the state of mind and a kind of positive, intellectual excitement that accompanied the author in writing this book. This book would not have been written but for kindness, support and comments from the two such joyful scholars – Professor Miroslaw Karwat from the University of Warsaw and professor Barbara Krauz-Mozer from the Jagiellonian University, whose daily work and intellectual attitude constantly show – not only to the author of this book – what the passion for learning means.[2]

---

1 S. Márai, *Dziennik (fragmenty)*, Spółdzielnia Wydawnicza „Czytelnik", Warszawa 2008, p. 31.
2 The current publication has been based on:
Filip Pierzchalski, Morfogeneza przywództwa politycznego. Pomiędzy strukturą a podmiotowością sprawczą, Wydawnictwo Naukowe Uniwersytetu Kazimierza Wielkiego, Bydgoszcz 2013.

Contents

Introduction 9

1. **Multi-dimensional understanding of the political sphere** 19
    1.1 Political reality in dialectical perspective 19
    1.2 Methodological tools for the theory of politics 21
    1.3 Syndromic understanding of the "matter of politics" 36

2. **Dialectical interdependence of agency and structure** 43
    2.1 Subjective approach to the political space..43
    2.2 Structural approach to the political space 52
    2.3 Complementarity of subjective and structural models 63

3. **Political subjectivity in the morphogenetic approach** 69
    3.1 Critical realism..69
    3.2 Morphogenetic approach...78
    3.3 Three-phase morphogenetic cycle..88
    3.4 Political agency in morphogenetic perspective 92

4. **Understanding political leadership** 101
    4.1 The notion of political leadership.. 101
    4.2 Political leadership paradigms and attributes of political leadership... 114

5. **The problem of the scope in political leadership**........................ 119
    5.1 Multi-level political leadership 119
    5.2 Micro-level political leadership theories 121
    5.3 Macro-level political leadership theories.. 132

6. Morphogenetic characteristics of political leadership 143

6.1 Determinants of political agency in leadership 143

6.1.1 Endogenous factors 144

6.1.2 Exogenous factors 147

6.1.3 Dialectic of conditions 149

6.2 Morphogenesis of political leadership 151

6.2.1 Leszek Miller's case – on the intensification of structured agent 156

Conclusion 171

References 175

List of Figures 185

Explanatory notes for key terms 187

Introduction

Scientific reflections on 'human agency vs. social structure' dualism in the broad sense of social sciences, including the political science of, have caused a lot of conflicting theoretical and methodological solutions. These conceptual differences clearly appear in extreme varieties of individualism and methodological holism, where we can notice the conflicting directives, procedures and mechanisms of scientific research on the explication of political reality. In the first case an individualistic tendency is used in the process of theoretical reductionist explanatory mechanisms, where every nomological description, explanation or prediction concerning politics is aimed only (and always) at an individual. In this variant, the primary object in the ontological and epistemological sense, through which one examines the world of politics, remains a single causative agent (the social part) which becomes the primary, and more importantly, the only element for explaining multiform dualism of agent-structure. In the second case there is a shift from individualist justifications of politics for the benefit of a comprehensive overview of the political space dominated by theoretical and research holism. Here we can see the scientific denial of the fundamental assumptions of methodological individualism with regard to the matter of politics for the benefit of constructing a detailed explanation based on multi-level, aspectual and syndromic analyses of politics, which take into account the dynamic emergent specificity of a particular political space (social entity). In this variant, differently interpreted and defined social entity and the exact complexity of higher order and/or structural configuration becomes the primary element for explaining the dualism of agent-structure. In other words, the diversity of form and content of the holistic research perspective, as antagonistic one towards the individualistic approach, raises the question of importance of supraindividualist change factors (independent of an individual causative subject) in the creative context of adequate nomological knowledge on the complexity of the subjective and structural relationship.

Undoubtedly, the described conceptual and methodological inconsistencies in the duality of agent-structure originate from historiosophic dispute over universals, where individual researchers of social phenomena have tried to settle the issue of the primordial category in relation individual ↔ society. In these discussions the topic of potential reality and knowability of an indiviual and social being, in which the problem of creating designates for such names, was defined as: the collective, group consciousness or collective action[3]. This speculative dilemma was voiced also in numerous theoretical and methodological disputes, where scientists attempted to scientifically settle the issues of reasonableness, appropriateness or usefulness of the research of two separate explanatory schemes, i.e. nominalist-individualist (resultant assumptions of sociological nominalism and methodological individualism) and realist-holist (the synonym combining realism with sociological methodological holism)[4].

For the development of sociological thought the dispute between an individual (social part) and society (social entity) is associated mainly with the wider sociological thought including two different ways of epistemological considerations. On the one hand, we can speak here of an individualistic approach, which treats people as a "sum" of human beings, which means, on the one hand, the supremacy of research and primitiveness explaining the individual being in relation to the social being. As John W. N. Watkins proposed in his the research directive:

> According to this principle, the ultimate constituents of the social world are individual people who act more or less appropriately in the light of their dispositions and understanding of their situation. Every complex social situation, institution or event is the result of a particular configuration of individuals, their dispositions, situations, beliefs, and physical resources and environment. (…) If methodological individualism means that human beings are supposed to be the only moving agents in history, and if sociological holism means that some superhuman agents or factors are supposed to be at work in history, then these two alternatives are exhaustive[5].

Many representatives of this orientation of research, in which the conceptual core of the scientific investigations constitutes the foundation of psychologism and nominalism include: precursors microsociololgy (the classical authors of microsociololgy include *inter al.*: Ferdinand Tonnies, Georg Simmel, Charles

---

3   G. Rodriquez-Pereyra, *Resemble Nominalism. A Solution to the Problem of Universals*, Oxford University Press, Oxford 2002; Ch. Landesman (ed.), *The Problem of Universals*, Basic Books, London 1971; G. Guigon, G. Rodriquez-Pereyra (ed.), *Nominalism about Properties*, Routledge, New York 2015.

4   J. Zahle, F. Collin (ed.), *Rethinking the Individualism-Holism Debate: Essays in the Philosophy of Social Science*, Springer International Publishing, London 2014; R. A. Sibeon, *Rethinking Social Theory*, Sage Publications Ltd, London 2004; D. Layder, *Understanding Social Theory*, Sage Publications Ltd, London 2006, pp. 190–301.

5   J. W. N. Watkins, *Historical Explanation in the Social Sciences*, "British Journal for the Philosophy of Science" 8 (2) 1957, pp. 104–117; S. Lukes, *Methodological Individualism*, [in:] D. Matravers, J. Pike (ed.), *Debates in Contemporary Political Philosophy. An Anthology*, Routledge, London 2003, pp.12–21.

Horton Cooley, Florian Znaniecki); representatives of interpretative sociology (verstehende *Soziologie*[6]) researchers associated with empirical microsociology (school of human relations, Jacob L. Moreno's sociometry); advocates of microtheoretical paradigm in social research (Peter Blau and Georg C. Homans and their theory of exchange, rational choice theory of James S. Coleman, network theory by John Scott[7]).

By contrast, the collectivist perspective treats the society as a whole, which is not only a simple sum of its components, but it is more than just a social unit. In other words, the collectivist narration by assumption authorizes one to reject the nominalist view of the whole society because, in some circumstances, the said whole is irreducible to previously identified and defined parts and/or units. Using Émile Durkheim argumentation means that the research situation in which the world community cannot be translated and explained only on the basis of atomistic argumentation (individualistic), because it is the world *sui generis*:

> Let us apply this principle to sociology. If, as is granted to us, this synthesis *sui generis*, which constitutes every society, gives rise to new phenomena, different from those which occur in consciousnesses in isolation, one is forced to admit that these specific facts reside in the society itself that produces them and not in its parts – namely its members. In this sense therefore they lie outside the consciousness of individuals as such, in the same way as the distinctive features of live lie outside the chemical substances that make up a living organism. (…) Social facts differ not only in quality from psychical facts; *they have a different substratum*, they do not evolve in the same environment or depend on the same conditions[8].

In this sense, the collectivist approach constitutes the antithesis of the individualist orientation, where the reality of various definitions of the social entity is acknowledged (collective subject, the collective, collegial body, leadership team etc.), which in given conditions becomes the primary, or even the key and necessary descriptive and explanatory element for the scientific analysis of politics. Among many representatives of the orientation of research, inter al. the following examples are worth mentioning: the structural and functional analyses of Talcott Parsons[9]; structuralism, especially the one of Louis Althusser, where the

---

6 E. Nagel, *The Structure of Science: Problems in the Logic of Scientific Explanation*, Hackett Publishing Company, New York 1979.
7 B. Roberts, *Micro Social Theory*, Palgrave Macmillan, New York 2006.
8 É. Durkheim, *The Rules of Sociological Method*, The Free Press, New York 1982, pp. 39–40.
9 T. Parsons, *The Social System*, The Free Press, MacMillan, New York 1964; T. Parsons, *Social Structure and Personality*, The Free Press, Collier-MacMillan Ltd. London 2007.

question of automatism and overdetermination of structures are mentioned[10] or the systemic perspective of Niklas Luhmann (the idea of *autopoiesis*[11]).

At the same time, there was a large group of theorists in the social sciences, who questioned, even rejected completely, the legitimacy of the antagonism between the part and the whole of society. Among these thinkers, the synthesizing strategies prevailed, which instead of binary thinking, chose the idea of creating a multi-layered patterns of triangulation. Based on various analytical tools, the researchers attempted to join contradictory research orders (planes). It was a synonym for an intellectual escape "forward", where the dilemma of individual vs. society was considered to be an aporetic situation (conflict which cannot be solved, the situation with an inscribed, indelible contradiction), to which research programs which in principle abandon the part-entity logic for the benefit of multivariate or complementary inferences became the only scientific recipe and answer. It is impossible to mention all the theoretical and methodological standings, which tried to "overcome" the individual vs. society dichotomies. Important synthesizing approaches that certainly deserve special attention include: the Hegelian speculative logic (the transformation of quantity into quality and vice versa; the idea of the negation of negation; the interpenetration of the opposites; or subjective-objective coincidence[12]), Marxism (Marxist interpretations of the human being, where, on the one hand, we can talk about objective entanglement of the agent in society, on the other hand, it emphasizes the relative autonomy of an individual[13]); figurative sociology of Norbert Elias (the idea of the process understood as a rejection of reifiying concepts of "society" and an "individual" to create multivariate and multi-faceted "models, structures and processes of space-time", in which part and the whole complement each other[14]); program of structural microsociololgy pushed through by Jacek Szmatka (the theory of

---

More in: K. von Beyme, *Die politischen Theorien der Gegenwart. Eine Einführung*, Sringer Fachmedien, Wiesbaden 2006, pp. 122–136.

10 L. Althusser, *For Marx (Radical Thinkers)*, Verso, London 2005, pp. 87–128.
11 N. Luhmann, *Social Systems*, Stanford University Press, Stanford 1995; N. Luhmann, *Intorduction to systems theory*, Polity Press, Cambridge 2013, pp. 70–83.
12 F. Engels, *Collected Works*, vol. 25: F. Engels, *Anti-Dühring, Dialectics of Nature*, International Publishers, New York 1987, pp. 110–135, 356–362.
13 K. Marx, *Capital*, Volume I, International Publishers, New York 1967, pp. 289–90; G. Carchedi, *Behind the Crisis. Marx's Dialectics of Value and Knowledge*, Koninklijke Brill NV, Leiden-Boston 2011 pp. 22–31.
14 N. Elias, *The Society of Individuals*, The Continuum International Publishing Group Inc., New York 2001.

the relationship between microstructures and macrostructures) and the idea of the dual property structures of Piotr Sztompka (the structure as simultaneous behaviour shaping factor for individuals being at the same time shaped by this behaviour[15]). This is not different in the morphogenetic perspective presented by Margaret S. Archer (the concept of analytical dualism).

From the point of view of political theory and the dispute between the above mentioned styles of thinking, it is nothing but an attempt to analytically solve the dilemma of the status, role, importance of agency etc. of the agent, individual being, as well as collective being, in a specific socio-political space. Additionally, it is often a moment of occurrence of theoretical alternatives with regard to the complex and multifaceted individual ↔ society relationship. In this perspective, the very process of conceptual research gains importance, in which, on the one hand, analytical and methodological primitiveness, secondary character or complementarity of the two sides in part ↔ entity relationship are determined, on the other hand, the degree of determination, impact, influence, relationships etc. of that relationship is detailed.

In such conditions, causative subjectivity (human agency, agent) is understood in this book as proposed by the sociological tradition: driving force of the entity; subjective sense of control over the social environment and/or socio-structural space; economic alienation; motivation effect. At the same time we cannot forget that the term "causative subjectivity" obviously raises the question of whether there is subjectivity other than causative? Yes, there is – e.g. cognitive subjectivity, which (even if it comes down to meditation, contemplation, mental speculation, self-reflection but also a form of activity) is not a direct practical ability to transform the reality. Additionally, perpetration can be direct (the entity as a direct perpetrator of the event, creator, producer and organizer of the event, the only and ultimate decision-maker, etc.) or indirect (the entity as a co-creator of the work, co-decision maker, co-perpetrator/accomplice of a product, etc.). It is therefore justified to reverse the relationship: is non-subjective agency possible? The answer to this question will also be positive, i.e. in the social practice we can distinguish between involuntary perpetration, which is associated with the inadvertent cause of specific events, situations and states of affairs perpetrated by an individual or collective agent. In this state of affairs the researcher realizes that the political reality rarely deals with isolated causative force where the entity becomes the sole agent of change in the social world. In most cases,

---

15 P. Sztompka, *Sociology of Social Change*, Blackwell, Oxford & Cambridge 1993, pp. 191–200.

the causative agent has a primarily complex nature, which means that it takes different intensity and form, as well as depends directly or indirectly on various socio-structural conditions.

The same regularity can be noticed in relation to the concept of "structure", which on the one hand, refers both to the social systems treated as an entity "impersonal" (complement to the subject, systemic and a complex determination of its existence in the social world), on the other hand, it is synonymous with social groups, communities or communities that are not only the system of relations or circumstances (e.g. management teams, team leadership, collective bodies, etc.). In this case, we also have to deal with the "practical blur" of the dichotomy between the subject and structure, where the latter may, but does not need to, be non-humanist ("non-subjective"). In most cases, it is a kind of reconfiguration of subjective agency and supraindividual mechanisms that create the structure.

Historiosophical dichotomy "causative subject vs social structure" also applies to the phenomenon of political leadership, where there are two completely different explanatory approaches, i.e. micro- and macroanalyses. In some ways, the two research schemes of research actually exemplify the transfer and replacement of speculative agent ↔ social structure relations for diverse ones in form and content in the political practice of leadership, where competent researchers use various underlying assumptions and methodological directives for scientific explication of complex meanderings of modern political leadership. In this perspective, it seems fully justified to take theoretical and methodological research on the issue of leadership in politics in combination with intellectual dualism: agent vs social structure.

The first research goal of this publication is an analytical attempt to combine, precisely adapt and use the dichotomy-entity structure in relation to leadership, which is formed at the interface between the leader/leaders (subjective leadership) ↔ followers (socio-structural environment). Only on the surface may it seem that such a scientific association of two so different research problems with respect to the range and subject matter has been misunderstood or misinterpreted by the author, but this work in principle has to be the proof of the accuracy of such explanatory research approach where the problem of adduction in politics is explained through the agent-structure relationship; where the political leadership is shown in a new conceptual and theoretical light, with the help and thanks to research tools previously used only to explicate the notion of political subjectivity; process where leadership becomes mainly a multidimensional dialectical relationship between the leading agent and the structural conditions.

In this sense, the subject of study in this work comes down to a detailed analysis of the current theoretical and practical dilemma, which takes the form of a question: Who/what is the carrier and expresses subjective leadership? Is this leading agent, ie. the leader as such – an outstanding above average, charismatic individual? Or just the opposite – it is a social group, a broadly organized entity and/or complexity of a higher order, in which it is difficult to clearly identify the individual leader. In other words, is the leadership always personified, which is associated with the mechanism to embody a particular politician, ruler, political or moral authority? Or is it just the opposite? – It is the result of some interaction, depending on whether the continuum of relatedness resulting from the "inter-subjective game" within the whole society, where *summa summarum*, thorough insightful investigations, leadership turns out to be a multiform cooperation of individual entities. As in networking leadership, where we deal with the distribution of influence between both formal as well as informal social actors, which only appears to be impersonal, self-perpetuating and autonomous leadership. Or perhaps we deal with cooperation in leadership on a large scale, where political leadership is identified with a single, complex subject of leadership?

These research questions are to some extent a consequence of the historical observation of the development of the formation and functioning of the mechanisms of leadership, where, on the one hand, individual surges and initiatives of leadership took place, in which the key roles and importance were played by a single leader/political authorities. On the other hand, we can talk about the spread (blurred) leadership, where it is difficult to predict and define the individual agent of leadership, whose power, influence or impact on the external environment would be strong enough and clear so the leadership would be the domain of a single leader.

In the first case we are talking about personalized leadership, where authority and esteem the leader in the overall properties determined the quality and mechanism of political leadership, for instance, historical descriptions made by Thomas Carlyle, who insisted that only the outstanding units, the so called heroes were able to bear the fate of the world. According to the thesis:

> In all epochs of the world's history, we shall find the Great Man to have been the indispensable saviour of his epoch; – the lighting, without which the fuel never would have burnt. The History of the World, I said already, was the Biography of Great Men[16].

---

16 T. Carlyle, *On Heroes, Hero-Worship, and The Heroic in History*, Longmans, Green, and Co., New York 1906, p.13.

Following this line of reasoning, it can be said that the process of leadership is the same as the personification of leadership, where the description and explanation of the complex and multivariate relationships of leadership is based on the separate entity of leadership, where the structural context plays a secondary, complementary role.

On the other hand, in the second case it is a depersonalized mechanism of political leadership, the subjective-psychological disenchantment that basically abandons the clear identification and determination of leadership in favor of contextual supraindividualist, even multifactorial grounds of leadership in politics. This results in a holist look at the leadership, which recognizes the role and the importance of the relational aspects of power and/or leadership; where the process of leadership is considered to be a synthesis, consisting in the scientific coincidence of subjective and objective factors, where the relation of leadership is the result of endogenous conditions (intrinsic, internal perpetration of political leaders), as well as endogenous (supraindividualist, external structural driving forces determining the process of leadership); where in the historiosophical study a simplistic research regularity occurring in the explication of complex leadership can be seen, i.e. at the beginning of explaining certain political events, the existence of a complex political agent is assumed; where leadership is spontaneous and irreducible to a single perpetrator, only *post factum* does it reverse the direction of the historiosophical narration when an attempt is made to distinguish a specific leader of those events by causal or heroic means (e.g. a leader and or the main character of the revolution, a key decision-maker, an outstanding catalyst for change).

The second, no less important research goal of this publication is a detailed discussion of the morphogenetic/static perspective in terms of the importance of cognitive-conceptual approach of this research, as well as its methodological usefulness. This is why specific research tools related to morphogenetic nomological analysis will be meticulously presented, verified and evaluated. Not without reason the theoretical standing proposed by Margaret S. Archer has been quoted in this work, who in the 90s of the twentieth century, based on assumptions of critical realism, presented the original concept of subjectivity, especially in the spirit of analytical dualism. Archer defined also the mutual influence and/or multi-level bilateral relationship between the subject and the social structure. From this point of view, there are two key original works by Margaret S. Archer, *Realist Social Theory: The Morphogenetic Approach* and *Being Human: The Problem of Agency*, which provide an overall morphogenetic/static interpretation.

It should be added that Archerian theoretical and methodological instruments originate from critical realism understood as a coherent epistemological concept which proposes ontological standing called layered ontology (stratified ontology), where the social and political reality is examined by analytical procedure of separating specific planes of research and their mutual or relational reconfiguration (the reciprocal influence and/or determination between the micro, meso and macro levels), among which there is the phenomenon of emergence understood as the formation of a qualitatively new properties within the structural complexity[17]. In addition, critical realism identifies with the idea of dual ontology, where the agent-structure dichotomy does not mean "inalienable" theoretical and practical antagonism, but multi-dimensional and – more importantly – complementary dual relationship in terms of scope and content. According to Roy Bhaskar, a precursor of the modern critical realism:

> The model of the society/person connection I am proposing could be summarized as follows: people do not create society. For it always pre-exists them and is a necessary condition for their activity. Rather, society must be regarded as an ensemble of structures, practices and conventions which individuals reproduce or transform, but which would not exist unless they did so. Society does not exist independently of human activity (the error of reification). But it is not the product of it (the error of voluntarism)[18].

The starting point for the analysis of agent-structure dualism lies in the concept of morphogenesis, which Margaret Archer borrowed from Walter Buckley:

> Some of the connotations of these concepts of >>self-regulation<< and the like are misleading, whether applied to modern machines, men, or groups, since the tendency is to overemphasize the independence of the internal system at the expense of situational or environmental variables. For this reason it might be profitable to utilize more neutral terms for two basic processes of interest to us here, namely, *morphostasis* and *morphogenesis*. The former refers to those processes in complex system – environment exchanges that tend to preserve or maintain a system's given form, organization, or state. Morphogenesis will refer to those processes which tend to elaborate or change a system's given form, structure or state. Homeostatic processes in organisms, and ritual in sociocultural system are examples of >>morphostasis<<; biological evolution, learning and social development are example of >>morphogenesis<<[19].

---

17 A. Sayer, *Realism and Social Science*, Sage Publication Ltd., London 2000, pp. 10–29.
18 R. Bhaskar, *The Possibility of Naturalism. A Philosophical Critique of the Contemporary Human Science*, Taylor & Francis, London 2005, p. 39.
19 W. Buckley, *Sociology and Modern Systems Theory*, Prentice Hall, New Jersey 1967, pp. 58–59.

Of course, such a definition of morphogenesis differs from many previous exemplifications occurring on the basis of natural sciences, especially in developmental biology and evolutionary biology where morphogenesis was identified as the development, progress and change within the cellular structures of living organisms[20].

It should be noted that the morphogenetic method for diagnosing the socio-political world in the course of the research work was heuristic set of research tools that were actually able to respond to the contemporary perturbations arising from the progressive complexity of political space and to the high complexity of leadership practices. It can be argued that the importance of explanatory concept of morphogenesis / morphostasis in theoretical sociology as proposed by M. Archer as well as her contribution to the development of research on methodological tools in theoretical politics are precisely aimed at synthesizing topics by fine delineation of analysis and research planes. At the same time, in accordance with the dialectic strategy, against eclectic thinking, attempts are made to show the multi-level mutual infiltration of subjective and structural activity.

The structure of this work has been designed to fulfill the primary aim of the research, which is precise and systematic explication of the concept of political leadership in morphogenetic context. In other words, the book is to systematize and refine knowledge of contemporary theorists and methodologists on scientific political grounds especially in the field of:

1. Significance of theoretical and methodological synthesizing strategies, i.e. the idea of a dual ontology in the dialectic spirit in the context of contemporary research on the subject-structure duality.
2. Precise discussion of the subject-structure duality in the context of studies on leadership, where nomological explanation of leadership in politics is placed in multi-level perspective, according to the agent-structure dialectic.
3. Presentation of main theses, assumptions, methodological directives, and research planes proposed in the morphogenetic/static approach.
4. Indications of methodological advantages and benefits arising from the use of sophisticated morphogenetic tools for scientific analysis of political leadership.
5. Enrichment and expansion of recent analyses in the field of theoretical politics with new threads and prospects of research and interpretation relating to the field of political leadership which is still being explored.

---

20 K. S. Thomson, *Morphogenesis and Evolution*, Oxford University Press, Oxford 1988.

1. Multi-dimensional understanding of the political sphere

1.1 Political reality in dialectical perspective

Dialectic understood as a complementary way of analysis and comprehension of reality has been a heuristic research tool for many theoreticians or methodologists within the scope of political science. Not only does it refer to the flagship issues of dialectic contradictions within the society, state or in supranational structures, which are even intensified in the contemporary globalised world but most importantly it refers to the cohesive research orientation. This orientation helps to create a dialectic model of political reality based on diachronic, holist and multi-level analysis of its individual components. In this sense, dialectic is a strictly defined strategy of research where – as Roy Bhaskar argued – there is a possibility for a multi-level explanation of the subject matter of politics, including facts, states of affairs or political processes:

> As it is, at the level of generality at which *Dialectic* is inevitably pitched, only very general maxims can be derived: "seek out contradictions in essential structures rather than, or at least in addition to, empirical regularities" – this is the way you will identify endogenous sources of change; "reconnect apparently unrelated phenomena at both intensive and extensive margins of inquiry" – to discover whether holistic causality is in fact at work; "treat geo-historical process and intra-activity as existentially constitutive". This is how indentifies the presence of the past or outside and of totality. Treat events as conjunctures; ideologies as both knowledge – discourse/power/normative intersects and compromise formation with reality (and spot categorical errors within them)[21].

Additionally, conducting research in political reality from dialectic perspective is not based only on the agreed and established set of theoretical concepts (such basic theoretical assumptions include inter al. the assumption of the systematic nature of the political world; the essential nature of the political system, the phenomenon of the unity of contradictions involving temporary coexistence of contradictory tendencies in a given system), but is based on the dialectic method which has been devised and is still being improved, which can be and very often is used by numerous theoretical approaches in social sciences. In this understanding dialectic is defined inter al. as:

---

21   R. Bhaskar, *Dialectic: The Pulse of Freedom*, Routledge Taylor & Francis Group, London, New York 2008, pp. 375–376.

1. Specific way of thinking and/or reasoning where dialectic conclusion is aimed at persuasion and cogency[22].
2. Theoretical and cognitive system thanks to which the researcher gets a specific spectrum of theoretical and methodological tools which facilitate conducting analyses at various levels (at micro, meso and macrosocicial level) or of various reach (i.e. creating research theories for single facts, behaviours or processes, i.e. middle-range theory and also creation of complete theoretical systems or scientific laws, the importance of which in the course of verification and falsification becomes irrefutable and the explanatory value becomes universal).
3. Specific societal model or societal metaphor where the society as such is defined in holist-structural categories, i.e. multilayeredness, interactivity and dynamics within a given community (research on the relationship between objects or elements constituting an entity) as well as the external environment and the endogenous processes happening within the society. It is also a constant emphasis on the primary rule or "propeller" of any scientific cognition is an objective phenomenon of dialectic contradictions (unity of contradictions), which constantly determine any nomological analyses. Given this assumption when we notice the role, function and meaning of various types of antagonisms (conflicts) on an individual, group, national and supranational plane, there is a chance to build respective explanation, a plausible description and an adequate scholarly forecast.
4. Useful paradigm applied in social sciences where by accepting specific theoretical presuppositions we obtain a pattern for conducting scholarly research i.e. a method of thinking, analysing and explaining the surrounding reality that is determined by directives and methodological theses. At the same time

---

22 Dialectical reasoning is: "clearly differentiated from analytical reasoning because it is not formally valid but is only reasonable or probable, e.g., reasoning by example. We cannot then consider the conclusion reached by dialectical reasoning as assured without an expressed or tacit agreement from the interlocutor. This condition shows that dialectical, unlike analytical reasoning, does not come forth impersonally or automatically. Furthermore, the premises of such reasoning are almost never evident or hypothetical. It is only in eristic dialogues, where through recourse to sophisms, we attempt to place the adversary in difficulty, say what he may, that premises play an unimportant role. On the other hand, with critical or dialectical dialogues, premises and the interlocutor's agreement are essential". More in: Ch. Perelman, *The New Rhetoric and The Humanities. Essays on Rhetoric and its Applications*, Reidel Publishing Company, Dordrecht 1979, p. 74.

dialectic is here the starting point for the practical application of the dialectic method that is characterised by relatively big explanatory and predicative power[23].

5. Starting point for detailed analysis of various political phenomena – in particular those relating to the structural changes interpreted in dialectic perspective where any dynamics of the specific political regime is interpreted as a mutual interdependence between the microlevel and macrolevel of the structure; where there is the bilateral determination between the subjective activity (voluntarism) and the societal surrounding (structuralism). An example for this type of viewing the political sphere may be the neo-Marxist concept of *structural selectivity* by Bob Jessop, where he highlights that the real borders for the system foundation in the state lies in the strategic fights between various societal powers, which leads to the mutual determination and dialectic multi-lelevel interdependence between specific subjects ("carriers" and creators of the structures) and the very structure (structure interpreted as an element which limits, controls, modifies the activities of societal agents)[24].

1.2 Methodological tools for the theory of politics

One has to consider first the dialectic method in the context of forming scholarly explanations with respect to the political reality, which constitutes a starting point to seek a decent solution for a multi-level dilemma: subjective activity vs to-date societal structure where the direct research objective lies in providing a meticulous proof for mutual dialectic relationships between various forms of human activity (agency) and the societal surrounding. We should not forget that the cotemporary political space is characterised by specific objective, more importantly – quantifiable regularities and/or conditions which, on the one hand, become the foundation for empirical observation and identification of dialectic mechanisms, on the other – they affect the research process itself. Such indisputable features of political reality include:

1. Complexity and temporariness of the political space – these are the essential determiners of politics without which a scholarly description, classification, explanation or forecasting with respect to facts, events or political processes will be always inadequate. Both tendencies are basically the starting point for

---

23 P. Sztompka, *Sociological Dilemmas. Toward a Dialectic Paradigm*, Academic Press, New York 1979, pp. 327–332.
24 B. Jessop, *State Theory: Putting the Capitalist State in Its Place*, Polity Press, Cambridge 1990, pp. 260–266.

each intellectual consideration over the political *praxis*, where the selection of suitable paradigm is secondary (in general all the effective paradigms in social sciences are exceptionally consistent with these two determiners. The difference lies only in the way of interpretation or the acceptance range and acquisition of assumptions concerning the progressive complexity and changeability of the social and political world) or the level of analysis (in this perspective it is not important whether eg. it will be the microtheoretical level referring to an individual, their behaviour, preferences, interactions or macrotheoretical level which analyses societal entities, their specificity, multitude of intraelemental relationships, etc.). An axiom of complexity is very important and it states that the political space is a complicated, contextualised, syndromic, multi-dimensional area which, apart from the constant change and movement characterising this area, is characterised by unpredictability, emergence or turbulence.

2. Subjective character of politics – progressive complexity of the political reality results from inter al. an increase in the interactions between agents thanks to which it is said nowadays that the activities of various political agents have a non-quantitative dimension. It means a situation in which any changes, their quantity and quality, directly depend on the so called agency coefficient. In other words – complexity of politics is connected with political activities and decisions of individuals, social groups and large masses.

In the first case we can speak about two key determiners which define the matter of politics – complexity and temporariness. The former contradicts the traditional mechanistic world where science was dominated by precise, seemingly infallible cause-and-effect thinking [according to the principle of causality: *The same cause always products the same effect*, or any similar (and preferably refined) one. In this sense we can talk about the doctrine of causal determination or causalism, where: "everything has a cause"; „nothing on earth is done without a cause"; "nothing can exist or cease to exist without a cause"; "everything that has a beginning must have a cause"[25]. This was replaced by a group of views and philosophical and theoretical schools which emphasised the unpredictable (unquantifiable), complex randomised, highly complicated and emergent character of reaity. In this view, complexity, understood as dynamically structured point of reference meant:

---

25 M. Bunge, *Causality and Modern Science*, Transaction Publishers, New Brunswick, London 2009, p. 4.

In complex systems, the behavior of single element is often completely unknown. In this case, the degrees of complexity of stochastic processes must be distinguished. The outcomes of a stochastic process (e.g. coin tossing) are distributed with different probabilities which are characterized by different probability distribution functions[26].

Complex societal systems in real world should be connected with the emergence of non-linear social behaviours, which may generate chaotic situations (non-linear beahviours mean situations in which minor changes within a given social system and/or entity may cause disproportionate effects and/or results with respect to the initial situation or initial assumptions. A good example is the so called butterfly effect where seemingly unimportant factor, artefact or event may trigger even chaotic, uncontrollable and unpredictable avalanche of events which cannot be controlled or prevented). In this sense, non-linear social behaviours are just nothing else than series of single behaviours that emerge randomly; which are devoid of any pattern or plan. Such status occurs most often in dynamic complex systems where the multitude of reactions and/or interactions leads to non-linearity at various structural levels of relationships (chaotic moments mean permanent dynamics and progressive complexity of a given societal system)[27].

Non-linearity menas the application of the Roman maxim by Terentius „Omnium rerum vicissitudo est" (everything changes); acceptance of non-closed forms both in the nature and in social practice; emphasising complexity and dynamic diversity in the world; sensitivisation to initial conditions of emerging complexities; emphasising the possibility of emergence of many, very often different results and/or dynamic patterns during each research. Thus we can speak about at least three planes for the interpretation of non-linearity used in theoretical considerations in broadly understood social sciences:

1. Spatial non-linearity – analysis of complexity inlvolves the use adaptive computational modelling at methodological level in which the conclusions are formed on the basis of the so called "computational experiment" understood as an analogy towards the empirical experiment. Such studies are usually based on conclusions formulated on the basis of quantifiable experiments, and not analytical solutions. For example, the research conducted by John H. Miller and Scott S. Page, who through the development of model simulations using

---

26 K. Mainzer, *Thinking in Complexity. The Computational Dynamics of Matter, Mind and Mankind*, Springer-Verlag, Berlin 2007, p. 9.
27 E. Elliott, L. D. Kiel, *Nonlinear Dynamics, Complexity, and Public Policy. Use, Misuse, Applicability*, [in:]R. A. Eve, S. Horsfall, M. E. Lee (ed.), *Chaos, Complexity, and Sociology. Myths, Models, and Theories*, Sage Publications, London 1997, pp. 65–67.

the tools of spatial mathematical computing examine inter al. the non-linear (diversified) distribution of votes in respective constituencies.
2. Temporal non-linearity – complexity is understood through a dynamic system, where the emphasis is placed on variation during the test of the subject matter (the study of social phenomena on the basis of vector fields or phase analysis, on the basis of which it is proposed to set out the research hypotheses). It is an approach in which the core of the research focuses on the individual empirical data interpreted as a collection of individual units and/or time sequences. An example of the application of this approach can be empirical research in economics (model analysis of the dynamics of exchange rates).
3. Functional non-linearity – the complexity of identical non-linearity is functionalized, i.e. with highlighting that not all defined functions in the area of complexity are solid. It may even trigger a situation which stimulates the complexity of variation and / or non-linearity function (an example of this way of thinking is the analysis of the field of neural networks)[28].

It should be emphasized that non-linearity reflects the endogenous dynamics of the complexity which in political subject matter is associated with a high degree of activity of subjects expressed with an unquantifiable number of interactions between the subjects:

> The crucial point of the complex system approach is that from a macroscopic point of view the development of political, social, or cultural order in not only the sum of single intentions, but the collective result of nonlinear interactions. (…) Nonlinear system of individuals with intentional behavior may be more complex than, for instance, a physical system of atoms or a chemical mixture of molecules[29].

However, the concept of emergence is equally important phenomenon impinging on the present state of the political science. Historical reflection on emergence indicates that we can actually speak of at least several meanings (interpretations) in relation to this phenomenon[30]. From the point of view of research into the world of politics, and because of its complexity, Conwy Lloyd Morgan's insights

---

28 D. Richards, *Political Complexity. Nonlinear Models of Politics*, The University of Michigan Press, Michigan 2000, pp. 1–20; J. H. Miller, S. E. Page, *Complex Adaptive Systems. An Introduction to Computational Models of Social Life*, Princeton University Press, Princeton 2007.
29 K. Mainzer, *Thinking…*, p. 373.
30 W. Strawiński, *Jedność nauki, redukcja, emergencja. Z metodologicznych i ontologicznych problemów integracji wiedzy*, Fundacja Aletheia, Warszawa 1997, pp. 171–194.

on emergency of evolution seem particularly important. They also include the description of new qualitative changes in the natural and social world:

1. The universality of evolution: there is an evolutionary process that runs through all of nature- the physical, chemical, organic, social and psychological domains; evolution is a multi-factors process, with different factors or combinations of factors producing evolutionary advance in different domains; evolution is creative of new entities, properties and relations among those entities.
2. The level structure of reality: reality is composed of entities which can be arranged in levels that are distinct and irreducible; higher levels include some things, properties or relations which do not occur in lower levels; higher levels depend on the lowers levels for their raw material; entities at different levels can interact, either directly or mediately.
3. The whole/part relationship: some wholes have properties that none of their parts have; in these cases, the novel properties of the whole cannot be predicted solely on the basis of the knowledge of the properties of the parts; the properties of the whole can be understood and explained in terms of those of the parts and some additional assumptions; wholes at one level can be parts of wholes at other levels[31].

Thus, it can be said that the phenomenon of emergence in its basic form is a characteristic of real, existing properties of given reality, which is an ontological feature. By underlining the complexity of the phenomena in the observable world we can talk about the new regularities – new types of properties – occurring at higher levels of complexity, which are a direct cause of a new quality. At the same time, these properties are unpredictable (not reducible to the elements constituting complexity). Hence, the scientific understanding and acceptance of emergent processes in the social world is tantamount to approval of the following claims:

1. *Emergence of complex higher-levels entities* – systems with a higher-level of complexity emerge from the aggregation of lower-level entities in new structural configurations (the new "relatedness" of these entities).
2. *Emergence of higher levels properties* – all properties of higher-level entities arise out of the properties and relations that characterize their constituent parts. Some properties of these higher, complex systems are "emergent", and the rest merely "resultant".

---

31 D. Blitz, *Emergent Evolution and the Level Structure of Reality*, [in:] P. Weingartner, G. J. W. Dorn (ed.), *Studies on Mario Bunge's Treatise*, Rodopi B.V., Amsterdam-Atlanta 1990, pp. 157–158. About the level of reality in: C. Emmeche, S. Køppe, F. Stjernfelt, *Explaining Emergence: Towards an Ontology of Levels*, "Journal for General Philosophy of Science", vol. 28, 1997, pp. 83–119; P. E. Meehl, W. Sellers, *The Concept of Emergence*, [in:] H. Feigl, M. Sriven (ed.), *The Foundations of Science and the Concepts of Psychology and Psychoanalysis*, University of Minnesota Press, Minneapolis 1976, pp. 239–252.

3. *The unpredictability of emergent properties* – emergent properties are not predictable from exhaustive information concerning their "basal conditions". In contrast, resultant properties are predictable from lower-level information.
4. *The unexplainability / irreducibility of emergent properties* – emergent properties, unlike those that are merely resultant, are neither explainable nor reducible in terms of their basal conditions.
5. *The causal efficacy of the emegents* – emergent properties have causal powers of their own – novel causal powers irreducible to the causal powers of their basal constituents[32].

In such conditions, emergence, or rather an emergent – understood as a basic unit of emergence – acquired the status of a fully fledged category (theory) in science, which in a synthetic understanding boils down to the following theses:

1. Emergence occurs in different ways in different contexts, ie. differently in relation to physical systems or biological or mental-cognitive systems, yet differently in the case of social systems and artifacts. In this respect, there is even no agreement among scholars, on which is a basic unit of emergence, ie. there is no consensus on what *emerges*. Emergent can be either a structure, as well as property, information, pattern of behavior, correctness and finally – a given standard.
2. Emergence arises mainly in multi-level hierarchical systems. Different levels of organization correspond to different kinds of rights and/or the correctness of the theory formulated in the theoretical languages of various orders. Each level in the hierarchical system it is characterised by a distinct type of cause and effect relationships.
3. Emergence is the result of the natural tendency of reality for an increase in organized complexity in hierarchical systems. Hierarchically structured world means that more complex units are formed from simple units. However, complex systems can combine with other structural systems of higher level of organization.
4. An important feature of emergents is their coexistence with the results. This means a situation in which emergents responsible for the relative qualitative discontinuity. The results, in turn, guarantee the quantitative continuity. Additionally, emergents are *unpredictable* even on the basis of complete knowledge of the events preceeding them, systemic components to which they are entitled or the rights of defining the behavior of these components[33].

---

32 J. Kim, *Making Sense of Emergence*, "Philosophical Studies", vol. 95, nr 1–2, 1999, pp. 3–36.
33 R. Poczobut, *Między redukcją a emergencją. Spór o miejsce umysłu w świecie fizycznym*, Wydawnictwo Uniwersytetu Wrocławskiego, Wrocław 2009, pp. 75–77.

From the point of view of wider social sciences, including political science, the acceptance for the concept of emergence means treating society as a comprehensive, complex and dynamic system. It is a system that, on the one hand, consists of a large number of interactive components forming a densely interconnected network connections, on the other hand, the overall operation of that system cannot be located in any single component, but rather it is distributed across the system[34]. Concluding, both the properties and emergent processes in the socio – political sphere have the following distinguishing features:

1. They are real – they are true properties and processes that are not idealisations, on the contrary, they are characteristics of a given political matter.
2. Emergence induced within the larger social community – it is characterized by the non-additive entity, i.e. those which cannot be reduced only to the whole entity.
3. They are not reducible – they cannot be moved out and distributed based on individual characteristics, i.e human individuals.
4. They are unpredictable – they cannot be deduced from other properties or processes.
5. They have a subjective character – political subjects constitute the driving force behind these properties and processes in holistic understanding, the so-called large groups understood as an organized entity.

In other words, we are talking about basic assumptions of emergent sociological structuralism, whose main thesis refers to the presence of emergence at various levels of integration of social reality. Hence emergence is interpreted as a *qualitative diversity of phenomena:*

> It manifests in the existence of certain areas of social reality known as levels, which are characterised by relative homogeneity inside but in which one is qualitatively different from the other. Between these levels there is "a smooth transition". Their properties are characterized by a significant, qualitative difference, a fundamental qualitative autonomy. Qualitative properties of individual structures and social processes are *discontinuous* at different levels of integration of the social world. So the emergent reality is characterised by discontinuity of properties and this is why we are talking about the multi-level reality. Therefore the emergent property is assigned to very large areas of

---

34 R. K. Sawyer, *Social Emergence. Societies As Complex Systems*, Cambridge University Press, New York 2005, pp. 21–26.

reality rather than to individual features or events and thus emergence is regarded as an absolute general feature of societal reality[35].

Precise illustration of the emergence of a particular social structure is a diagram 1, which demonstrates the essential significance and/or functions of emergent properties in the context of constructing nomological explanations or predictions on the increasingly complex political world. It should be emphasized that the diagram is based on two fundamental positions that are the starting point for its proper interpretation:

1. Emergent ontological thesis – if the scientific analysis of social reality is, as always (and only) to study the real existing objects and/or beings, not their ideas, projections and sensory interpretation, this emergent ontological thesis assumes that the social world is made up both of individual entities (ontology of parts), as well as with social entities (ontology of entity). The study of progressive complexity of society takes place in the *ontological imbalance*, where between the entities and the social unit there is the ontological primitivity of the latter. This means the situation in which the whole ontology, precisely a detailed analysis of the dynamics occurring between objects at higher levels of organization (complexity), is the foundation and the natural determinant for constructing adequate explanatory mechanisms for social reality (ontological appreciation of entity beings is a comprehensive scientific justification of emergence).
2. Emergent epistemological thesis – in order to learn about the political world in detail we cannot ignore a holistic point of view, where by specific recognition of relationships between the elements within the complexity and more specifically –by identifying emergent unpredictable changes within the dynamic social structure – a coherent picture of reality is formed (gnoseological anti-reductionist activities limit cognition of temporal societal structures; they emphasize cognitive intransferability to their components).

---

[35] J. Szmatka, *Małe struktury społeczne. Wstęp do mikrosocjologii strukturalnej*, Wydawnictwo Naukowe PWN, Warszawa 2007, pp. 31–43. A similar view on emergence was presented by Stefan Nowak: „The advocates of this orientation voice the view that the reduction described above, at least in relation to some properties and regularities of the functioning of the whole, is not possible, since new properties *emerge* at every level of system complexity and these are not reducible to the properties of elements". More in: S. Nowak, *Methodology of Sociological Research. General Problems*, D. Reidel Publishing Company, Dordrecht/Boston 1977, p. 425.

Diagram 1: Phenomenon of emergence in analitically distinguished societal structure (S)

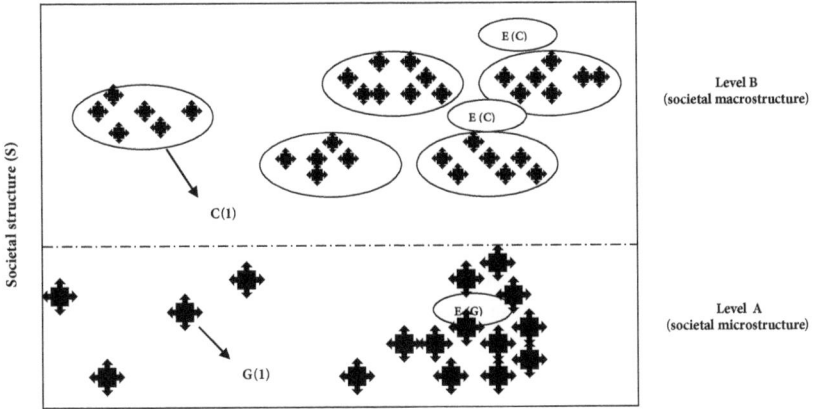

Source: own work

The diagram shows the formation of the phenomenon of emergence **E(G)** and **E(C)** on different levels of the social structure (S), ie. both at microtheoretical level [emergence as a consequence of increased interaction, correlation and/or mutual determination between the active groups **G(1), G(2)...G(n)**] and at macrotheoretical level [emergence as a consequence of increased interaction, correlation and/or mutual determination between the active complexities of higher order **C(1), C(2), C(3) ... C(n)**]. In addition, emergence of **A** and **B** in an analytically separate social structure **(S)** allows us to draw three basic statements about the peculiarities of the socio-political environment:

1. Temporal nature of complexity – highlights that the functioning of the social structure (S), where **E(G)** and **E(C)** spontaneously arise, is the empirical evidence of temporality and progressive complications of that entity. This means that a situation in which intrastructural dynamism, both between the groups as well as between the complexities of higher order, and multi-channel interaction with the environment is a *sine qua non* for the phenomenon of emergence of **A and B levels**. According to the statement that where we are dealing with a static social structure, there is no place for emergence [emphasizing that the presented societal structure (S) treated as a dynamic entity is subject to, inter al., such mechanisms as: autopoiesis –the production and/or reproduction of independent substructures within the structure; balancing between entropy and negentropy – a simultaneous elimination and production of various intrastructural configurations].

2. Additive-emergent character of the increasing structuring – a multi-channel observation mechanism structuring[36] the social structure (**S**), and more specifically, empirical proposals on deepening complexity at the meeting point of: data of the group [**G(1), G(2)** ...**G(n)**] and complexities of higher-order [**C(1), C(2), C(3),** ...**C(n)**] and overall structural change of **A** and **B**. In this arrangement, the emergence of a qualitatively new features and properties on social structure (**S**) maytake and very often takes an additive form. In other words, social structure (**S**), understood as a dynamic social unit, is not a mere sum of the elements and/or substructures included in its composition, but it means more – it negates aggregative definition of the social structure for the benefit of additive definition, where in transferability and irreducibility of the structure to substructures is the cause of the emergence of substructures, which is associated with the justification for the process of qualitative structuring unpredictability.
3. Subjective nature of complexity – indicates that the presence of emergent changes in the societal structure (**S**) is strictly associated with the perpetration by the subject, ie. the real activity of the group [**G(1), G(2)** ...**G(n)**], or the complexity of higher order [**C(1), C(2), C(3)**...**C(n)**]. Merging of unpredictability/irreducibility of the subjective factor with the evolution of social structure (**S**) is an indirect proof for the practical indeterminism which thus *a posteriori* becomes an inherent feature of any complex structure [here it is the empirical fact that undermines the legitimacy of a strong causality principle, where a certain cause always leads (and only) to a specific effect. In this sense, the negation of rigid causality implies a situation in which there is no deterministic axiom, ie. if the cause or effect is the actual activity of the multitude of symptoms, there is no guarantee of strict cause and effect consequence. There is rather a gap for probabilistic irreducibility of behaviors, activities or decisions, which means *inter al.* the lack of clear prediction or retrodiction].

Another parallel to the complexity of the objective correctness of modern political practice is the temporality of political space, which is an additional premise which makes the multifaceted phenomenon of complexity real. In this respect, the key issue seems to be the diachronic and/or sequential interdisciplinary

---

36 In this perspective the connotation "increasing structuration" is generally equivalent to "structuration" proposed by Anthony Giddens. But structuration is understood here as "structuring of social relations across time and space, in virtue of the duality of structure", i.e. as feedback between the structure and its constituents. More in: A. Giddens, *The Constitution of Society. Outline of the Theory of Structuration*, Polity Press, Cambridge 1990, pp. 16–25.

research, which is an ideal complement to academic descriptions, explanations or formulations of short-term and long-term forecasts relating to various types of non-linear political processes. In principle, it is possible to talk about the increasingly popular trend of research in the political science, which boils down to the indisputable conclusion that modern society should be viewed primarily as a *dynamic social field* and more specifically as:

> Process; not as a rigid quasi-object, but as a continuous, unending stream of events. It was recognized that a society (group, community, organization, nation-state) may be said to exist only in so far, and only as long, as something *happens* inside it, some actions are taken, some changes occur, some processes continue to operate. Ontologically speaking, society as a steady state does not and cannot exist. All social reality is pure dynamics, a flow of changes of various speed, intensity, rhythm and tempo[37].

In the interdisciplinary study of the dynamic range of socio-political scope and more specifically, in the interpretation of society as a structured entity, which is subject to multi-variant and constant change, there are three basic research problems, which very simply constitute the starting point for a holist and structural explanations of temporal complexity of politics:

1. Internal mobility of the substructure – it is the mobility of individuals within a given social group, community or an organized community. The fact that many groups and/or organized communities within the macrostructure are liquid in nature is syndromic here, which in fact means multi-level movement of units in analytically separated substructure, affecting there definition of borders and affecting the internal shape of the substructure [mobility can be conditioned inter al. by: the change of the social status (career advancement and/or wealth); macroeconomic indicators (unemployment); self-motivation units (change of the political party dictated by the desire to gain a lucrative position); qualifications (gaining licence, degree or certificate)].
2. Mobility of the substructure on macro-structural scale – it is the mobility of the population, community or organized community within the macrostructure, i.e. in a given society. This phenomenon of origination, processing and disappearance of various types of collective political actors within analytically separate complexity. In most cases, a matter of constant antagonism is based on the development of the dominant position of the company in a broader social structure (mobility of substructure is interpreted as a the competition between the subjects the success of which depends largely on the flexibility of

---

37 P. Sztompka, *The Sociology of Social Change*, Blackwell, Oxford & Cambridge 1993, p. 9.

the internal structure of the status, resources, leaders allowing the organized community a rapid and effective implementation of goals, needs, and interests).
3. Interaction between social differentiation in certain sub-structures and their relative position or status in different macrostructures – the issue of mobility and intergroup competition. Social differentiation in sub-structures is reduced to the mechanism of recruiting the leaders of political and/or administrative organisation who – creating elite through formal and informal channels – influence the functioning of the macrostructure. However, the direct objective of competition for substructures is mainly the social support in any form (eg. political parties compete for voters or companies fight for customers) used to acquire the parent company and/or superior position in the macrostructure, which translates into the internal structure (eg. achieving market dominance legitimizes leadership, provides awards and splendor to the members. On the other hand, failure in competition leads to the leader replacement or to the so called internal opposition)[38].

From the point of view of progressive complexity, non-linearity and structural phenomenon of emergence occurring in political reality, heterogeneity of various social processes seems to be the key issue, which confirms *inter al.* such phenomena as:

1. Non-linear processes – processes the course of which is conditioned by qualitative jumps and/or breakthroughs, ie. after periods of quantitative growth in a given society, the so-called threshold limits are exeeded which are a premise for radical, even violent changes (it is the concept of revolution in Marxist terms, which is an expression of the growing tensions in time, antagonisms and class conflicts).
2. Omnidirectional (liquid) processes – processes whose nature is completely random, chaotic, almost devoid of any pattern or plan.
3. Morphogenetic processes – processes that lead to the creation of entirely new conditions, states of society, social structures (processes, where the effects are creative- innovative nature for the society)[39].

In order to sum up the question of temporalityas a political matter in a reasonable and representative way, interpreted as a convergent cause and/or necessary

---

[38] P. M. Blau, *Exchange and Power in Social life*, Transaction Publishers, New Brunswick, New Jersey 1986, pp. 284–312.
[39] P. Sztompka, *The Sociology of Social Change*, Blackwell, Oxford & Cambridge 1993, pp.12–23.

correlation for the complexity of the phenomenon, the inevitability of dichotomous cores should be emphasized (diagram 2), which have a direct impact on the shape and formula of the dynamic sociopolitical order.

Diagram 2: Image of the political space in a dynamic emergent tangle of processes

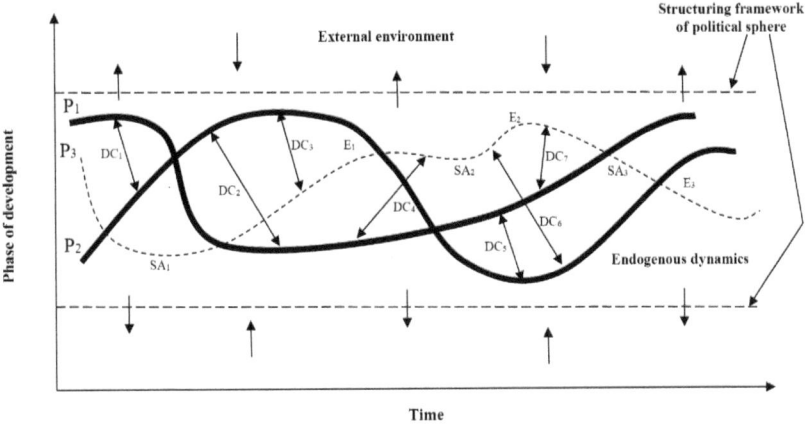

Source: own work

The diagram presents the political reality understood as permanent social change where the order and structure-creating space of politics emerges at the interface of endogenous changes and external environment dynamics. In this arrangement, the endogenous reference system means a dynamic emergent stream and/or combination of processes $P_1, P_2, P_3 \ldots P_n$, which with the plurality of reconfiguration and progressive time complexity produce the space of politics. At the same bundle of processes $P_1, P_2, P_3 \ldots P_n$, is nothing else than the dynamic interdependence, sometimes constant (linear and/or deterministic processes. An example fr the above could be the process P_1 or P_2, in which we have to deal with the practical application of the principle of causality and predictability; where there is no room for a chance and the probability of occurrence of a specific event, fact or the state of affairs is very high and is conditioned by the initial state of the process), and sometimes this probability may be just random (nonlinear and/or liquid, even chaotic, and to some extent emergent processes. An example would be the process P_3, in which there is a case, an element of uncertainty and risk, where the probability of a scientific extrapolation is negligible), but which constitutes the basic building blocks for political space. At the same time, a stream of processes $P_1, P_2, P_3...P_n$, i.e., the sequences of events, both of these random (indeterminisic) as well as those planned (deterministic), are conditioned and/or function based on the *dichotomous cores* $DC_1, DC_2, DC_3...DC_N$. Therefore, the political space is not so much changing in the time sequence of events, which is undeniable, but above all *dichotomous cores* $DC_1, DC_2, DC_3...DC_N$ which decide that the matter of politics incudes different types of antagonisms, occurring both in endogenous reference system, as and also outside the system; they are a confirmation of the claim that "the driving force" of the political matter in the subjective-objective conditions is some form of tension and/or contradictions, which automatically generates temporality and can lead to the formation of the structures of higher order. Of course, antagonisms in the political space are explained hereas the appearance, performance and/or reproduction by the very political matter, and more specifically – by different political actors (participants of collective life), as well as by products of these subjects (alienation of the products of symptoms, which begin to function in the public space regardless of the creator), opposing tendencies, factors, phenomena, properties, goals, needs, reasons, values, norms, laws, regulations, legal provisions and interests that directly impinge on the shape and form of a given society. This state of affairs means a situation in which the *dichotomous cores* $DC_1, DC_2, DC_3...DC_N$ may lead inter al. to:

1. Positive vs. negative co-operation – i.e. to gradable reaching a compromise or conflict between the party (parties) and counter-party (counter-parties) of antagonism inside the political space. In this perspective, we have to deal with two extreme situations, where the *dichotomous cores* $DC_1, DC_2, DC_3...DC_N$ lead to the elaboration of sensible and/or latent consensus, possibly overt and/or covert struggle, and with the entire repertoire of intermediate situations.
2. Emergence – i.e., the dynamics of endogenous and cross-border changes at the interface of the external environment and the political space which provokes permanent tensions and contradictions that are the substrate and/or the ontological basis for the emergence of *emergent*, i.e. factor, property, structure causing emergence. This creates the phenomenon of emergence in a process dynamics $E_1, E_2, ...E_n$.
3. Randomness – an inherent feature of a dynamic series of processes $P_1, P_2, P_3 ... P_n$, in addition to multidimensional relativity and gradable complexity indeterminism is also emphasised, which means the existence of unpredictability or irreducibility of the processes, behaviors, states of affairs, etc. in the course of changes between $P_1, P_2, P_3 ... P_n$. This situation facilitates the actual

existence of a single case, a set of cases and/or situations of accidental SA_1, SA_2,... SA_n as the resultant interactions between *dichotomous cores* DC_1, DC_2, DC_3...DC_n (case here is closely related to the concept of necessity, it is the antithesis of the necessity understood as a constant consequence, rigid sequence of events or established coexistence and repeatability of functional dependencies between certain parameters).

It should be added that the political space explained from the perspective of dynamic- emergent series of processes P_1, P_2, P_3 ... P_n, except for the fact that it is a construct based on the mechanism of the internal dynamics resulting from relational multivariants among *dichotomous cores* DC_1, DC_2, DC_3...DC_n (endogenous changes which are the source in induction, stimulation, extinction, layering and delamination of intrastructural antagonisms), is also the result of internal turbulence and external circumstances which interact continuously with the changing political reality (these are exogenous change-inducing factors which directly or indirectly stimulate, shape, model etc. interior political space).

In the latter case, we can talk about objective-subjective character of political reality, which means that analytically separated subject and/or subjects constitute an indisputable justification for nomological studies of political science. Although this statement contains a hidden naive reductionism, which always reduces the solely syndromic nature of the object of study of political science to the subjective factor, in the case of this study this procedure is extremely necessary and explanatorily useful. However, in the context of morphogenetic analysis of the political leadership it is *sine qua non* because by continuous emphasis that most of the facts, states of affairs, processes or properties that occur within political practice cannot happen or occur without subjective activity. This means a situation in which politics is based on two nodal statements to which reference has been made in the following chapters:

1. Superiority of anthropocentric-activist nature of politics – any explanation of different types of patterns in the area of political practice involves, as always (and only) the analysis of the subject in the totality of its properties and its products. In this sense in the research process an abstractly separated entity becomes the primary explanatory element of any scientific analysis so, in the context of many functioning paradigms and theories in the social sciences, a broadly defined economic plane is indispensable for adequate descriptions or explanations. The very definition of the entity, its semantic, ontological and epistemological justification or research aimed at defining the attributes and traits, is secondary here (this may be: an actor, a single self, subjective existence, netizen, a social group, social class, union, nation, etc.). On the other

hand, activist perspective is crucial here, which means that the subject in the whole scope of their properties affects the environment; they become a kind of the "starting point" and, at the same time, the "point of arrival" for scientific decisions relating to the world of politics.
2. The subjective-causal model of political practice – constantly emphasizing that the subject actually has the so-called political and\or causal force, which in research practice indicates a situation in which the so-called subjective factor is the justification for most of the quantitative and qualitative changes taking place within the political space; measurable and effective research tool for a variety of phenomena occurring in the political reality.

1.3 Syndromic understanding of the "matter of politics"

Detailed analysis of the determinants of politics shows that the requirement of scientific accuracy, generally, any reflection of political science is conditioned to a large extent by the adoption of both dynamic and emergent perspectives as well as thinking in terms and perspectives of subjectivity. This thread was to serve as theoretical and empirical justifications for measurable correctness co-creating a scientific picture of political reality that directly impinge on the definite description, explication and prediction of today meanders of politics. In addition, looking at politics, including the complex process of leadership from the perspective of subjective change factors, the phenomenon of non-linearity, unpredictability, additivity or dynamic-emergent properties and features having structural and subjective sources, results in at least four proposals relating to the subject of research (cognition) of political science:

1. Subject of research in political science is not a forever defined and strictly established research area with clear and irrevocable limits shaped in the spirit of scientific formalism or positivist demarcation (the most common effect of applying the line of demarcation is a methodological mechanism to reduce the complex matter of politics to a single phenomenon, a factor, aspect, process, feature, etc.). The subject of research in the science of politics is rather temporally relativized, which in turn is associated with the existence of many equivalent objects of cognition and/or areas of research which are inherently different in terms of content and form (they potentially have the same scientific value).
2. The contemporary object of study of political science usually is syndromic in nature, which means that individual competent researchers of political phenomena are gradably aware of epistemological pluralism with regard to determining the scope of the science of politics, including contextual, multi-factorial nature of the matter of politics, where the object of study becomes:

A series of phenomena forming a conglomerate or complex of unique quality that the elements co-creating it lose their unique properties in this configuration gaining traits determined by the entity but also *vice versa*: outside this configuration they do not possess these features (...). Political nature of social phenomena is nothing but a combination of factors in terms of various origins and formal affiliation (e.g. technological, economic, religious, artistic) that are historically variable, but always involved in terms of social balance, disturbed by the conflict between the interests, views and particular aspirations in any matter and integration requirements and the social consolidation[40].

3. Syndromic character of the political space means that in political science, in principle, it is impossible to talk about the existence of such a state of affairs in which we can talk about clear, timeless, non-cancellable, complete in content and form conclusions of theoretical and methodological nature, which would lead to the monopoly and domination of one orientation, schools, network of concepts and research perspective. In such hypothetical circumstances, a fossilized space for theoretical research would arise, which in fact would be a denial of the theoretical and methodological development in the political science[41].

4. Epistemological and methodological pluralism in the science of politics is also reflected in perception and defining of the object of study. In such circumstances it depends directly on at least two factors: the enquiring subject (subjective choice and research assessment relating to perception, understanding and definition of the matter of analysis); matter of analysis (the problem of availability, measurability, translation, transferrability, frequency and verification; descriptive possibility or application of the selected research tools, including formal and logical set of tools, advanced techniques – hermeneutic interpretation, etc.).

It should be noted that the conclusions about the modern perception of the object of research of political science are largely a consequence of self-awareness of competent investigators of political phenomena, which is expressed by critical

---

40 M. Karwat, *Syndromatyczny charakter przedmiotu nauki o polityce*, [in:] K. A. Wojtaszczyk, A. Mirska (ed.), *Demokratyczna Polska w globalizującym się świecie*, Warszawa 2009, pp. 175–188; M. Karwat, *Polityczność i upolitycznie. Metodologiczne ramy analizy*, „Studia Politologiczne", vol. 17, 2011, pp. 63–88.
41 The contemporary political science is characterised by the *celebration of diversity*, whih means status equality and rightful charcter of often differing theoretical and research perspectives. More in: D. Marsh, G. Stoker (ed.), *Theory and Methods in Political Science*, Palgrave Macmillan, New York 2002, pp. 3–17.

reflection, a deep understanding and the acceptance of such objective conditions of modern scientific practice as:

1. Research conventionalism – meta-assumption leading to the claim that any settlement in scientific practice is based on some socially articulated convention, i.e. on the subjective decisions of a particular researcher-theorist and/or the circle of scholars[42]. This means a situation in which there is no "clean" and strictly objective or supraindividual experience, knowledge, explanation or prediction in science, because the starting point and, at the same time, the conclusive point in scientific explorations depends only on the enquiring agent. It is a particular researcher and/or a group of scholars, who at all times are responsible for the overall research process, which undoubtedly involves the separation and definition of the subject of research; its conceptualization and operationalization with the use of specific research tools, including conceptual grids, indicators, indexes, inferential schemas forming conventional construct of research; the actual analysis and/or empirical measurement; scientific evaluation. In this perspective, all nomological analyses in political science are considered from the persective of social constructivism, which is crucial to the achievement of intersubjective agreement between scholars (an attempt to achieve semantic, theoretical, communicative, etc. agreement between the competent researchers in the framework of an academic discipline or within a designated area of knowledge, in which different epistemic cultures collide frequently[43]); there were *a priori*, wishful postulate of the unity of science is undermined for the benefit of cognitive and research heterogeneity in which there is a semantic fluency of meanings as well as mutual exclusion (negation) and disparity between given theories and methodological directives.

---

[42] An example of conventional character of research practice is creation of stipulating definitions in accordance with Kazimierz Ajdukiewicz's argumentation: "Now if a definition of a word is a postulate in that language to which it belongs, then such a definition is termed stipulating in that language. We say so because such a definition is based on a stipulation concerning the denotation of the word to be defined (…) A terminological convention is neither a statement nor a proposition that would state or deny something, it is merely a declaration of will which lays down something. As such, a terminological convention is not subject to any appraisal from the point of view of its truth or falsehood". More in: K. Ajdukiewicz, *Pragmatic Logic*, D. Reidel Publishing Company, Dordrecht-Boston 1974, pp. 70–71.

[43] K. Knorr Cetina, *Epistemic Cultures. How the Sciences Make Knowledge*, Harvard University Press, Cambridge 1999.

2. Epistemological relativism – means the relativity, multiplicity and historical volatility of practice and scientific research, as well as the products of these practices (empirical theories, scientific models, research techniques, etc.). This means a situation in which the semiotic plane (language considerations, including research operations related to the development of definitions, concepts, categories, etc. or denotation and connotation of the names or terms), ontological plane (the so called basal determination of reality/lack of reality of given research subject matters) epistemological plane (cognitive structures related to cognitive limitation) and availability or cognizability of the research object of study) and methodological plane (theoretical and practical settlements which involve selection/adaptation of the explanatory methods and techniques for the previously specified object of analysis) is directly dependent on the individual and not on the arbitrary decisions of the enquiring subject[44]. For example, for the semiotic plane, which becomes the starting point for taking a thorough scientific reflection, it will attempt to intellectually challenge the concept of immanent truth (disqotativey) based on linguistic nominalism, where it is difficult to talk about stability, versatility and irrevocability of semantic concepts – it even leads to the phenomenon of ambiguity/polysemy diversified in the form and content (liquidity of meanings) or cognitive-explanatory conflicts between scholars-interpreters. In this sense, we can talk about the phenomenon of "language games", which in practice results in a scientific semiotic heterogeneity, ie. progressive linguistic diversity. These arereferred to as Wittgensteinian different ways of life – *Lebensform*– which means that:

> There are *countless* kinds: countless different kinds of use of what we call >>symbols<<, >>words<<, >>sentences<<. And this multiplicity is not something fixed, given once for all; but new types of language, new language-games, as we may say, come into existence, and others become obsolete and get forgotten. (…) Here the term >>*language-game*<< is meant to bring into prominence the fact that the *speaking* of language is part of an activity, or of a form of live[45].

---

44 A. Schütz, *On Multiple Realities*, "Philosophy and Phenomenological Research", vol. 5, no. 4, pp. 533–576. On epistemological relativism, inter al. in: M. Hollis, S. Lukes (ed.) *Rationalityand Relativism*, MIT Press, Cambridge 1982; H. Siegel, *Relativism Refuted. A Critique of Contemporary Epistemological Relativism*, Springer Science+Business Media B.V., Dordrecht 1987.
45 L. Wittgenstein, *Philosophical Investigations*, Basil Blackwell, Oxford 1973, p. 11. In an extreme form language heterogeneity leads to solipsism, which is encapsulated in the premise: "The world is my world: this is manifest in the fact that the limits of language (of that language wchich I alone understand) mean the limits of my world." It means

Summing up the previous considerations, we have to make a few comments on today's scientific practice in widely understood social sciences. From the point of view of this argument, this procedure is necessary because the scientific attempt to describe and explain the determinants of contemporary politics, i.e. the complexity and the related temporality, clearly indicates the inalienable objective and multi-facetedness of these phenomena. In fact, we can talk about *meta-attribute* for all political phenomena, where the modern researcher/methodologist is not able to identify the following aspects: one equitable method or position in the theory of politics; certain and indisputable decisions; irrefutable evidence; comprehensive and complex reasons. The more we deal with the *phenomenon of fragmentation of knowledge*, which, paradoxically is not an accusation because modern science – more precisely laws, theories or explanatory diagrams used in the political science – are not able to compensate for semi-justifications, statements, forecasts, etc. In general, it is difficult to speak today in the social sciences with hard and irrefutable empirical evidence which are uncontested and arbitrary. In this respect, the key seems to be a critical self-awareness of individual researchers, including methodologists and theorists concerned with explaining the world of politics, who, as the starting point in research, should accept three conditions:

1. Fallibilism – belief that every element of our knowledge is essentially contestable, because knowledge itself, including scientific knowledge, is prone to error (is fallible), which is connected with the fact that every scientific knowledge is uncertain, but probable (constitutive feature of fallibilism is irremovable indeterminacy and variability of human cognition[46]).
2. Equal theoretical and methodological pluralism – an attitude that the researcher who not only sees, but from a distance is also able to fully accept the phenomenon of ideological pluralism and the research pluralism in the community of scholars. In the case of political science this means a situation in which there is a multi- factual and theoretical accumulation undertaken through a variety of research issues which are embedded in given a research strategies.

---

that the agent in the entirety of his or her characteristics, in particular in the context of the use of specific language sets limits on his or her own and is the self-limitation for cognition, interpretation, explanation or understanding of the world. More in: L. Wittgenstein, *Tractatus Logico-Philosophicus*, Routledge Classics, London & New York 2002, p. 68.

46 Ch. S. Peirce, *Philosophical Writings of Peirce*, Selected and Edited with an Introduction by Justus Buchler, Dover Publications, New York 2011, pp. 42–59.

At the same time, many aspects, understood as a meta-attribute of the political space has been used to explain the complexity and temporality. In this arrangement it can be stated that the two determinants are immanent qualities and/or characteristics that exist in the socio-political world, which translates as follows into the practice of research:

1. Scientific analysis of political science should include a component of complexity and/or multi-levellness, where, by analytical evolution of the different levels of analysis (micro, meso and macrostructural) and their dialectical interdependence and determinationstic way to the regularities that govern the political matter, one can perceive and explain the regularities which govern the matter of politics.
2. Politics for the theorist and methodologist is also the study of non-linear processes, where by accepting the complexity and unpredictability of the political practice, one accepts the process of irreducibility of characteristics or facts that may lead to phenomena such as disorder (deterministic chaos), emergence at higher levels of complexity and scale-free network structure.

2. Dialectical interdependence of agency and structure

2.1 Subjective approach to the political space

Historical and philosophical disputes over the issue of agency – structure indicate the presence of constant theoretical and methodological tension in this scientific dilemma, the un ambiguous solution of which is impossible to find. Numerous discrepancies as to the dichotomous relationship can be seen both in different fields of knowledge, as well as within a given discipline, which are apparent differences between individual researchers, often representing a distinct epistemological approach[47]. The essence of the dispute boils down to answering the following questions: who/what has a greater impact, influence, significance, driving force, causal force, level of alienation etc. in explaining agent-structure relationships? Is there an agent (individual or collective)in the totality of its properties? Or vice versa, i.e. an essential explanatory link only (and always) social structure/environment, which is the only and direct determinant for the direction of, or changes in the functioning of the entity.

In the first case we can talk about the appreciation of subjective factor, where by the psychological anthropocentric attitude an attempt is made to indicate the descriptive and explanatory primitivitiveness of abstract agent in political reality. At the same time one cannot forget that the term "agent" refers in this case not only to the individual (single agent, individual perpetrator, the manufacturer, the creator of changes, etc.) but also to the collective agent (the real existence of human teams, both formal as well as informal, which operate on the basis of complicity, participation, cooperation, a sense of connectedness, of belonging, or the convergence of interests, etc.). The second case emphasizes the leading role of the structure factor, where the objectivity and inevitability of impact of structures on the subject indicates the primitiveness of theoretical and methodological structural conditions.

---

47 Discrepancies in interpretation in sociology might be an example here where the problem agent-structure has been examined by such researchers as Robert Merton – functionalist approach, Ervin Goffman – dramaturgical approach, combination of the so called humanist sociology with symbolic interactionism and with functionalism or Anthony Giddens – structuration theory.

Confirmation for historiosophic agent-structure dilemma lies certainly indifferent types of analysis of political science which are trying to point to this unique, correct, often foreground factor of political change. In such circumstances, the most one-sided arguments come to the fore and are equated with binary thinking, which translates into the notion of agency. In other words, the main problem in the social sciences is a multiple-answer question – who/what "makes history"? On the one hand, it underlines the key role of the activity of individuals (personal determination) on the other, the key role of primary importance the structural conditions that determine people (non-human determination)[48]. According to the statement:

> The two antagonistic formulas of a »natural-human process without a subject« and »ever-baffled, ever-resurgent agents of an unmastered practice« are both claims of an essentially apodictic and speculative character – eternal axioms that is no way help us to trace the actual, variable roles of different types off deliberative venture, personal or collective, in history[49].

An individual quantifiable human being seems to be crucial for the subjective approach who becomes a direct factor (perpetrator) of the change in the socio-structural contemporary surrounding. In this understanding, agency, according to Anthony Giddens:

> [...] presumes that to be an agent is to be able to deploy (chronically, in the flow of daily life) a range of causal powers, including that of influencing those deployed by others. Action depends upon the capability of the individual to »make a difference« to a pre-existing state of affairs or course of events[50].

The result of agency understood in such a way is, on the one hand, the transformation, on the other reproduction of certain social forms, i.e. the socio-political, cultural systems, public institutions. At the same time, we have to keep in mind that the experience of agency is not something homogenous for an agent, on the contrary –it is a gradable bundle of feelings. Therefore we can say that the sense of agency and/or "making a difference" leads to three types of experiences in the same body: freedom of choice (a sense of self-determination, where the

---

48 A. Callinicos, *Making History. Agency, Structure, and Change in Social Theory*, Brill, Leiden-Boston 2004, pp.1–33. On historical antinomies in social sciences, including the problem of agency-structure inter al. in: J. C. Alexander, *The Antinomies of Classical Thought: Marx and Durkheim*, University of California Press, Berkeley 1982.
49 P. Anderson, *Arguments within English Marxism*, Verso, London 1980, p. 21.
50 A. Giddens, *The Constitution of Society. Outline of the Theory of Structuration*, Polity Press, Cambridge 1990, p. 14.

"I" is the source of thought, judgment and action); feelings of control/influence (conviction as to the real possibility of subjective execution of control in given areas of life); efficacy/competence (the feeling that one is able to take and bring some action to fruition to enable the objectives and prove effectiveness or confirming competence)[51]. This definition corresponds to the concept of subjective factor suggested by Piotr Sztompka, where he emphasized the importance of the two domains, i.e. the personal and structural domain in the creation of social life. He emphasizes, however, that the activity of subjects (individual and collective subjects) – quantifiable actions, factual actions and decisions – lead to the scientific study of the society, and more specifically – of the community which is subject to a permanent and multilateral processes of change. It is connected with the acceptance of the following theses:

(1) That society is a process an undergoes constant change;
(2) That the change is mostly endogenous, taking the form of self-transformation;
(3) That the ultimate motor of change is the agential power of human individuals and social collectivities;
(4) That the direction, goals and speed of change are contestable among multiple agents, and become the area of conflicts and struggles;
(5) That action occurs in the context of encountered structures, which it shapes in its turn, resulting in the dual quality of structures (as both shaping and shaped), and dual quality of actors (as both producers and products)
(6) That the interchange of action and structure occurs in time, by means of alternating phases of agential creativeness and structural determination[52].

Against this background, critical realism presents an interesting research prospect based on analytical dualism[53]. For researchers representing such an epistemological standing, an idea of agency fits in each issue of agent-structure duality, which emphasizes the simultaneous autonomy and interdependence of the two areas of activity: the personal and structural; where it departs from the scientific anastomosis (Giddensian duality) structure and subjective agency and heads for

---

51 M. Kofta, *Człowiek jako przyczyna zdarzeń*, [in:] M. Kofta, T. Szustrowa (eds.), *Złudzenia, które pozwalają żyć: szkice z psychologii społecznej*, Warszawa 1991, pp. 169–203.
52 P. Sztompka, *The Sociology of Social Change*, Blackwell, Oxford & Cambridge 1993, p. 200.
53 Critical realism, as a new epistemological position in science was launched in the 1920s of the 20th century. Today authors identifying with the mainstream of research include inter al .: Bhaskar Roy and Margaret S. Archer. The latter author, based on the thesis of critical realism, developed the morphogenetic theory. More on this subject in Chapter 3 of this publication.

one, as far as consistent, object of study for the analytical separation of the two orders (domains) and indication of their permanent mediation and mutual interaction. In this sense, the scientific analysis of political practices take the following basic theorem as their starting points:

1. That structure necessarily pre-dates the action(s) leading to its reproduction or transformation;
2. That structural elaboration (changes in social world – emphasis. F. P.) necessarily post-dates the action sequences which gave rise to it[54].

Additionally, perpetration in critical realism is an attribute of individuals as well as social groups operating in a given socio-structural environment. It is the property inscribed in the human condition, which according to Margaret S. Archer, is directly linked to human reflexivity. In other words, the essence and core agency is always (and only) reflexivity, defined as internal conversation of the agent adopting the form of "dialogue between different phases of the ego"[55]. Hence:

> It is proposed that »reflexivity« be incorporated as a personal property of human subjects, which is prior to, relatively autonomous from and possesses causal efficacy in relation to structural or cultural properties. (…) In other words, »reflexivity« is put forward as the answer to *how* »the causal power of social forms is mediated *through* human agency«. Our internal conversations perform this mediatory role by virtue of the fact that they are the way in which we deliberate about ourselves in relation to the social situations that we confront[56].

Archerian conformist approach contradicts the structuring idea where the society functions on the basis of mindless imitation of subjects with regard to the existing norms, values, procedures, general social beliefs or practices. On the contrary – there are no social practices without human reflexivity, which is an essential point of reference for *homo sapiens*. Jeffrey C. Alexander spoke in a similar vein: for him action and perpetation (agency), however, constitute two different forms of social activity. Alexander emphasized that the perpetration of the subject is synonymous with their creativity, spontaneity, competence, self-reflexivity. Yet, the action symptoms usually take the form of mechanical steps, routine habits, and even restorative repeatability. In such an interpretation perpetration is in some way a

---

54 M. S. Archer, *Realist Social Theory: The Morphogenetic Approach*, Cambridge University Press, Cambridge 1995, p. 15.
55 M. S. Archer, *Being Human: The Problem of Agency*, Cambridge University Press, Cambridge 2000, p. 228.
56 M. S. Archer, *Making our Way through the World: Human Reflexivity and Social Mobility*, Cambridge University Press, Cambridge 2007, p. 15.

negation of action, because it means gradable ability of subject/-s for autonomous and reflective activity against the elaborated rules and effective procedures, social conformism or commonly imposed cultural codes[57].

At the same time, the definitions which focus on the essence of subjectivity in the same subject, its features psychophysical, cognitive capabilities, driving force for the manifestation of own predispositions, talents, goals, plans or intentions seem to be crucial for the subjective approach to the political reality. In this way, we have to deal with the mechanism of the personification of social structures, where the core of any social structure lies always (and only) in human beings and relations between them. Such an analysis is conducive to psychological research perspective[58] through which subjectivity is manifested, among others, by self-awareness and self-knowledge (orientation-cognition); indication of the criteria of good and evil and the ability to evaluate oneself according to these criteria (emotional-motivational sphere); the ability of self-control and agency, i.e. to control oneself, control actions and development and to take responsibility for one's own actions (executive sphere)[59].

The mechanism of subjective out-of-body experience (OBE) of entities within analytically separate political space (diagram 3) is an illustration of subjective experience agency, wherefrom a psychological point of view, two complementary processes are shown in order to generate actual subjectivity, i.e. endogenous constitution of subjectivity (the situation forming auto-subjectivity, where the individual "I" becomes a fully-fledged agent) and exogenous strengthening of subjective agency (obtaining the personal influence and control over the external environment).

---

[57] J. C. Alexander, *Action and Its Environments: Toward a New Synthesis*, Columbia University Press, New York, 1988, pp. 210–218.

[58] In other words, we can talk here about one of the types of theoretical explanation dominated by (methodological individualism). In this case methodological individualism attempts to place the focus of determinacy in the psychological realm, so that all explanation of social phenomena could be reduced to psychological terms, i.e. attributes of individuals. More in: E. Nagel, *The Structure of Science. Problems in the Logic of Scientific Explanation*, Routledge & Kegan Paul, London1961, pp. 540–546.

[59] M. Jarymowicz, *Psychologiczne podstawy podmiotowości. Szkice teoretyczne, studia empiryczne*, Wydawnictwo Naukowe PWN, Warszawa 2008, pp.10–11.

Diagram 3: Subjective approach to political reality

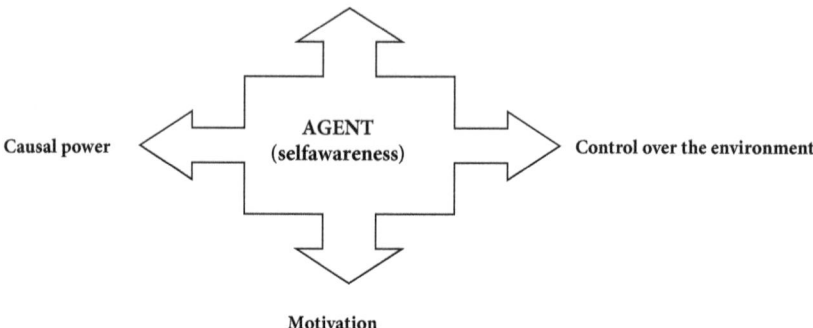

Source: own work

The diagram shows the dynamic process of the formation of subjectivity, where analytically separate entity within the specified ambient conditions is subject to two complementary processes, i.e. internal empowerment and external empowerment. In the first case we are dealing with the phenomenon of subjective self-awareness, where the agent defined by the state of self-awareness can define oneself, learn or assess oneself against others, the environment, as well as with respect to oneself. In this option, we can talk about the subjectivity only if essential self-reflection takes place, which is associated with the will to be an agent.

On the other hand, in the second case we are dealing with the process of disclosure of the inherent strength (energy) of entities, including self-awareness elements, in the external environment, where the realization of agency means:

1. Subjective OBE – the development of human capacity. Alienation interpreted as a measurable indicator of man's dominion over the forces of nature can be understood in two ways: as individual autocracy, i.e. as self-determination and/or fulfillment of individual agents (extensive development of human power, spiritual dispositions and self-knowledge through which unrelieved and objectified agent is formed. In other words, it is an embodiment of the personal potential for oneself and outside one's borders – in the external environment); as the production of collective social forms, which are distributed among the population as a whole (transfer of the subjective potential

by both the individual as well as collective agents for the benefit of the entire community)[60].

2. Causal power – in this approach the agent in political reality is characterized by gradable agency, which means that the effects of various actions or decisions taken by the agent result "directly" from the agent, i.e. have the source of agency. In other words, the results of various activities in the social world are not dependent on changes and/or external variables, but mostly based on the agent, their energy, ingenuity, activity and aspirations (in some cases gradable causality is synonymous with human causality, i.e. the individual causality[61]). At the same time it should be added that in political practice we rarely deal with an isolated causal force, where the agent becomes the primary or sole actor of change in the social world (keeping the causal logic is the only and fundamental strength of the causal relationship between the subject and the environment). In most cases causality of the agent is complex, which means that it takes different forms and intensity (managerial, executive, aiding perpetration, partisanship, incitement, etc.), as well as dependent directly or indirectly on different socio-structural conditions (the form and quality of the driving force of the agent depends on the needs, functions and adaptive changes or innovation; the agent provides a particular effect in a strictly defined set of circumstances).

3. Control over the environment – belief and self-conscious entity towards the control over the contemporary reality, where through the rational, conscious and sovereign action (idealistic attributes of any action, which in practice are usually relative and gradable[62]) and under certain conditions and by appropriate means an agent satisfies needs, interests, aspirations and ambitions (here, throughout the activity of individual agents, there is a potential, as well as a real ability to influence and control the external environment, where the agent does not exist "for the world", but it is the world that exists "for the agent").

4. Motivation effect – intentional and/or intended call by the specific effects from the external environment. When the agent observes measurable impact of their activity or activities in the socio-political space, the sense of agency

---

60 Z. Cackowski, *Człowiek jako podmiot działania praktycznego i poznawczego*, Warszawa 1979, pp. 90–121.
61 E. Mayr, *Understanding Human Agency*, Oxford University Press, New York 2011, pp. 36–45.
62 Humanist interpretation developed by "the Poznań school", inter al. by Jerzy Kmita. More in: J. Kmita, *Essays on the Theory of Scientific Cognition*, Springer Science, Business Media B.V., Dordrecht 1991.

increases, which in turn leads to an increase in internal motivation (lack of internal motivation to act means passive – not creative, reception and functioning in the environment).

It is worth referring to praxeological interpretations on agency, which has distinct characteristics, and more importantly, is not limited to the above described perspectives. In the praxeological meaning of perpetration it is related to the operation. In this sense:

> To act – or at east to act on reflection – means to change reality in a more or less conscious manner; to strive for a definite goal under given conditions by appropriate means in order to pass from existing conditions to conditions corresponding to the adopted goal; to include into reality factors determining the passage from a system of initial conditions to be determined to a system of definite final conditions. The action thus to be brought about requires triple determination: 1) determination of the goal, 2) determination of conditions involving reality, 3) determination of means adjusted both to the chosen goal and to existing reality[63].

In praxeology, agenthood is identified with is threefold relationship occurring between a specific perpetrator (operator), any impulse (act of bigger and /or smaller effort performed by the perpetrator; impulse as such is directional, intentional, is an impulse towards something), work (due to any reason which is an impulse of any kind; an event which changes the thing or the state of a thing). Hence:

> The agent of an event is the perpetrator whose free impulse is the cause of that event. (…) Every impulse is directional and intentional; it is an impulse Ahmed at something; we, of course, are always agents not only of what we intended, but, in so many instances of precisely what we did not intend[64].

Causative relationship that exists between the acting agent/perpetrator and broadly defined environment is stressed here, where the latter is potentially and actually dependent on the impulse of any perpetrator. The perpetrator and/or an accomplice are primarily creators of the works, which means that:

> A result is always an event, and an event is always either a change of something or a state of something. Now, by the product of a given agent with respect to his given free impulse, we mean any object (or thing) the state of, or change in, which was the result of that agent with respect to that free impulse[65].

---

63 T. Kotarbiński, *Praxiology. An Introduction to the Sciences of Efficient Action*, Pergamon Press, Oxford 1965, p. 10.
64 Ibid. pp. 17–18.
65 Ibid. p. 29.

In such circumstances, the manifestation of subjectivity, whether individual or collective, is a state of dependence of something/someone on the perpetrator variously defined, and precisely on any impulse of the same perpetrator. At the same time, one should remember that subjectivity understood as the action of the perpetrators, as well as products of the same action may be more or less conscious, i.e. any perpetration is characterized by a gradable expediency and rationality of the agent.

From the previous analysis it can be concluded that a subjective perspective at the political area which is in principle an anthropocentric-psychological approach, is basically a reduction in the cognitive sense as well as in theoretical and methodological ones. In this variant, the duality of subject vs. structure is described and explained through the perspective and/or the predominance of one component – the agent as such. In addition, the epistemological orientation emphasizes that the polymorphic political reality during the test should take the subjective stance both in input and output position. Most often such attitude in research is based on a subjective analysis of social issues, where science-based claims for explaining theses are related to the individual agent and, more specifically, to its activity, behavior, motivation and introspection; where society as such is analyzed through the prism of the overall social structures, but in the context of these entities it belongs to the whole structure; where the leading roles are played by actors and the interactions between them, and not by the structural-functional image and/or correlative society.

Subjective perspective means aiming explanations of the political practice at the individualist settlements (single agent), where many aspects of cognitive and research relations at the junction of the subject-structure are ignored. In such conditions, single causality is conceptually and analytically "separated", even excessively appreciated against multivariate analyses of political science. It should be added that such theoretical and methodological process does not notice how important the accuracy is with regard to the phenomenon of an individual agent. It does not notice certain regularity on the objective level (needs, interests, conditions for their implementation) as well as on the subjective level (consciousness of agent – knowledge, feelings, aspirations). Individuality is not something "carved from the whole" or something emerging from the "outside" of the properties of the environment. It is rather the configuration product of structural, processual, situational and unique predispositions of an individual, which anyway also gain specificity due to the uniqueness of these determinants. In other words, this means breaking the monopoly power of agents, where researchers emphasize that despite distinct ontological and explanatory nature of the agent it is always a component and/or an inalienable part of an existing social structure.

Subjective look at the political area with the help of the reductionist mechanism paves the way for psycho-personal flashbacks and justifications, where subjectivity is usually a subjective determination of boundaries and draws a field of impact unit within the external environment; where subjectivity is synonymous with the separate status (position) in the political area; where the achievement of subjectivity is gradable, which means:

1. Scaled self-awareness – graded agent orientation, where the maximum level of self-awareness is the full and throughout the awareness of agent's own "I", self-control cognitive-causal self-control, the possibility of intellectual and decision-making opportunities, including propensities to many intra-subjective restrictions as well as structural restrictions. At the opposite pole there is a minimum level of self-awareness that negates the maximum.
2. Scaled power and influence of external subjective graded orientation, where the maximum power and influence is the complete alienation and control of "I" over a piece of external reality, the causal course of events, as well as the facts, events or processes involving the agent. At the opposite pole there is the minimum power and influence of the agent, which negates the maximum.

2.2 Structural approach to the political space

The initial perspective for the structural policy is an axiom relating to the originality of the social structure as a whole (timeless social skeleton) and the duplication of the dynamic interaction of symptoms included in its composition. In this sense, there is no public social structure where a hypothetical loss of the structure, if not impossible, would mean the formation of amorphous, even chaotic collection of individuals. In this perspective, the social structure is an inalienable attribute of every social organization, which is associated with the fact that it is a system of relations between people, social groups, organizations or institutions common both in microscale, as well as in the macroscale (social structure takes various forms and is synonymous with such phenomena as: the hierarchy, distance, inequality, roles, positions, divisions and social stratification)[66].

---

66 Contemporary social science shows at least three ways by which structure is defined: 1. Macrosocial perspective defining structure as the pattern underlying the history of human societies; 2.Microsocialanalyses defining structure as persistent aspects of social behavior (structures are produced at the individual level and can, in principle, be explained by individual-level laws alone); 3. Multilevel view – this approach is concerned

Such epistemological stance emphasizing the role and importance of different types of structures in the process of shaping the political reality includes automatically the issue of duality of social agent or object, where the structural perspective enriches its value, even absolutizes the structuring process (imperialism of the social object) while depreciating also the "understanding sociology", particularly the statements regarding the activity of agents (imperialism of the subject)[67]. At the same time we cannot forget that the concept of "structure" in relation to "agent" in the widely understood social sciences was, and still is, defined in a different way. Therefore, the "structure" can be understood, on the one hand, as something external to the agent (structure explained as "impersonal" or "non-subjective" social system), on the other hand, the economic structure, in which agents play a fundamental role (structure interpreted as existing, relationship linked together between the agents, which combined by bond and/or a sense of community formed a given structural integrity. Most often the structure exhibits the complexity of higher order, which is not only a system of mechanistic relationship or circumstances. Examples include management teams, team leadership, collective bodies, etc.).

No less important is the fundamental distinction between the synchronous (static) and diachronic (dynamic) structure. In the first case the research of the structure takes the form of analysis of the coexistence of items/phenomena or the coexistence of their properties. It is a scientific attempt to diagnose, describe and explain the structure of the whole and/or a fragment of social reality with the help of analytically generated synchronous section of that whole, where any structural dynamics is rejected, i.e. it is abstracted from the coefficient of movement, in favour of the study, among others, of co-existential or morphological laws (from the point of view of methodological procedures, static testing of structures is based on the rejection parameter of the time). The second case refers to diachronic structural studies, where the key to understanding and explaining specific structure (the social entity) is dynamic and variable over time of relatedness occurring between analytically distinct elements of that structure (parts of society). In this arrangement, diachronic perspective concentrates on the study of developmental, dynamic, causal laws, etc., that make up the overall picture of internal structural dynamics, as well as the continuum of dependence

---

with structure at both the micro and the macro level. More in: D. Willer, J. Szmatka, *Structural Formulations and Elementary Theory*, [in:] J. Szmatka, J. Skvoretz, J. Berger (eds.), *Status, Network, and Structure: Theory Development in Group Processes*, Stanford University Press, Stanford 1997, p. 274.

67 A. Giddens, *The Constitution of Society. Outline of the Theory of Structuration*, Polity Press, Cambridge 1990, p. 2.

and the influence of the external environment[68]. For agent-structure duality it means a research situation in which agents, both individual as well as collective, apart from being an essential component of the structural entity, additionally become the causative factor of such a structure (the agent as such plays a double role here– an instrument and creator of structural changes of socio-historical processes, revolutionary changes, etc.).

Considering the category of subjectivity through the perspective of structure certainly has its historical and theoretical base, which is expressed in structural-functional thinking. In most cases, these considerations are based on methodological holism, where all scientific explanations of socio-political reality are always (and only) based on the analysis of a particular social unit and on the elements comprising this reality. Thus, structuralism in social studies as a method of exploring and explaining the phenomena, processes or states of affairs accepts the study of synchronous dynamic structures and their invariants (diachronic structuralism). In this sense, the purpose of scientific analysis is first to clarify the directly unobservable structures, dependencies or accuracy occurring between analytically separate levels of the whole society. It should be remembered that the static and dynamic testing of structures, despite the fact that they are standing against each other in a certain opposition, should be treated as complementary in their content and scope, which in practice means a more accurate scientific description or a more adequate explanation or prediction. This complementarity is necessary because it results from the double view of social reality, which means that:

> However, for knowledge, understandably, not only the discovery and formulation of the laws of motion and development of the reality to be investigated (developmental laws, dynamic and causal laws) are important, but also discovery and formulation of the laws of the structure of the relatively isolated systems that find themselves in a state of relative equilibrium. (…) Reality is indeed in constant motion and change; it nevertheless experiences states of a relative equilibrium of the elements, i.e. of a part of that whole that we call reality. From this also follows the double view of reality and the doubleness of its uniformities: It is both dynamic and static, changing and (relatively) unchanging; at the same time dynamic (causal) and synchronic (coexistential, morphological) laws rule it. The formula which we have here is not »either – or«, but »both – and«[69].

---

68   A. Schaff, *Structuralism as an Intellectual Current*, [in:] J. J. Wiatr (ed.), *Polish Essays in the Methodology of the Social Sciences*, D. Reidel Publishing Company, Dordrecht 1979, pp. 105–120.
69   Ibid., pp. 121–123.

No less important element in the wider structuralist orientation is the visibility of structural automatism, which in this case is synonymous with antihumanist vision of relations and socio-political processes, where the structuralist "rejection of the subject" takes place. An example of such theorizing are the views of Louis Althusser and Étienne Balibar, who while interpreting Marxism came to a different, more precisely non-dialectic, even anti-Marxist, hypostatization on the products of social interaction (overinterpretation of historicism). In this arrangement, an agent, both individual as well as collective, became only the "bearer of social categories" and/or "the result of the structure activity" or "unconscious executor" of existing social relations. This means that the situations of theoretical research, in which the structure interpreted as autonomous instances of the social formation, are primarily a combination of structural type, in which the agent is nowhere to be found (localizable):

> The real subject of each component history is the *combination* on which depend the elements and their relations, i.e. it is *something that is not a subject*. In this sense we can say that the first problem for a history as a science, for a theoretical history, is the determination of the combination on which depend the elements which are to be analysed, i.e. it is to determine the structure of a sphere of relative autonomy, such as what Marx calls the process of production and its modes[70].

In this interpretation, the duality of agent-structure is in the whole of its traits and characteristics is reduced to one element, i.e. omnipotent structure, which, being a configurable whole is, on the one hand, something "absent", on the other hand, something "inherent" to the subject. Louis Althusser provided most complete definition of superiority of automatism and structures towards individual and collective agents:

> Structure of the relations of production determines the *places* and *functions* occupied and adopted by the agents of production, who are never anything more than the occupants of these places, insofar as they are the »supports« (*Träger*) of these functions. The true »subjects« (in the sense of constitutive subjects of the process) are therefore not these occupants or functionaries, are not, despite all appearances, the »obviousnesses« of the »given« of naïve anthropology, »concrete individuals«, »real men« – but *the definition and distribution of these places and functions. The true »subjects« are these definers and distributors: the relations of production* (and political and ideological social relations). But since these are »relations«, they cannot be thought within the category *subject*[71].

---

70 L. Althusser, É. Balibar, *Reading Capital*, Verso, London & New York 2009, p. 250.
71 Ibid., p. 180. Such logic leads Althusser to the thesis of structural causality, which replaces linear causality. According to him: "If the field of economic phenomena is no longer this planar space but a deep and complex one, if economic phenomena are

In other words, any agent that can be defined and identified in the socio – structural area of their existence, performs the role or function owing to the current structural configuration where social, political or economic relations pre-exist in these agents, i.e. their existence, rank, importance or status are directly dependent on the structural conditions. Here, the agent (defined social part) is secondary to the structure (defined social entity) in ontological, epistemological and methodological terms.

In turn, the functionalist approach in social studies focuses on indicating the participation of any components of the social system in maintaining society as a whole (analysis of the feature of the entity/social structure, thanks to which this entity/structure maintains consistency and relative balance. The concept of function, however, can be interpreted, among others, as: function in the sense of activity or task-performance of an object or entity; function in the sense of relation of interdependence with activities of other entities; function in the sense of interdependence of special quality, especially in regard to ends, such as maintenance of a system; function in the sense of consequences of structures or structural items[72]). The following distinguishing features can describe the general characteristics of functionalism:

1. It presupposes the existence of real, lasting social structures, but functionalism subordinates the term "structure" to the concept of function (in this sense it emphasizes that a structure can be multifunctional so it can perform various functions; on the other hand, the function can be fulfilled by various structures).
2. It analyses unity and social objectives of the entity (the entire social system as such).
3. It tries to find functional equivalents and correlations between the existing states of affairs in a particular social system.
4. It captures the multifaceted causal explanation, i.e. not in a rigid relationship "specific cause-effect", but taking into account the multiplicity of causes and effects[73].

---

    determined by their *complexity* (i.e. their structure), the concept of linear causality can no longer be applied to them as it has been hitherto. A different concept is required in order to account for the new form of causality required by the new definition of the object of Political Economy, by its »complexity«, i.e. by its peculiar determination: *the determination by a structure*". Ibid., p. 184.

72 W. W. Isajiw, *Causation and Functionalism in Sociology*, Routledge, New York 2010, p. 72.
73 K. von Beyme, *Die politischen Theorien der Gegenwart. Eine Einführung*, Sringer Fachmedien, Wiesbaden 2006, pp. 122–136.

It should be remembered that the concept of structure in the broadly defined social sciences, including the political science is ambiguous, which manifests itself in the freedom of interpretation and numerous connotative discrepancies among competent researchers. In order to facilitate a reliable and representative way to make explication of this concept it should be stated that the social structure is defined in at least three ways:

1. As the geometry of the system and/or type of general abstract form.
2. As a type appropriate to the reality scope of elements and compounds forming relatively permanent and coherent set.
3. As an organized set of dependencies, which involve different types of agents.

In the first approach the social structure means the geometry of the system and/or some kind of abstract forms, which are present in a variety of social objects. At the same time, this form is directly dependent on the approach which researchers take in researching socio-political phenomena, i.e. through the selection of a research perspective there is a possibility to define social structure in a different manner. Therefore, in the typological distinction one can specify the following social structures:

    1. Long-range social structure– whole variety of phenomena from the analytically dedicated level of social reality (such structures exist at all levels of the multilevel social reality, i.e. at the micro level – small groups; meso level – local communities, as well as macro level – great social groups or big social systems). These are the hidden and deep structures, i.e. they are some what an invisible, internal skeleton events for this category (the phenomena of a given level of reality), but they really exist in the social world, but from the point of view of the researcher they are fuzzy and anti-substantial.

    2. Short-range social structure– the whole variety of phenomena from the same levels of reality that are substantial, real and concrete. These entities exist inside an object (social group social process), and are therefore a basic skeleton and/or the backbone of given social objects with which it is possible to identify and clarify the specific characteristics and properties of respective elements of the social object (the social group), as well as the characteristics and properties of the subject as a whole (mode of operation)[74].

On the other hand, in the latter case, the social structure is synonymous with the world in which there is no place for random tangle of phenomena, on the

---

74 J. Szmatka, *Małe struktury społeczne. Wstęp do mikrosocjologii strukturalnej*, Wydawnictwo Naukowe PWN, Warszawa 2007, pp. 34–37.

contrary – it is a reality with numerous areas characterized by relative stability and internal governance. Hence, the social structure is type-specific elements of reality; elements and compounds between them that make up a relatively permanent and consistent collection and/or internal correlation. But this complexity of reality is expressed precisely by the social structure in which one can distinguish between three layers and/or spheres, and each of them characterizes the type of element and the compounds relevant to these elements:

1. The first layer – the social structure is presented as a collective consciousness and is defined by quantitative and qualitative features of this community (the conditions, in which a community exists; ways of living within the community). In this case we are talking about a substrate material in all its aspects – as time, space, size and density of population, its economic, social or civilizational conditions – where the substrate material limits the community and/or designates what occurs in the community and what can be implemented.
2. The second layer – the social structure mixes with the elements of culture which create the right people to the world of signs, meanings, and values. In this sense, it refers to the sphere of cultural commonality (the symbolic sphere), where the system of accepted meanings, recognized values, truths, rules, standards or aesthetic codes sets a specific range and a hierarchy of aspirations for all members of the community. In this way, the cultural and symbolic spheres create the order and structure.
3. The third layer – the social structure consists of elements through which the structure is realized in the active form of human society, i. e. the sphere of social activity, and more specifically, the activities and events with entities that shape the relationship between people and create an organization of collective life[75].

In the case of the third interpretation, the social structure, apart from the cultural structure, creates a comprehensive environment and/or general social framework for human existence. Here, the social structure is seen as a key element of a larger whole, i.e. social system, which performs specific functions for the integration and maintenance of homeostasis of that system (a functional analysis, where it is emphasized that the researchers of social phenomena should concentrate all their explanatory efforts on the analysis of inter al.: function/dysfunction of the social system, the requirements and the mechanisms by which functions are

---

[75] P. Rybicki, *Struktura społecznego świata, Studia z teorii społecznej*, Państwowe Wydawnictwo Naukowe, Warszawa 1979, pp. 167–170, 543–544.

fulfilled in the system; context of functional or structural constraints of the social system[76]). At the same time, the social structure may be defined as "an organized set of social relationships in which members of the society or group are variously implicated" and the cultural structure "organizes a set of normative values governing behavior which is common to members of a designated society or group". It should be added that the functioning of the social structure is analyzed in this context in the light of the theory of anomie (loss and/or lack of standards), where the internalization level of certain goals, values and standards by individuals making up the society testifies to the emergence of anomie or lack thereof. In this sense, symbiosis and convergence of cultural practice, including aspirations, needs, goals of individuals to practice institutional is a sign of conformity and integration of members of the public with generally accepted models of education, codes of aesthetic or canon of values, where there is full socialization and absorption mechanism of institutionalized patterns of society as a whole by community members as their own. This refers to the relative social stability, where the goals, values and socially assigned functions are clearly defined, and the behavior of the agents belonging to the society is under control, and, to some extent, predictable. While the gap between culture and structure leads to anomie and/or aberrant behavior, which are a sign of disagreement as to the standards, objectives or cultural values functioning in the community and socially structure the operational capacity of members of that community. Therefore:

> Cultural values may help to produce behaviour which is at odds with the mandates of the values themselves. On this view, the social structure strains the cultural values, making action in accord with them readily possible for those occupying certain statuses within the society ad difficult or impossible for others. (…) When the cultural and the social structure are mal-integrated, the first calling for behavior and attitudes which the second precludes, there is a strain toward the breakdown of the norms, toward normlessness. (…)Simple anomie refers to the state of confusion in a group or society which is subject to conflict between value-systems, resulting in some degree of uneasiness and a sense of separation from the group; acute anomie, to the deterioration and, at the extreme, the disintegration of value-systems, which results in marked anxieties[77].

Various theoretical and methodological concepts with regard to what social structure really is generate consequences of such definitional ambiguity. In this context, four concepts of social structure can be distingushed:

---

76 R. K. Merton, *Social Theory and Social Structure*, The Free Press, New York 1968, pp. 104–109.
77 Ibid., pp. 216–217.

1. Patterns of aggregate behaviour that are stable over time – where the social structure is defined as the persistent pattern of behavior and/or specific product of individual and aggregate behavior of different types of political agents (social structure perspective through the prism of methodological assumptions of individualism).
2. Law-like regularities that govern the behavior of social fact – in which the explanation of the social structure is based on the rejection of the psychological perspective, including behavioral perspective, in favor of a holistic perspective, where the social structure is seen as something completely independent (released) from the perpetration of political agents. An example of the anti-individualist and/or anti-reductionist approach to the question of the existence of the social structure is at least functional structuralist proposal by Talcott Parsons who, in the spirit of sociologism, shows versatility and stability of the social structure in relation to individual behaviours. In this perspective, the social structure:

   Stands between the cultural system including its religious components on the one hand, the personality system on the other. And the focus of the set of interconnections is the set of values institutionalized in the society and internalized in the personality. Crucial as social values are in the dynamics of the social system, in the nature of the case they cannot be the sole determinants of processes on the society. These also are a function of the resources that are available for the implementing of values and goals, including the organizational resources. They are a function of many processes of internal adjustment within the society by which various strains and tensions can be handled[78].

3. Systems of human relationships among social positions – social structure is explained through the prism of relationship and/or links between actors/agents that come together in numerous, often innumerable social interactions (such recognition of the social structure exists especially in the Marxist tradition, in symbolic interactionism, network theory or sociological realism). In this view:

   Social structure is a nexus of connections among [human actors], causally affecting their actions and in turn causally affected by them. The causal effects of the structure on individuals are manifested in certain structured interest, resources, powers, constraints and predicaments that are built into each position by the web of relationships. This comprise the material circumstances in which people must act and which motivate them to act in certain ways[79].

---

[78] T. Parsons, *Social Structure and Personality*, The Free Press A Division of the Macmillan Company, New York 1970, pp. 297–298.
[79] D. Porpora, *Four Concepts of Social Structure*, [in:] M. S. Archer, R. Bhaskar, A. Collier, T. Lawson, A. Norrie (ed.), *Critical Realism: Essential Readings*, Routledge, London 1998, p. 344.

4. Collective rules and resources that structure behaviour – here the structure is interpreted both as base and resources where the explanation of the social structure is based both on the subject, i.e. the individual causative agency as well as on objective social structure. In other words, it is the agent-structure connection (approximation), where a full explanation of a particular social structure always comprises two elements, i.e. it cannot ignore any part (the theory of structuration by Antohny Giddens is an example, on the one hand, the social structure is constituted by agents, and more particularly, its activity, on the other hand, the same structure determines the quantity, quality, character or the personal type of activity)[80].

In fact, the last concept concerning the formation of the social structure is an attempt to overcome the duality of structure versus agent where structuration theory as proposed by Anthony Giddens, which assumes the starting point for the duality of structure. In this system, the constitution of agents in the sociopolitical space, as well as the structure of that space are not just two independent processes, but they testify to duality. This means a situation in which we can speak of two-element relationship between the structure and the social system, which is accompanied by a process of structuration (diagram 4).

Diagram 4: The Duality of Structure by Anthony Giddens

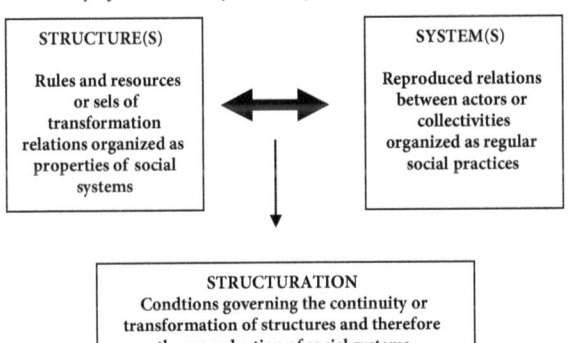

Source: own work based on A. Giddens[81]

---

80 D. Elder-Vass, *The Causal Power of Social Structures. Emergence, Structure and Agency*, Cambridge University Press, Cambridge 2010, pp. 76–86.
81 A. Giddens, *The Constitution of Society. Outline of the Theory of Structuration*, Polity Press, Cambridge 1990, p. 25.

The diagram shows that the structure understood as "consistently organized set of rules and resources" is permanent and non-spatial; structure in which there is "absence of the agent." At the same time, it is a social system, in which the structure is embroiled, includes reproduction in time and space relationships between agents, which are key human activities, namely resources and rules structure used by actors/agents. Therefore, the structure itself is not just "external" to the parties, but it is also a source of restrictions, freedom, creativity and causal force of these agents (structural properties are both in the middle of the process, as well as the result of the activity of symptoms; they constitute the elements that make permanent generation of causative operations possible)[82]. Structuring is an equally important element in this diagram, which means the continuous structuring of social relations in time and space under the structure duality. In this perspective, structuring means continuous reproduction of society through the transformation and/or change within the dependencies of structural system. It should be remembered that any change within society, i.e. within the social system, is associated with the causative operation, which is situated "between" limitations (e.g. moral or structural limitations) and opportunities posed by a particular structure. From now on we can talk about the natural duality of subject-structure, where there is a constant tension between the activity of individual entities and the structural stimulation; where, on the one hand, the agent as such is a "powerhouse" of any changes within the social structure (according to the thesis – nothing without the agent, all about the agent), on the other hand:

> Human societies, or social systems, would plainly not exist without human agency. But it is not the case that actors create social systems: they reproduce or trans form them, remaking what is already made in the continuity of *praxis*. The span of time-space distanciation is relevant here. In general (although certainly not universally) it is true that the greater the time-space distanciation of social systems – the more their institutions bite into time and space – the more resistant they are to manipulation or change by any individual agent. This meaning of constraint is also coupled to enablement. Time-space distanciation closes off some possibilities of human experience at the same time as it opens up others[83].

Summing up, it is clear that the structural perspective of politics which only assumes valuing the structural conditions in fact attempts to belittle the role and importance of the agent. In most cases, structural approach to the matter of politics

---

82 Ibid. Also on this subject in: P. Baert, F. Carreira da Silva, *Social Theory in the Twentieth Century and Beyond*, Polity Press, Cambridge, pp. 159–169.
83 A. Giddens, *The Constitution of Society. Outline of the Theory of Structuration*, Polity Press, Cambridge 1990, p. 171.

shows that no serious scientific analysis of political reality can "get rid" of the agent as such, and more specifically the activity of agents, which is the core of every political practice. Besides, the structural perspective does not mean level ling the subjective factor – it is the opposite –it involves adopting a completely different epistemological and methodological perspective, in which the leading role is played by objective and structural aspects and/or holist view of political reality. In this arrangement the foreground does not extend forever (and only) psycho-personal flashback or considerations, but the justification referring to compounds, compositions, hierarchy position and relationships within a given structure (analysis of patterns, relationships, policies, resources, positions, antagonisms, statuses or social roles). In this way, not only is unbridled subjective OBE of agents and/or their unfettered causal power manifested, but the environment and /or the surrounding is rather presented, which fulfill the potential and actual agency. Of course, there are considerable differences associated with defining the social structure as such, but it can be assumed that this semiotic ambiguity is conditioned mainly by the progressive complexity and temporality of the whole society. In addition, structural political perspective means:

1. Holistic multifactorial thinking, where economic activity is not the only but one of many factors included in the scientific explanation of political reality.
2. Extending the research perspective by structural and functional dependencies, where the social entity (including the concept of subjectivity) is analyzed in various relationships, invariants, levels and contexts, which means rejection of microreduction understood as a mechanism of artificial simplification of any explanation to the analysis of the agent as such.

2.3 Complementarity of subjective and structural models

The current explication of the duality 'economic activity vs current social structure was limited to two separate reasons and/or group of arguments, where through a detailed presentation of different theoretical and methodological categorical or subjective approaches or social structure primitivism were indicated. Despite the accuracy of certain statements or justifications in relation to political reality, it is clear that both the subjective as well as structural perspective is just a naive reductionism, where there are attempts to reduce such a highly complex and multidimensional problem of agent-structure interdependence to the two groups of factors, i.e. subjective-psychological (economic analysis) and objective-structural (structural analysis). Each of the answers mentioned so far is the scientific shortcut. In fact, this approach rejects the dialectical method of explanation of the multifaceted issues 'agent versus structure'.

In this system, one should consider the strategy of synthesizing in the dialectical spirit, where dialectic becomes an authenticating premise for the concept of dual ontology assuming the reality and know ability of the political reality of both agents (individual agents and/or public parts), as well as of the social groups, collective bodies, management teams, great human communities (collective agents and/or the social entities). In other words, the ontological dialectic forming process of agent-structure dualism leads to a scientific strategy for synthesizing while rejecting thinking in terms of alternatives (be it the agent or the structure) in favour of dialectical complementarity (agent and structure). Dialectical method here is the intellectual mechanism for "synthetic overcome", where, on the one hand, it connects to the plane of individual agents with structural ones and vice versa, on the other hand, it shows the relative separation of the two spheres. According to the theorem:

> Both ontological dichotomies outlined earlier – structure-action and continuity-change – inspire theoretical syntheses. One important line of theoretical development is the theory of agency, taking up the first opposition (of structure and action) as it main preoccupation; another line is historical sociology, focusing on the second opposition (of continuity and change). From different points of departure they gradually converge on the common image of society as a dynamic process in which people, by their own actions, persistently produce and reproduce the context of their existence, social structures which later become the initial conditions – constraining or facilitating – for further actions. Social life as a process of structural emergence via actions, and the tension between actions and structures as the ultimate moving force of the process are the ideas that form the core of recent theories of agency, as well as of historical sociology[84].

Undoubtedly, the direct inspiration for the adoption and application of dialectical explanatory diagram originated from the theses worked out by the "Poznań school", which based on Marxism presented an original way of analyzing

---

84 P. Sztompka, *Evolving Focus on Human Agency in Contemporary Social Theory*, [in:] P. Sztompka (ed.), *Agency and Structure. Reorienting Social Theory*, Routledge, London & New York 2014, p. 35. Another example of dialectic synthesis of classical sociological antinomies, including agent-structure distinction is the functional approach. More in: J. C. Alexander, *Formal and Substantive Voluntarism in the Work of Talcott Parsons: A Theoretical and Ideological Interpretation*, [in:] P. Hamilton (ed.), *Talcott Parsons. Critical Assessments*, vol. II, Routledge, New York 1992, pp. 153–172; B. Agger, *The Discourse of Domination. From the Frankfurt School to Postodernism*, Northwestern University Press, Evanston 1992, pp. 57–72.

the political space. This refers to a coherent theoretical and methodological interpretation, which is based on theoretical historicism which successfully pointed inter al. research tools such as: directive interpretation of the humanities; directive subjective-objective coincidence; theoretical assumptions of political holism or abstract method based on the formulation of the idealisational laws and the process of their concretization in the formation of scientific explanatory statements[85].

In order to overcome the above reductionist mechanism, which boils down to the glorification of the agent or structure, in the context of a detailed analysis of politics it should be borne in mind that each time the starting point of scientific research on the social and political reality should consist of the two key determinants – complexity and temporality. In principle, acceptance and recognition of such determinants of politics automatically, almost *apriori*, sets a different conceptualization of the problem of economic activity – it replaces the social structure. We could say that the two differentiators release a dialectical way of thinking, where both the agent and the structure are shown in the dialectic micro and macro-social processes. This state of affairs means that the researcher sees the political reality not as a homogeneous social environment in which individuals, groups or communities are the predictable community with clearly defined objectives, needs and values, but as a complex space of flows and/or fluctuations in the dialectical dependence and dichotomous cores (see. diagram 2).They are a sign of the emergence of mobility. In this perspective, the public is not being fossilized, given once and forever, but changeable – it is a task, an assignment where general social framework for order creation is constantly redefining; the demarcation line at the intersection of the external environment – the internal structure becomes blurry, almost transparent and cross-border.

At the same time the heterogeneity in the world of politics makes it difficult to clearly identify one most important factor, with which any scientific analyses will be conducted. On the contrary, we have to deal with the "liberation" and/

---

85 Among numerous works of the „school of Poznan" the following works are particularly important: L. Nowak, *Property and Power: Towards a Non-Marxian Historical Materialism*, D. Reidel Publishing Company, Dordrecht 1983; L. Nowak, *The Structure of Idealization: Towards a Systematic Interpretation of the Marxian Idea of Science*, D. Reidel Publishing Company, Dordrecht 2010; J. Topolski, *Methodology of History*, D. Reidel Publishing Company, Dordrecht 1976; J. Kmita, *Problems in Historical Epistemology*, D. Reidel Publishing Company, Dordrecht 1988.

or complete rejection of monistic perception by individual researchers in the broadly defined social sciences including political science. The mechanism of negation of monistic perception (one-dimensional perception) is also reflected in the agent-structure duality. In this sense, the agent independent of the structure and vice versa is subject to criticism. It also indicates that we cannot artificially separate the two spheres of political space because the process of mutual agent-structure condition is so tightly bonded together that in the analysis it is difficult to isolate two supposedly different research approaches. This procedure is fundamentally false, which is associated with the fact that it is doomed to explanatory failure. Peter L. Berger and Thomas Luckmann very well captured this relationship:

> Since society exists as both objective and subjective reality, any adequate theoretical understanding of it must comprehend both these aspects. As we have already argued, these aspects receive their proper recognition if society is understood in terms of an ongoing dialectical process composed of the three moments of externalization, objectification and internalization. As far as the societal phenomenon is concerned, these moments are *not* to be thought of as occurring in a temporal sequence. Rather society and each part of it are simultaneously characterized by these three moments, so that any analysis in terms of only one or two of them falls short. The same is true with the individual member of society, who simultaneously externalizes his own being into the social world and internalizes it as an objective reality. In other words, to be in society is to participate in its dialectic[86].

In this perspective, properly conducted research in political science should be based on multivariate analysis of two contexts that talks about the unbreakable bond and/or the context of the unity of the agent (the study of subjective aspects of human action, i.e. the order of values and/or axiology and knowledge and/or cognitive and praxeological aspects of a given agent) and the objective context (the study of specific functional structure, the element of which is the action taken and/or performed by the agent, which is linked to objective circumstances of activity). The moment of capturing multi-level objective-subjective dependence in the political world can be seen very clearly in the Marxist materialist dialectic, where the concept of social development can be explicated by the following traits of reality as such which function among active players:

---

86 P. L. Berger, T. Luckmann, *The Social Construction of Reality. A Treatise in the Sociology of Knowledge*, Penguin Books, New York 1966, p. 149.

1. Autodynamism – means putting the mechanism of change within the system given; emphasizing that the changes in the socio-political reality make up the interaction of elements remaining in the various relationships, including contradictions (contradictions and/or conflict).
2. Activism – a subjective-objective explanation of all social processes, where subjective aspects mean deliberate and conscious human activities and their incentive structures, and their results constitute what could be called objective conditions of human activity (social process is objective, i.e. it has an external nature in relation to human action as well as subjective, i.e. it is a human creation).
3. Holism – deals with all the social processes through an overall perspective, where no part of the process can be analyzed in isolation from the structural and functional dependence within the whole society.
4. Essentialism – an indication that social development depends on various factors that affect particular elements of reality differently and/or with a different "strength"[87].

These differentiators prove that multichannel relationship between the entity (entities), understood as a separate element of the social entity exists and replaces the social structure, which in this case is the actual and specific multi-element relationship. This coupling is basically so strong that it is indelible, i.e. an agent cannot function without the objective external-structural conditions whereas the very structural conditions are just an empty and hypothetical frameworks, in which there are potential rather than real frameworks, procedures, rules, relationships, dependencies, bonds or antagonisms (according to the thesis, where the substrate is human, there is a proper matter of politics, i.e. the intersubjective rules, relations, antagonisms, relationships). Therefore, any attempt at omissions and/or repudiation of any component not only makes the researcher apply methodological reduction, but also hypostasize in isolation from the real agent-based structural relationship. Additionally, we can say that discussed differentiators

---

[87] J. Topolski, *Methodology of History*, D. Reidel Publishing Company, Dordrecht 1976, pp. 193–218; 225–230.

coincide with the assumptions and methodological directives of historical epistemology that highlights the coincidences of subjective factors that are diverse in form and content with the objective ones as the essence of any changes in the socio-political practice[88].

---

[88] According to the thesis: "Social praxis consists of the totality of subjectively-rational human actions which, together with the accompanying system of objective socio-economic conditions (determined by the nature of relations of production and the level of development of the productive forces), forms a dynamic hierarchical functional structure relative to the property of reproducing existing objective conditions and/or producing conditions of a new type, with the provision that: (i) the various type of social praxis, or independent sections of the social division of labour, form functional substructures which are directly or indirectly subordinated to that substructure consisting in the fundamental »material« praxis, namely production and exchange; (ii) every type of social praxis includes a successive substructure: its socio-subjective context, i.e. the set of beliefs whose observance by individual participants in social praxis of a given type is a necessary condition for its providing adequate answers to the demands addressed to it by social praxis as whole". More in: J. Kmita, *Problems in Historical Epistemology*, D. Reidel Publishing Company, Dordrecht 1988, p. 16.

3. Political subjectivity in the morphogenetic approach

3.1 Critical realism

So far, the analysis of the problem of agency-structure in the political science has shown that in practice scientific and research issues are often the basic contradictory statements[89] in the matter of politics. Among the many topics covered in the first and second chapter, we can also see those associated with mutually exclusive ontological theses or contradictory statements concerning scientific sources of political cognition (differences resulting from the individualistic and holist approach). But from the point of view of further parts of the work, especially due to the detailed presentation of the morphogenetic approach, the realistic approach seems to be crucial[90].

The starting point for the presentation of the assumptions in critical realism[91] understood as an important and useful epistemological perspective in the social sciences is to consider a realistic initial strategy proposed by Roy Bhaskar with regard to the study of society who:

---

89 Basic statements are the current theoretical statements and/or systems of judgements of reality (scientific theories), which – apart from common knowledge–create *background knowledge*. More in: K. R. Popper, *Conjectures and Refutations. The Growth of Scientific Knowledge*, Routledge and Kegan Paul, London 1963.

90 Realism means many different philosophical concepts. Thus realism is mentiond in the dispute over universals; theory of perception; development of science; language. More in: S. Haack, *Realism*, [in:] I. Niiniluoto, M. Sintonen, J. Woleński (eds.), *Handbook of Epistemology*, Springer-Science, Business Media, B.V., Dordrecht 2004, pp. 415–436; R. N. Boyd, *The Current Status of Scientific Realism*, [in:] J. Lepin (ed.), *Scientific Realism*, Univeristy of California Press, London 1984, pp. 41–82.

91 The term critical realism was proposed in the 1920s of the 20th c. by the group of American philosophers who were critical about the naïve realist theory of perception and opposed idealism. This group included inter al.: Roy W. Sellars [*Critical Realism: A Study of the Nature and Conditions of Knowledge* (1916)]; George Santayana [*Realms of Being* (1927)]; Arthur O. Lovejoy [*The Revolt Against Dualism* (1960)]. Nowadays critical realism has been elaborated anew and propagated in science by inter al.: Roy Bhaskara [*A Realist Theory of Science* (1975)]; Margaret S. Archer [*Realist Social Theory: The Morphogenetic Approach* (1995)]; Andrew Collier [*Critical Realism: An Introduction to Roy Bhaskar's Philosophy*, (1994)] Andrew Sayer [*Realism and Social Science* (2000)].

Want[s] to distinguish sharply, then, between the genesis of human actions, lying in the reasons, intentions and plans of people, on the one hand, and the structures governing the reproduction and transformation of social activities, on the other, and hence between the domains of the psychological and the social sciences. The problem of how people reproduce any particular society belongs to a linking science of »socio-psychology«. It should be noted that engagement in social activity is itself a conscious human action which may, in general, be described either in terms of the agent's reason for engaging in it or in terms of its social function or role[92].

In other words, realistic view of the political world means coupling a realistic epistemology, where reality is independent of the learning agent (the negation of the idea of constructivist and postmodernist assumptions) with a critical attitude to the methodology of research. In the political science, realistic position means primarily the acceptance of the thesis of the political independence of political knowledge[93]. Hence the critical realists emphasize that different types of events, states of affairs or political processes are the result of specific, and more importantly, identifiable causal forces. At the same time, it does not mean that we can easily and clearly describe or explain all the causal relationships that constitute certain political phenomena. The state of the scientific inability to relate to the fact that causality (quantifiable causes/effects) is impossible to be directly captured and diagnosed in the political space in many moments because there are the so called deep structures that are essentially unobservable (no direct perception), which could mean a poor explanatory effectiveness of theoretical and methodological instruments in scientific analysis. Moreover, the adoption of realistic-critical perspective of research in political science is associated with the acceptance of the following statements: (1) although the political phenomena exist independently of our interpretation, our interpretation in a gradable way determines the results of observation of descriptions or explanations of these phenomena; (2) scientific knowledge about politics is prone to errors and conditioned theoretically. Therefore, if a scholar is to identify and explain the various

---

92 R. Bhaskar, *Societies*, [in:] M. Archer, R. Bhaskar, A. Collier, T. Lawson, A. Norrie (ed.), *Critical Realism: Essential Readings*, Routledge Taylor & Francis Group, London, New York 1998, p. 216. In another place Bhaskar writes that critical realism: „understood as consisting of transcendental realism as a general theory of science and critical naturalism as a special theory of social science (which includes the emancipator axiology entailed by the theory of explanatory critique)". More in: R. Bhaskar, *Dialectic: The Pulse of Freedom*, Routledge Taylor & Francis Group, London, New York 2008, p. 2

93 A. Sayer, *Realism and Social Science*, Sage, London 2000, p. 11.

cause-effect relationships operating within a political reality, they must firstly – understand the outside world, and secondly – the social structure of that world[94].

Complementing ontological and epistemic assumptions, differentiation was described by Bhaskar, who analytically identified three overlapping domains of reality as such, i.e.: real, actual and empirical (diagram 5). In this sense, the reality of the domain contains the actual domain (events or non-events generated by the causal mechanism) and empirical (observable and experimental events), which means that "reality" is synonymous with "causality". Therefore, real are only those generative mechanisms that are defined as both diverse forces of causal social structures as well as the specific activity of agents (actors) included in these structures. But researchers during scientific analyzes are not able to directly observe most generative mechanisms. In such conditions, the only proof of existence of such causal forces are observable results (effects) of generative activity[95].

Diagram 5: Bhaskar's three overlapping domains of reality

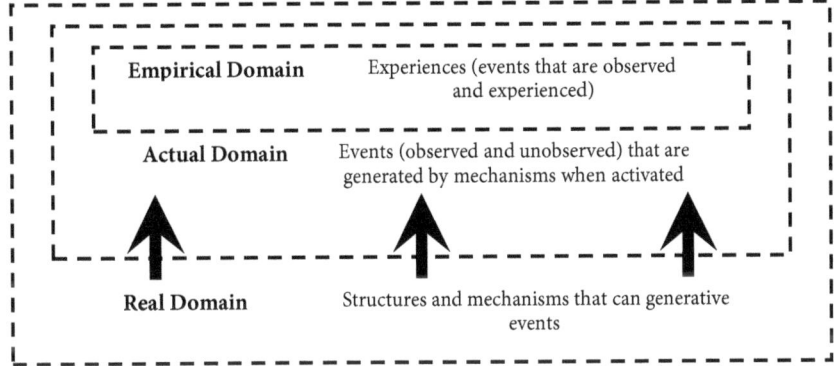

Source: own work based on J. Mingers[96]

In other words, the political reality, understood as an object of study, is an entity and/or structural complexity of higher order, which is the result of three

---

94 D. Marsh, P. Furlong, *A Skin not a Sweater: Ontology and Epistemology in Political Science*, [in:] D. Marsh, G. Stocker (eds.), *Theory and Methods in Political Science*, Palgrave Macmillan, London 2010, pp. 204–206.
95 R. Bhaskar, *A Realist Theory of Science*, Routledge, London & New York 2008, pp. 46–52. Also in: J. Mingers, *Systems Thinking, Critical Realism and Philosophy: A Confluenceof Ideas*, Routledge, New York 2014, pp. 10–47.
96 J. Mingers, *Systems Thinking…*, p. 19.

components (levels) – empirical, factual and real. Hence, the political space for critical realists is a comprehensive, complex and dynamic integrative entity, which cannot be reduced to the elements comprising it. This means that being a multi-entity it has a specific ontological independence, which is associated with the fact that it cannot be reduced to quantifiable elements comprising it. On the contrary, it is an entity, within which there is a specific causality and emergent properties[97]. It is clear that in this approach, the political space is understood as a complex, dynamic complexity of multi-level internal dependencies where inter al.: the macro analytical insight is appreciated in the structural and systemic spirit (research on the macro scale); the primordial ontological and epistemological and methodological character in a scientific reflection on the political phenomena is emphasized; assumptions and directives of methodological holism are used in analyses of political science (although holism, understood as a strict methodological approach is subject to numerous conceptual modifications, we can talk about a few converging methodological directives for this research perspective). Therefore the following assumption have been distinguished:

1. The social world can be analytically divided into social entities (groups, social classes) and social components (individuals). Both components and entity really exist, and more importantly, they have the same ontological status.
2. Explaining the properties of the whole society only the statements describing properties of these entities should be used, which means the lack of space for mechanistic reduction in the individualistic spirit.
3. The social entities are "governed by" their own laws, and more importantly – have emergent properties that are independent and autonomous in relation to the components[98].

We can also talk about the distinction made by Margaret S. Archer about the social world in a similar way to Bhaskarian model of the three domains of reality. Describing the current condition and the state of scientific and sociological affairs, Archer wrote that the social world can be ranked according to three complementary orders (natural, practical, social) and the corresponding forms of knowledge (embodied, practical, discursive). The rationale for creating this typology was to draw attention to the importance of the order of practical science, where for

---

[97] D. Elder-Vass, *The Causal Power of Social Structures. Emergence, Structure and Agency*, Cambridge University Press, New York 2010, pp. 44–45; R. K. Sawyer, *Social Emergence. Societies as Complex Systems*, Cambridge University Press, New York 2005, pp. 93–94.
[98] J. Szmatka J., *O holizmie i indywidualizmie w naukach społecznych*, „Studia Filozoficzne", nr 7 (128), Warszawa 1976, pp. 17–39.

practical dimension humanism revindicated. It is in that moment when a human being becomes a reflective agent in relation to the structural environment, which means that the category of subjective reflexivity becomes imperative for theoretical research for various types of sociological analysis; human agency is a crucial theoretical and practical component in order to explain the meanders of the social world, especially for such phenomena as the social change (morphogenesis), the performance of agency in individual/collective socio-structural conditions[99].

Certainly, the realistic approach of social reality can also be the starting point for the analysis of entity-structure dualism, which highlights the important role and contribution of critical realism in the intellectual and theoretical development of this research problem[100]. In this sense, critical realism suggests ontological stance referred to as stratified ontology, where the political reality is analyzed in the perspective of analytically separate levels and of the relationship between them (the relationship between the micro, meso and macro levels), among which there is emergence understood as the formation of a qualitatively new phenomena (properties) on various levels of complexity. However, realism implies, on the one hand, a large explanatory power of causal explanations (analysis of what the real works boils down to, the research on the actual sequences of cause and effect in the political space, which are synonymous with the social change; it is an analysis based on structure and/or multiplicity and interdependence of real objects, phenomena or processes through the perspective of the causality principle even in a mechanistic attempt to explain the matter of policy). On the other hand, it refers to the interpretative orientation (definite description and explication of political phenomena are inextricably linked with the elaboration and acceptance of meanings –it is a constitutive feature of these phenomena)[101]. This means a situation in

---

99   M. S. Archer, *Being Human: the Problem of Agency*, Cambridge University Press, Cambridge 2010, pp. 155–190.

100 In this work critical realism is a derivative of sociological realism, not realistic standpoint in art., literature, film or neocriticism (kind of neokantism).

101 A. Sayer, *Realism and Social Science*, Sage Publication Ltd., London 2000, pp. 10–29. Stratified ontology first, in critical realism it is another justifying premise for the concept of emergence; second, it confirms theses put forward by Mario Bunge on the scientific analysis of reality. Bunge claims: 1. That reality is arranged in levels; 2. That something qualitatively new can emerge from a lower level (emergence); 3. He points out the distinction between a real world and a conceptual one, between our descriptions of it and the factual reality; 4. He criticizes empiricism for its reduction of reality to the observable. More in: B. Danermark, M. Ekström, L. Jakobsen, J. Ch. Karlsson, *Explaining Society: Critical Realism in The Social Sciences*, Routledge, New York 2002, p. 5.

which researchers divided the study material into primary qualities – the quality corresponding to the objective and/or independent properties of the learning agent (epistemological realism) and secondary qualities – the quality corresponding to subjective interpretation and/or dependent on social context, i. e. on the current discourse of meaning among the group of experts, cultural factors or self-consciousness of researcher (interpretationism).

It should be noted that critical realism seeks to establish a general theory and/or meta-theory of relationship: the current social structure –causal agency. Therefore the following can be confirmed after Justin Cruickshank:

1. Critical realism can resolve the structure-agency problem using the notion of »emergent properties«. (…) The emergent properties in this case concern social structure that are created by the actions ofindividuals, but which then exert a causal influence over individuals, although individuals retain the power to alter social structures.
2. While emergent properties (for Margaret S. Archer: cultural, structural and human emergent properties – emphasis F. P.) are all interconnected in reality, Archer argues that we need to separate them analytically in order to study their interplay, and this leads her to argue for »analytic dualism«. This analytic dualism underpins Archer's »morphogenetic method«, whereby she argues that research, first of all, should posit a description of the structural factors; then discuss the socio-cultural agency of groups; and then conclude by describing how the structural factors have been modified (giving as »morpghogenesis«), or reproduced (giving as »morphostasis«)[102].

These arguments basically confirm that critical realism postulates a close agent- structure relationship, in which emergency is the main merging explanatory element. This point of view is fully consistent with the thesis of synchronic emergent power materialism proposed by Roy Bhaskar who argued that although the social structure is directly dependent on the actions of individuals and/or different types of entities, it is reducible to these individuals and is therefore independent of them (realism is identified as emergentism). This results from combining the potential and real capabilities of individuals (emphasis on the microtheoretical paradigm) with the concept of emergence (emphasis on the macrotheoretical paradigm). As Margaret S. Archer pointed

---

102 J. Cruickshank, *Underlabouring and unemployment. Notes for developing a critical realist approach to the agency of the chronically unemployed*, [in:] J. Cruickshank (ed.), *Critical Realism: The Difference That it Makes*, Routledge, New York 2003, pp. 112–113.

out, Bhaskar's strategy is rendered by Transformational Model of Social Action (TMSA), the intellectual foundations of which constitute the following statements: societies are irreducible to people and to a theoretical model of their connection; social forms are a necessary condition for any intentional act; their pre-existence establishes their autonomy as possible objects of investigation; their causal power establishes their reality; the pre-existence of social forms will be seen to entail a transformational model of social activity; the causal power of social forms is mediated through human agency. These arguments suggest that TMSA interpreted as a conceptualization of the problem of agent-structure is a form of mediation between the structure (an attempt to answer the question of how structure affects the perpetration) and the actors/agents (an attempt to answer the question of how actors transform the social structure); is a theoretical and conceptual system which defines interaction (duality) between the activity of the agents and the specific social structure[103]. The starting point of the duality of socio-political practice is in this case Bhaskarian model which links communities and individuals (diagram 6), when we deal with, on the one hand, the structural impact on individuals and/or members of the public (socialization process), on the other hand, with the impact and/or influence of these units by numerous interactions and activity of individual entities on the whole society (the processes of reproduction/transformation of the structures).

Diagram 6: Bhaskar's model of the society/individual connection

Source: own work based on R. Bhaskar[104]

---

103 M. S. Archer, *Realist Social Theory: The Morphogenetic Approach*, Cambridge University Press, Cambridge 1995, pp. 137–154. According to Archer, in TMSA model, one can find a very high affinity to the theory of structuration by A. Giddens, where this theory is an example of central conflation, understood as dual junction of the structure and agency into one entity (research issue). More in subsection 3.2. in this chapter.

104 R. Bhaskar, *The Possibility of Naturalism. A Philosophical Critique of the Contemporary Human Science*, Routledge, London & New York 1998, p. 40.

The model linking the society with individuals (diagram 6) has been enhanced by Bhaskar and took the form of TMSA, where, dual dependence on the agent-structure of the social practice follows through the component of temporality and the phase transition from point 1 to point 1' (diagram 7).

Diagram 7: Bhaskar's refined transformational model of structure and praxis (TMSA)

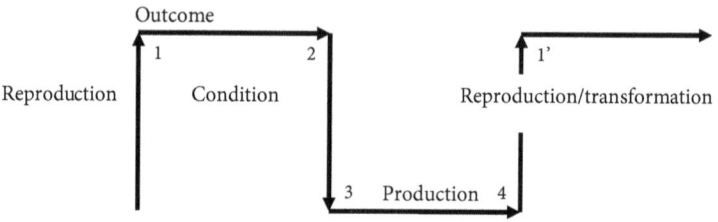

Source: own work based on R. Bhaskar[105]

It is clear that the beginning of the scientific considerations in the transformation model of social actions (TMSA) is the current state of the structural characteristics (point 1 and 2), which is a consequence of inter al. factors such as the involvement of entities in the social space; phenomenon emergence at different levels of complexity; (intended or unintended) consequences of previous actions taken by the agents. Only by identifying those conditions, i.e. the actual structural characteristics is it possible to conduct a thorough analysis of agency, which is expressed in the production process, and more specifically, in mediation and/or relatedness of specific agents in the structure (point 3 and 4). In this case, the objective perpetration expressed in the diagram of production process affects the social structure by many channels, which thus undergoes transformation and transfiguration (reproduction), which promotes the formation of new structural characteristics (point 1')[106]. Hence, the question of the historical-temporal fusion

---

105 Ibid.
106 In TMSA model we deal with conceptual analogy to the theory of structuration by Anthony Giddens, where he spoke about the duality of structure, which results from the continuous reproduction of social time and space (reproduction means creation of the social life). In this perspective "The social systems in which structure is recursively implicated, on the contrary, comprise the situated activities of human agents, reproduced across time and space. Analysing the structuration of social systems means studying the modes in which such systems, grounded in the knowledgeable activities of situated actors who draw upon rules and resources in the diversity of

activity of entities in the structural conditions is brought to the fore, where social structure has strong ontological reasons (social structures are "grounded" in space and "located" in time). Additionally, TMSA divides the social process into stages, which facilitate the observation and analysis of changes within the sociopolitical system, in which there are numerous processes of mediation, i.e., the relationship between social practices, which cannot be reduced to interpersonal interaction between agents[107].

It should be added that processes occurring at the interface of society ↔ individuals in TMSA model indicate the objective duality of socio-political practice, which is expressed in the historical, emergent and mediation character of the relationship between individuals and the formation of the general social order. In this perspective, society is perceived as a social unit subject to constant transformation, which is based on the activity of the agent(s). In turn, the perpetration of symptoms is seen as a key factor in transforming the material conditions of society, precisely – as the main building blocks of structural relations in society. Therefore TMSA model represents a relational concept of social structures, where the researcher focuses on the structural conditions for action in a given society, which is associated with the following analysis:

> Differential allocations of: (a) productive resources (of all kinds, including for example cognitive ones) to persons (and groups) and (b) persons (and groups) to functions and roles (for example in the division of labour). In doing so, it allows one to situate the possibility of different (and antagonistic) interests, of conflicts *within* society, and hence of interest-motivated transformations in social structure[108].

Summing up the discussion above it can be said that critical realism, interpreted as an epistemological stance relating to the agent-structure relationship is based on several principles, which can include such statements as:

1. The distinction between transitive and intransitive objects of science: between our concepts, models etc. and the real entities, relations and so forth which make up the natural and the social word.

---

action contexts, are produced ad reproduced in interaction". More in: A. Giddens, *The Constitution of Society...*, p. 25.
107   In TMSA we should formulate two theses: that structure essentially pre-dates the action(s) which transform(s) it; and that structural elaborations essentially post-dates those actions which have transformed it. More in: M. S. Archer, *Realist Social...*, pp. 156–157.
108   R. Bhaskar, *The Possibility...*, p. 45.

2. The further stratification of reality into the domains of the real, the structural and the empirical. The last of these is in a contingent relation to the other two; to be (either for an entity or structure or for an event) is *not* to be perceived.
3. The conception of causal relations as tendencies, grounded in the interactions of generative mechanisms, these interactions may or may not produce events which in turn may or may not be observed.
4. In addition to these ontological claims, and related to the first one, we have the rejection of both empiricism and conventionalism above. The practical expression of this epistemological position is the concept of real definition. Real definition, which are important for both realist and rationalist philosophers of science, are neither summaries of existing verbal usage nor stipulations that we should use a term in a particular way. Although they are of course expressed in words, they are statements about the basic nature of some entity or structure (...)
5. Finally, and related to (3) above, the realist conception of explanation involves the postulation of explanatory mechanisms and the attempt to demonstrate their existence[109].

In addition, proponents of critical realism often tend to integrate different theoretical and methodological stances. An expression of this research strategy is the appreciation of interpretationism when trying to create adequate descriptions or explanations about the world of politics. Such merging elements can also be seen in the case of the agent-structure duality, where the critical realism is trying to move beyond traditional intellectual dichotomies.

3.2 Morphogenetic approach

Morphogenetic/static approach developed by Margaret S. Archer remains important in the contemporary theoretical and methodological debates on the relationship agent vs. social structure. The starting point of the scientific analysis of the dualism of agent-structure here is the concept of morphogenesis that Archer adopted from Walter Buckley[110]. It turns out that in the case of morphogenesis and morphostasis interpreted as contradictory, but complementary

---

[109] W. Outhwaite, *Realism and Social Science*, [w:] M. S. Archer, R. Bhaskar, A. Collier, T. Lawson, A. Norrie (ed.), *Critical Realism: Essential Readings*, Routledge, London 1998, p. 282.

[110] For the author morphogenesis meant: "Morphogenesis will refer to those processes which tend to elaborate or change a system's given form, structure or state. Homeostatic processes in organisms, and ritual in sociocultural system are examples of »morphostasis«; biological evolution, learning and social development are example of »morphogenesis«". More in: W. Buckley, *Sociology and Modern Systems Theory*, Prentice Hall, New Jersey, 1967, pp. 58–59.

processes occurring at the interface of the social system it is the external environment that has a major impact on the whole social space. In principle, one can say that morphogenesis and morphostasis illustrate the internal dynamics and variability of specific structures which through intersubjective interaction undergo numerous transformations within the designated social complexity. Therefore, on the one hand, there is a process of a subjective character, inducing changes and/or stimulating and regulating the movements of structure forming (morphogenesis), on the other hand, there are processes of stabilization (morphostasis) for the maintenance of relative homeostasis which is associated with restoration of the internal structure and governance between the elements (the parts of) the social complexity. Generally, morphogenenesis, according to Dave Elder-Vass, includes processes that contribute to the creation and development of the agent(s) in the social space; subsequent modification of such an agent (agents) in accordance with the structural range and/or scale on which the agent (agents) gradably depends. This process coincidence is basically a sign of the dynamics of social structures, where there is not enough stable intrastructural compound, but with the desire to reach structural balance between the elements of the structural entity, which are positioned in constant tension towards each other. But such structures include the potential changes that could lead to many results and/or effects, i.e., among others, to convergence between the specified elements, relationships and subjective activities forming part of the structural space or even to the disintegration of the structure. In this sense, the social system, based on morphogenesis and morphostasis becomes an additive dynamic complexity, i.e. the irreducible complexity of higher-order, emergent properties, capable of improvement and a combination of structural (social system operating between the two states, i.e. between reaching balance and lack of balance)[111].

It is important to add that the above-defined concept of morphogenesis differs from the original understanding of the term inspired by life sciences, where morphogenesis is associated with the biology of development, and more specifically, with the evolution of biological organisms. In this perspective, morphogenesis is understood as chronologically progressive creative process of forms and structures of organisms in which the development, growth, differentiation and pattern formation (the plan) of specific organisms, understood as a biological entity, is

---

111 D. Elder-Vass, *The Causal Power…*, p. 37.

synonymous with complex morphogenetic mechanism[112]. Therefore, the term morphogenesis in biological evolution refers to the developing embryo, which:

> The developing embryo is dynamic, and forms all manner of shapes and structures. This is achieved through various different types of cell behavior. The term morphogenesis (creation of form) is used to describe how embryonic structures arise. Without morphogenesis, the embryo would never progress beyond a simple ball of cells, and dynamic processes such as gastrulation, embryonic folding and organogenesis would not be possible[113].

Reasons for the formulation of morphogenetic interpretation can be found in the criticism of duality of subjective agency and social structures that exist in various epistemological concepts. According to Archer, contemporary duality explication of agent-structure theories of sociology oscillates around three conflations[114], i.e. top-down conflation (downwards conflation) grassroots conflation (upwards conflation) and central conflation (central conflation). And all types of conflation (diagram 8) are in conflict with the morphogenetic recognition, where the complicated relationship between subjective perpetration and social structure is considered as model compounds stretched in time, i.e. as a three-part series of changes in which a transition is performed by social interaction (T^2–T^3) from structural conditions (T^1) to the structural elaboration (T^4).

---

112 N. J. Berrill, G. Karp, *Development*, McGraw-Hill, California 1976.
113 In this understanding most significant components of morphogenesis include, inter al. such processes as: different rates of cell proliferation; change of cell size; change of cell shape; cell death, cell fusion; cell-matrix interaction etc. More in: R. M. Twyman, *Instant Notes. Developmental Biology*, Taylor & Francis, Oxford 2000, p. 39 and subsequent.
114 Conflation in sociological theory means one-dimensional theorising. Such approach especially refers to agent-structure debate (in the history of sociology this issue was referred to as part/individual dilemma – entity/society; the problem of scope or micro-macro link), where *conflation* means – in theory – favouring the specific "side" of this dualism. Conflation in methodological sense means the use of reductionist mechanisms, where social reality is reduced either to the subjective level (methodological individualism) or to the structural level (methodological holism). More in: M. S. Archer, *Being Human…*, pp. 4–7; M. S. Archer, *Realist Social…*, pp. 6–7; J. Alexander, B. Giessen, R. Munch, N. Smelser (ed.), *The Micro-Macro Link*, University of California Press, Berkeley 1987; B. Roberts, *Micro Social Theory*, Palgrave Macmillan, New York 2006.

Diagram 8: The limited time span of conflationary theories compared with the Archerian morphogenetic approach

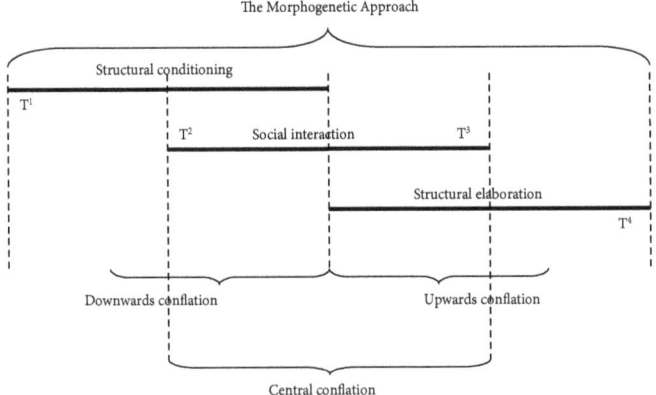

Source: own work based on M. S. Archer[115]

In the case of top-down conflation, socio-political reality is explained through the perspective of structural conditions (T^1), which are the primary actors in relation to their activities, actions or widely understood agency (social part is secondary in relation to the social entity at the ontological, epistemological and methodological level). In this perspective, people are causative individuals of the social structure (the agents of structures), where socio-cultural changes are the result of certain autonomous processes occurring in the structural space; where the causative entity never achieved full autonomy (independence) with respect to the structure; where the individual actors and social interaction (T^2) do not have the capacity to generate emergent properties; where emergence is formed on the upper, irreducible units, levels of complexity; where emergence is treated as an integral part of progressive complexity of the structure. At the same time, structural elaboration (T^3) depends only on the structure, where "future" of the political space is an extension of inherent structural trends, and is not dependent on the agency of individuals. While grassroots conflation (upwards conflation) is a kind of denial to top-down conflation, when the conditions and/or structural environment (T^1) are reduced to agency, and, more specifically, to a series of intersubjective activities of individual agents/actors – participants of the social structure (social entity is secondary in relation to

---

115   M. S. Archer, *Realist Social...*, p. 82.

the social part of the ontological, epistemological and methodological plane). In this variant, the structural properties (T^1) and the structural elaboration (T^3) comes down to the effects and/or results of activities, including actions and decisions of specific actors (T^2). In addition, it is assumed that the structural properties are reversible and depend directly on the subjective agency. Similarly, structural elaboration (T^4) is not determined and is dependent on any emergent structural properties, but mainly due to the causative subjectivity, which has an impact on and translates into structural conditions (here economic activity is a prerequisite for structural changes). On the other hand, central conflation means combining top-down conflation with bottom-up conflation, when an attempt is made to unite perpetration (the field of activity of agents) with the structure (the field of structural interactions). Strategy of standardization is, in principle, supposed to lead to multivariant connection of the two dimensions of social life so one plane contains in the other and vice versa.[116]

Examples of central conflation that manifests as agent-structure duality include at least two sociological theories: theory of habitus by Pierre Bourdieu and theory of structuration by Athony Giddens. In the case of the theory of habitus[117] analysis of the socio-political space is a detailed reproduction of the dialectic of the inside and of the outside, i.e. two overlapping and intertwining processes – interiorization of the outside and exteriorization of the inside. In this perspective, the study of political practice is primarily the analysis of habitus and stable dispositions occurring in the social environment, which mean:

1. Observation of social practice for the formation of the dialectic relationship between the social situation and habitus, which is defined as "sustainable and transferable systemic predispositions", which sustain, perpetuate and reproduce a defined order and structuring framework. Hence habitus – chronologically arranged series of structures – affects the objective harmonization of practices and products of society, which leads to a continuum of regularity

---

[116] M. S. Archer, *Realist Social...*, pp. 82–86.
[117] According to P. Bourdieu: "All I want to say here is that the main purpose of this notion (the concept of habitus – emphasis. F. P.) is to break with the intellectualist (and intellectualocentric) philosophy of action represented in particular by the theory of *homo oeconomicus* as rational agent, which rational choice theory has recently brought back in fashion at the very time when a good number of economists have repudiated it". In this understanding, habitus is "found in the socially constituted system of structure and structuring dispositions acquired in practice and constantly aimed at practical functions". More in: P. Bourdieu, L. J. D. Wacquant, *An Invitation to Reflexive Sociology*, Polity Press, Blackwell Publishers, Cambridge 1992, pp. 120–121.

and universalization of the habitus in the socio-political space (the role and importance of individual *habitus* increase with their social "rationality", which will entail that habitus is perceived as obvious and evident).

2. Analyses of habitus in terms of their subjective facilities, i.e. system of internalized structures, perceptual frameworks and methods of action common to all members of the group and/or social class, which are prerequisites for any objectification in the social life (an analysis of the phenomenon of homology, which arises between habitus members of the group, class, nation, etc.; it is interiorization of the same key structures by respective individuals)[118].

3. Research on the political reality as relational field (the space of objective relations "existing independently of the will and consciousness of individuals"), which hosts a permanent intrastructural configuration. More specifically there is a "game" between participants and/or players of the socio-political space. This "game" (exchange) depends on the size of capital resources, the strategy or the set of habitus. Thus, the field functions as a space for potential and active forces (the field is a kind of balance of current and potential forces):

> The field is also a *field of struggles* aimed at preserving or transforming the configuration of these forces. Furthermore, the filed as a structure of objective relations between positions of force undergirds and guides the strategies whereby the occupants of these positions seek, individually or collectively, to safeguard or improve their position and to impose the principle of hierarchization most favorable to their own products. The strategies of agents depend on their position in the field, that is, in the distribution of the specific capital, and on the perception that they have of the field

---

118 According to the thesis: "The proper object of social science, then, is neither the individual, this *sensrealissimum* naively crowned as the paramount, rock-bottom reality by all »methodological individualists«, nor groups as concrete sets of individuals sharing a similar location in social space, but the *relation between two realizations of historical action*, in bodies and in things. It is double and obscure relation between habitus, i.e., the durable and transposable systems of schemata of perception, appreciation, and action that result from the institution of the social in the body (or biological individuals), and fields, i.e., systems of objective relations which are the product of the institution of the social in things or in mechanisms that have the quasi reality of physical objects". More in: P. Bourdieu, L. J. D. Wacquant, *An Invitation to Reflexive Sociology*, Polity Press, Blackwell Publishers, Cambridge 1992, pp. 126–127.

depending on the point of view they take *on* the field as a view taken from a point *in* the field[119].

In turn, in the structuration theory by Anthony Giddens, we have to deal with the emergence of the duality of social structures (diagram 4), where through a process of structuration an attempt is made to merge the two levels – individual and structural – into one unit of analysis. In this sense, the socio-political space is characterized by duality, which lies in the fact that:

> Structures shape people's practices, but it is also people's practices that constitute (and reproduce) structures. In this view of things, human agency and structure, far from being opposed, in fact presuppose each other. Structures are enacted by what Giddens calls "knowledgeable" human agents (i.e., people who know what they are doing how to do it), and agents act by putting into practice their necessarily structured knowledge[120].

This means a situation in which social structures, as the so-called. "virtual" forms, exist in the form of ideas and patterns functioning in society and are explained as follows:

1. Rules – social structure is a set of rules that are "generalized procedures used in establishment/restoration of social practices." This means a situation in which participants actors of socio-political life must be provided with knowledge (must be knowledgeable) about these rules, which in the context of the functioning of the social practice, allows them to create different intersubjective interactions. Therefore, the structure understood as a set of "virtual principles" facilitates objective generation, processing and validity of the rules, patterns or diagrams, which contributes to their implementation among the participants of collective life.
2. Resources – social structure is explained on the basis of resources, which are the tool which "serves as a source of power in social interactions." In this arrangement, Giddens distinguishes between two main categories of resources: the authority (human resources – physical strength, agility, knowledge and negotiating expertise of agents that can be used to acquire, enhance or maintain power); allocation (physical resources – animate and inanimate objects, which can also be used to gain, reinforce or maintain power). Therefore, all participants of the socio-political reality have a different amount of and/ or have different access to specific resources, both human as well as natural

---

119 Ibid., p. 101.
120 W. H. Sewell Jr., *A Theory of Structure: Duality, Agency and Transformation*, "American Journal of Sociology" vol. 98, no. 1, pp. 1–29.

resources, which facilitates a detailed analysis of the structure through the perspective of active agents which, thanks to resources constitute causative power and causalpower[121].

It should be noted that the morphogenetic approach is critical to all conflationary sociological theories. It can rather be said that Margaret S. Archer is an advocate of distinguishable new research strategy, which she calls analytical dualism. It is intended to be an intellectual breakthrough, or even a significant counter-proposal to the existing scientific concepts relating to the issue of agent vs. structure. According to Archer, analytical dualism, on the one hand, the opposite of duality understood as a scientific junction between the structure and subjective agency (an alternative for different types of sociological stances identified with conflation, where the relationship between the agent's perpetration and the structure takes the form of a highly tortuous unity of areas), on the other hand, it is practical and methodological embodiment of realistic ontology present in the social sciences. Analytical dualism also stresses equivalent status and interdependent structure and agency together with their conceptual separation from research. This means a situation in which the researcher uses methodological principle, based on the rejection of the conflationary theorizing path (non-conflationary theorizing) for a detailed study of interaction between the structure and the agent (relationship sometimes incomplete, but necessary from the point of view of scientific explanation)[122]. Therefore, the stance is referred to as analytical dualism, despite the mutual and necessary determinants of structural symptoms often difficult to research includes a certain "independence" of individual elements of this dichotomy (i.e. distinctiveness in terms of the occurrence of emergence in the subjective and structural dimension), where in accordance with the thesis of John B. Thompson:

> Such an analysis would show that, while structure and agency are not antinomies, nevertheless they are not as complementary and mutually supporting as Giddens would like us to believe[123].

For the theorist, this means a situation in which the agent vs. structure relationship is not radically, even extremely, antagonistic, where there are no common elements in creating adequate explanations of the political practice. It is also

---

121 Ibid.
122 M. S. Archer, *Realist Social…*, p. 15.
123 J. B. Thompson, *The Theory of Structuration*, [in:] D. Held, J. B. Thompson (ed.), *Social Theory in Modern Societies: Anthony Giddens and his Critics*, Cambridge University Press, Cambridge 1989, p. 74.

criticism of the stances in which the two planes agent-relationship structure merge into a theoretical-conceptual entity, and/or indistinguishable theoretical basis, where the lack of demarcation as transparent borders, the position, function, role, significance, etc. either of entity or structure (rejection of merger of different methods, often irreducible and/or planes analytically separate levels of politics, where by the deliberate merger of various elements an attempt is made to, under the guise of adequacy, exhaustively describe, demonstrate and explain different types of agent-structure relationship).

In addition, the prospect of analytical dualism in research practice means two simultaneous conducts of research: remembering about analytical and theoretical approach, often practical distinction between the sphere of individual agents and structure; meticulous analysis of the agent-structure conditions of their mutual influence or mutual determination. Hence, it is possible to identify the structure due to its nature, and exactly irreducible, autonomous and relatively permanent character, but also due to agency. At the same time we can talk about a realistic approach to the socio-political reality, where the activity of the agent/s does not form a structure, but only reproduces (restores) or transforms it. Hence, the morphogenetic approach boils down to the study of a particular social space for the analytical separation of flows between the structure and the perpetration, which is expressed in the following formula: emergence ↔interplay ↔ outcome[124].

Illustration of analytical dualism in the dimension of research practice is certainly the morphogenetic/static perspective, in which, on the one hand, epistemological assumptions of critical realism are reflected, on the other hand, the essence of anti conflationary thinking is shown (diagram 9).

---

124 M. S. Archer, *Realist Social...*, p. 168. It is visible that emergence ↔ interplay (agency-structure) ↔ outcome sequence is a clear reference to R. Bhaskar's realism, more specifically to TMSA model (diagram 7), where social space is considered as a given structural state (1), where subjective reproduction (restoration) takes place and transformation – into a new structural state (1').

Diagram 9: Co-picturing Methodological Realism and the morphogenetic/static approach

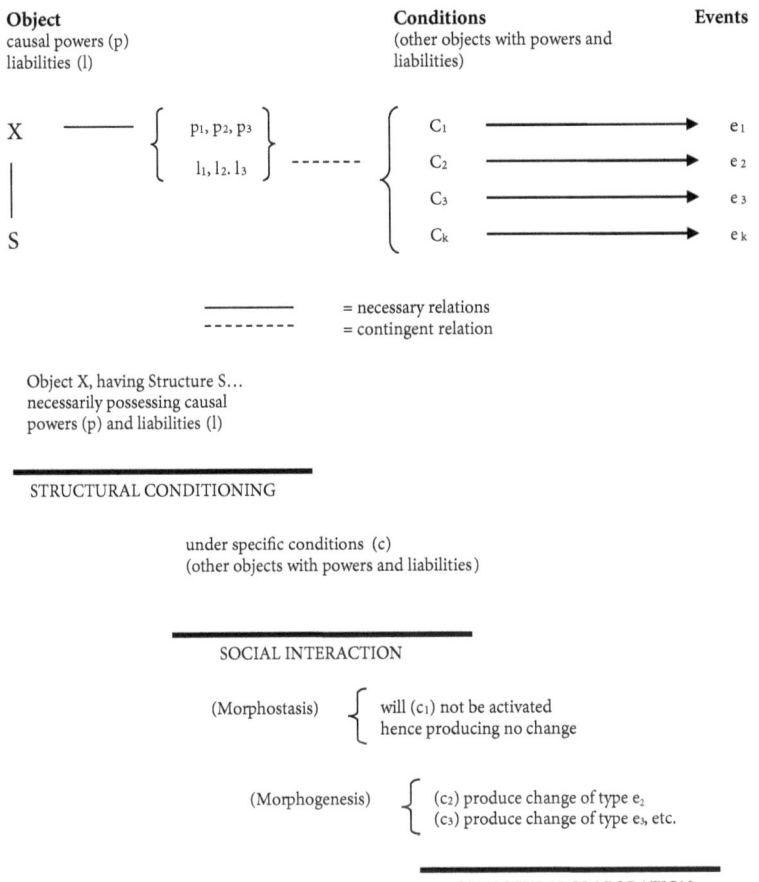

Source: own work based on M. S. Archer[125]

Diagram 9 shows the application of causality principle to analyze the political reality, where different objects (including agents) operating in space have a measurable structural force – the causal force with designated responsibilities, more precisely – commitments and tendencies caused by this force, which allow not only the potential but also a real change and/or reconfiguration of the existing environment (structural conditions). Therefore, relations within the

---

125 M. S. Archer, *Realist Social...*, p. 160.

structure and structural elaboration are based on the implementation of multi-variant sequences of cause-and-effect relationships that have a direct impact on morphostasis (maintaining structural stability) and morphogenesis (the occurrence of structure forming processes). Simultaneously, in Diagram 9 for practical causality morphogenetic approach was imposed in which multiple relationships between the structure and the constituent objects are shown. In this arrangement the shape, size, quality or quantity of intrastructural changes of the social structure are directly conditioned by the same structure, and more precisely, by the phenomenon of emergence occurring within it, which affects the course of establishing and/or generates specific structural conditions; social interactions that occur between different types of objects (agents) having a real driving force that stimulates, manufactures and finally "emerges" specific events, processes, states of things, structure, properties, etc.. In this context, there are two determinants of any change in the structure: based on structure as such, and based on objects (including agents) of its components. With the structural elaboration interpreted as the final phase processes of structure, one could pick two forms: morphostasis (sign of change; synonym mechanism stabilizing-balancing or maintaining the status quo within the structure); morphogenesis (syndrome formation of different types of transformations, production changes or the occurrence of completely new movements within the structure).

From a methodological point of view, it can be stated that the approach to morphogenetic research practice means the negation of the mechanism of reduction to explain the agent-relationship structure, where there is no one-dimensional explanation of the perpetration of subjective and social structure. It seems that the morphogenetic analysis supported by analytical dualism privileged and highlighted the fact of coupling between the agent and the structure, even trying to carefully separate the two spheres so that, in the research process, the multi-threaded relationship "agent-structure" is not merged into a single research problem (by highlighting two discernible spheres of research morphogenetic approach intellectually and theoretically attempts to overcome the central conflation, which is the lack of clear separation of the agent from the structure and vice versa).

3.3 Three-phase morphogenetic cycle

In fact, it can be concluded that the essence of the morphogenetic approach is expressed in relation to human agency to the social structure in time. We have to repeat that this multi-layered relationship – specifically dialectical interaction – the agent and structure expressed in the concept of analytical dualism is reflected in the three-phase morphogenetic cycle, which comprises the steps of forming a kind of *continuum*: the structural conditions; social interaction; structural elaboration (diagram 10).

Diagram 10: The morphogenesis of structure

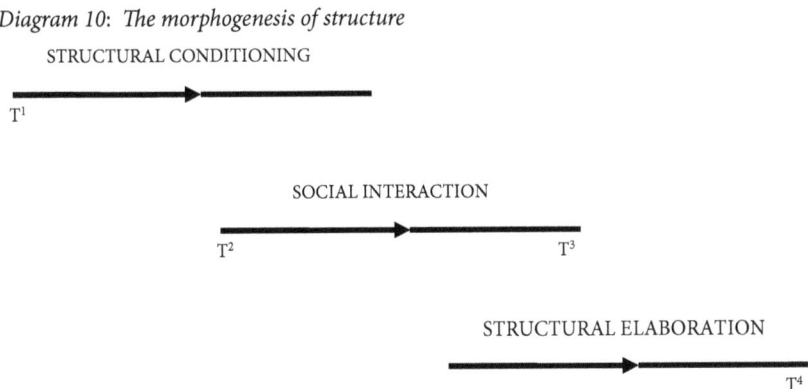

Source: own work based on M. S. Archer[126]

In the case of structural conditions (T^1) we are talking about the structural and social context, where different types of activities, including the causal activities take place. Of course, the starting points for the creation of structural conditions (T^1) are previous actions that shape subsequent conditions. Therefore, the structural conditions (T^1) have a direct impact on the articulation of interests, needs and aspirations of individuals, which is connected with the fact that all the activities of both individual agents and collective ones are determined directly by the earlier structured conditions. In turn, the sequence for social interaction (T^2–T^3) is to draw attention to the fact that different operators can (to gradable extent) influence events in social reality, more precisely – have a causal power to change certain structural and social terms. At the stage of interaction, (T^2–T^3) refers to the interaction between individuals or social groups based on their own abilities, resources (e.g. human resource base, managing centre), measures the values we are trying to pursue interests, needs, aspirations, goals etc. As a rule, it concerns two different types of intersubjective relationships, i.e. positive co-operation (cooperation and/or investigation consensus based on dialogue and debates) and negative co-operation (conflict and/or developing, stimulating and leveling differences and antagonism among the participants of interaction).

---

126   M. S. Archer, *Realist Social…*, p. 193.

But the structural elaboration (T^4), referred to as improvement or restoration of structural change lies in the continuum of structural conditions by the number of social interactions (T^2–T^3). In this system agents – the elements of the social structure – manage to adapt to the prevailing conditions of their own interests, needs and aspirations. This means a situation in which a change in conditions arises as a result of structural and/or social interaction result (T^2–T^3). At the same time, the process of change of structural conditions (T^4) is here referred to as morphogenesis and leads to a new structural configuration. At the same time, we have to deal with the reverse situation, when the study (T^4) does not lead to the structural elaboration but rather to structural reproduction, i.e. to morphostasis where the causal activities do not change the structural conditions.

Archerian morphogenetic cycle is a diachronic-dialectic illustration of connecting activity of the agent/s with the structure, where – by the threefold sequence – the socio-structural complexity is shown. At the same time, diagram 10 shows that every social system is a specific structural configuration, marked by such objective characteristics as:

1. Structural emergent properties – properties that cannot in any meaningful way be reduced to personal agency; properties that generate causality (causal forces) independent of individuals and/or elements included in a given social structure.
2. Cultural emergent properties – properties whose existence means that the social system is primarily a socio-cultural system, where the participants of public life are considered to be agents with gradable cultural competence. In this case, the emergence is synonymous with the practice of culture where the cultural context has a direct impact on the functioning of agents (e.g. the process of social integration), as well as the formation of the social structure.
3. People emergent properties – properties that are associated directly with the wider activity of individuals and groups. Of course, this activity can take many forms – from mobilization to cooperating to competition – which suggests that the participants of collective life are a factor causing emergence[127].

By pointing outcultural emergent properties, Margaret Archer expanded the morphogenetic cycle (diagram 10) by an additional component – the culture. In this sense, culture, next to agency and structure has become a central metatheoretical concept, so that there is a possibility to capture different relationships between the material and ideational (imaginary) sphere. What is more,

---

127 M. S. Archer, *Realist Social...*, pp. 172–190.

the morphogenetic analysis postulates relative autonomy of both spheres demonstrating their dialectic dependence at the same time[128]. It should be clarified that both structural emergent properties and cultural emergent properties may indicate the relative originality of social factors in relation to a specific agency. Margaret S. Archer proved this point of view in the following way:

> These results of past actions are deposited in the form of current situations. They account for what there is (materially and culturally) to be distributed and also for the shape of such distributions; for the nature of the extant role array; the proportions of positions available at any time and the advantages/disadvantages associated with them (…) In these ways, situations are objectively defined for their subsequent occupants or incumbents[129].

However, in other texts the author warns that the structural and cultural emergent properties are in some way independent of the entity (agency of emergent properties), and vice versa. More precisely, it means the lack of direct influence between emergent structural and cultural forces and perpetration, which is always mediated in human reflexivity[130]. This means a situation in which the reflectivity is located between the structure and subjective perpetration, mediating structural influence on an individual and deciding about what the answer would be subject to structural constraints and opportunities, which leads to a three-step model in which:

1. Structural and cultural properties *objectively* shape the situations that agents confront involuntarily, and *inter alia* possess generative powers of constraint and enablement in relation to

---

128 S. McAnulla, *Structure and Agency*, [in:] D. Marsh, G. Stocker (eds.), *Theory and Methods…*, London 2002, pp. 271–291.
129 M. S. Archer, *Realist Social…*, p. 201.
130 For Archer reflexivity is equivalent to internal conversation of an individual and/or agent which takes the form of a "dialogue between different phases of the ego"(she uses the definition as proposed by an American pragmaticist, Charles S. Peirce). Additionally Archer distinguishes between four types of reflexivity, i.e. communicative reflexivity (internal conversations need to be confirmed and completed by others before they lead to action); autonomous reflexivity (internal conversations are self-contained, leading directly to action); meta-relfexivity (internal conversations critically evaluate previous inner dialogues and are critical about effective action in society); fractured reflexivity (internal conversations cannot lead to purposeful courses of action, but intensify personal distress and disorientation resulting in expressive action). More in: M. S. Archer, *Being Human…*, p. 228; M. S. Archer, *The Reflexive Imperative in Late Modernity*, Cambridge University Press, Cambridge 2012, p. 13; M. S. Archer, *Making our Way through the World: Human Reflexivity and Social Mobility*, Cambridge University Press, Cambridge 2007, pp. 158–266.

2. Subjects' own constellations of concerns, as subjectively defined in relation to the three orders of natural reality: nature, practice and the social.
3. Courses of action are produced through the reflexive deliberations of subjects who subjectively determine their practical projects in relation to their objective circumstances[131].

3.4 Political agency in morphogenetic perspective

Before the category of political agency in morphogenetic perspective will be explained, it should be noted that subjectivity in the science of politics is defined as a relatively stable, gradated property for the various parties, including both individual and collective, by which certain activities address the needs, interests, values and goals. In this arrangement, the political agency is the result of meta-assumptions (within logical causation): activity → action → decide → subjectivity.

From a methodological point of view, political subjectivity considered through the prism of activist component means a situation in which explanation of the researched political reality boils down to the analysis of the causal power of the agent, where the polymorphous active participant in community life is the causative agent of processes and policy changes; where economic power is the same as causal potential for structure process of the agent; where throughout concrete actions and political decisions the agent modifies, stimulates or affects the existing environment –the social structure.

Given these assertions, we can say that the political agency is a term that in its scope of meaning refers to the characteristics of the real ontic agent and/or agents, which in the case of methodological research of political *praxis* means taking a realistic understanding of the categories of agency. In realistic perspective, analysis of subjectivity is nothing but a sensitive study of the tangent point between the two areas, i.e. the freedom of individual agents (perpetration) and material circumstances (structural environment). In other words, a detailed analysis of constant tension occurring between the unrestrained space of individual agents and/or human freedom and structured supraindividual space and/or objective-social determination, where existential conflict between the individual being and the external environment exists. This condition means that subjectivity is a property of various political actors that:

---

131 M. S. Archer, *Making our Way...*, p. 17.

[…]is not the primary feature of human being but a derivative existential effect of building its property In the process of ontic solidification of the whole agency structure and acquring autonomous and relatively independent position by this structure[132].

At the same time, political agency defined in this way can be considered on the basis of two explanatory diagrams (horizontal analysis):

1. On the agent's part as such– where agency is understood from the perspective of the intrinsic qualities and/or characteristics. Here, causal force and structure forming potential of agent(s) are the core of each nomological explanation for the world of politics, where the explanatory mechanism focuses always (and only) on the internal/endogenous conditions of each participant of collective life (for an individual agent it will be m.in.: personality traits, psychophysical characteristics, temperament, etc.. On the other hand, for a collective entity it will be inter al.: type of relationship and the relationship existing between the members of the group; type of hierarchy determining the location of the group members with respect to each other and relative to the environment; principles of operation, coordination and subordination of the group as the social entity, etc.). No less important aspect of this type of method is to emphasize that the political agency is as a result of participation in the events of the social agent. Here the agent is only a component of socio-political events, when a part of the set within which interactions take place. In this case, the agent is also the source of the impact and the recipient and therefore, subject and object of transformations taking place in a specific political reality (the agent is an active ingredient and regulator of multiple events).
2. On the social structure's part as such – where agency is defined from the perspective of the effect and impact of the existing external circumstances on the agent(s). In this way it emphasizes that the implementation of agency associated with the suprapersonal vision or is independent of the will, knowledge and experience of a particular agent (i.e. submitting the characteristics of the political system as an entity over the intrinsic characteristics). Therefore, in this scenario a major role in the design category of political agency plays a determinant existing *outside* agent, or more precisely all types of processes, events or socio-political relations, in which the political agent is involved in and/or under the influence of, be it consciously or unconsciously (existing events beyond the control of the causative agent, but which by its effects, more or less affect the ontological status and the real position of the agent in a given reality).

---

132   J. Lipiec, *Wolność i podmiotowość człowieka*, FALL, Kraków 1997, p. 65.

Where reference is made to the first level of analysis, any explanation related to subjectivity is built based on the individual basic decision, i.e. on a single agent, and only by this agent. Accepting an individualistic explanatory perspective in the context of agency means the application of mechanisms for the reduction of all types of social phenomena (explanation entirely by analysis of the parts). Methodological reductionism is focused only on a detailed analysis of individuals who, being the final components of different types of the whole society, become the only legitimate explanatory category. Here two elements are are brought to the fore:

1. Objective relational individual (single-agent of politics) and its subjective capacity for rational actions and decisions.
2. Potentiality of structuring individuals (single entity policies), or causal force of that agent, which is objective in nature.

At the same time, the analysis of the political agency at microtheoretical level is an example of the reistic-nominalist approach in the social sciences, including the political science, where the appreciation of the human oneself to his or her surrounding-community takes place. This is an example of the research, when one refers to the simplest elements of the social structure, i.e. to the individual political agent interpreted as the only certain and infallible element in the study of political science.

But for macrotheoretical level, or for multi-level analysis of structuralist explanations of the political agency are built on the basis of holist decisions (nomological explanation and any justification or research statements are based on *integrative entities*[133]). In such an arrangement, an attempt to explain the phenomenon of political agency is based on the community as a whole – in particular by its additive characteristics (explanation of some properties of the whole, which does not have any other features in addition to those shared by its elements together). Hence the really existing agent is not a single entity, but the collectivity of a higher order, which is constituted by the emergent properties (the expression of agency for those integrative ones are new qualities occurring

---

133 *Integrative entities* are entities of higher order which are characterized by a new quality and properties to which individual parts – elements included in their composition are not entitled. They emerge as a result of the interaction of part of a particular system of compounds. Hence integrativeness is the most important feature distinguishing characteristics of entire creations, which enables us to understand all the other specific characteristics of an entity. More in: M. Karwat, *Podmiotowość polityczna. Humanistyczna interpretacja polityki w marksizmie*, Państwowe Wydawnictwo Naukowe, Warszawa 1980, pp. 211–212.

within them that do not have the space for individual agents, but are produced at higher levels of complexity and are the result of the interaction part of the compounds in the particular system). Emergence as a phenomenon occurring at the level of agents is in this case a confirmation of the independent status of the ontological and epistemological societal entities. That is why society can be regarded as the complexity and does not represent only the sum of individual agents (society is not the sum of individual elements), but it is primarily a network of mutually conditioning and correlated relations between various agents.

Actually, by defining agency in the science of politics, as well as by the presentation of contemporary semantic-connotative perturbations relating to this concept we can return again to the morphogenetic approach, in which the issue of agency is being considered in the context of analytical dualism. According to Margaret S. Archer, the question of the practical dimension of agency is revealed primarily through the dialectic relationship and multi-level interaction between the agent and structure. An expression of this kind of thinking is a three-phase morphogenetic cycle (diagram 10), illustrating the temporal exchanges between analytically separate plane of the structural and individual agents. At the same time, the theory of morphogenesis stresses that any coupling between structural determinants and the perpetration is always (and only) made by human reflexivity. In this sense, Archer writes about the double morphogenesis where the human individual and/or agents shape(s) and is/are shaped by structural conditions. This means a situation in which the process of interaction between the agent and the environment as such undergoes structural bilateral (mutual) transformations. The consequence of such metathesis is, on the one hand, structural and cultural elaboration having its foundation in agent perpetration, on the other hand, the changes in the same agent(s), and more specifically in their identity, behavior, beliefs, etc., as a consequence of the environmental and structural impact[134]. In addition, reflexivity is the basis for the definition of agency, i.e. the position and status of individual agents in relation to a particular social structure. This is because reflectivity becomes the core of the separate sense of self and/or self-consciousness interpreted as an inviolable ontological element in agent vs. structure relation. The self along with personality, memory and emotional sphere is the essence of agency as such. Therefore, Archer classifies four correlated levels of humanity – selves, primitive agents, multiple agents and actors –which from the point of view of this work can be similarly used to define four descriptive levels of agency (diagram 11). Undoubtedly, this is a realistic interpretation, in which Margaret Archer tries to explicate as society based

---

134 M. S. Archer, *Realist Social...*, p. 190 and subsequent.

on an individual, where the first two levels – primary selves and agents – are determined by the continuum of reflexivity, which means self-awareness, but also an individual identity (continuous self). While the next two – multiple agents and actors – emerge as a consequence of the entanglement of a particular agent/s in the socio-structural reality, where changes on the level of subjective agency are made with the influence of the environment.

Diagram 11: Realism's account of the development of the stratified human being

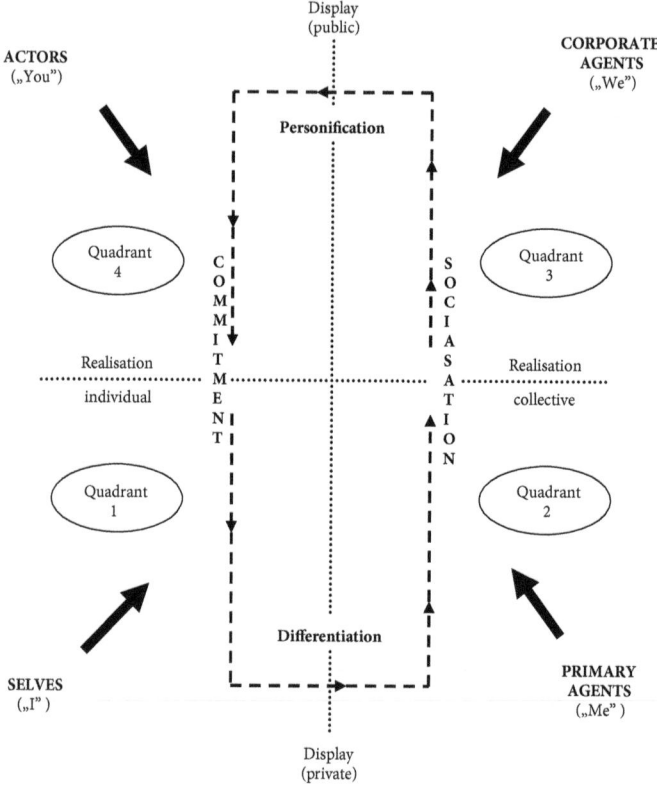

Source: own work based on M. S. Archer[135]

The starting points for understanding agency in morphogenetic terms are represented by quadrants 1 and 2, relating to both personal self (selves), as well as the

---

135 M. S. Archer, *Being Human…*, p. 260.

primary agents. In the case of individual self-agency refers to the gradual process of individualization, in which "subjective I"is formed, i.e. a subjective reflexivity, which is the first indication of the potential of subjective and real driving force in changing the existing external conditions (the self is here synonymous with individualist features, proving that individual agents are unique, as well as highlighting their unique self-consciousness, which emerges in social practice). Bearing in mind that the selves do not work in any social vacuum, but from birth they are objectively involved in the structural and cultural context (a mechanism independent of the will or desire of the agent). On this basis, the primary agent – "objective I", i.e. the self – unintentionally, often unconsciously, is located in the social distribution of resources as a key element of collective exchange and/or intrasystemic conversion. This means a situation in which "objective I" is a consequence of, inter al., such social processes as socialization of the individual, socio-economic stratification, sound historical and cultural foundation or addiction of the self to objective external conditions (in this case quadrant 2 is the carrier of individual and social identity, where "objective I" means the designation of places, role, functions, status of the new positions in the social distribution and allocation of resources. In turn, quadrant 1 is the introspective space in which self-definition and/or self-identification of the agent take place). In turn, quadrants 3 and 4 relate to collective agents (corporate agents) and actors. The formation of collective agents is based on a mechanism in which the individual agents get involved and participate in various collective action – in the collective arena (e.g. they take part in social movements and civil protests, represent the interests of social groups, layers and classes in public space, etc.; collective perpetration means that we can talk about the plane, "We"). In this case, the multipliable agents to be construed as an essential element are the causative agent stimulating and modifying a given structural space ("We" is the agent for the following regularities: how the agent is determined by external circumstances). In addition, "objective I" and "We" through public engagement directly affect the sphere of an individual entity. This determination is manifested by the creation of an actor ("You"), which in this way is subject to numerous transformations (redefinition) in relation to the "subjective I." Hence the actor ("You") is nothing but the personification of the agent, who underwent a kind of structural and social reconfiguration; who by the distribution of material resources and assets, the activity inside the structure and involvement in public affairs changes its position and/or status; who by the individual and social identity of constructs on the future foundation, and more specifically, on the new range of roles, positions, hierarchies; who by the mechanism of impersonation creates and / or designs a new realization of the individual, supported by the collective activity, ie. the collective agent. Therefore, the implementation for the individual agent itself consists of: crystallizing the "I" in the course of reflection and/or continuous conversation inside, where the personal self is manifested by declarations or articulate individual aspirations (quadrant 1 is synonymous with implementation of private individuality); the creation of a future actor ("You"), based on earlier declarations and aspirations, which represents an embodiment of the collective (quadrant 4 is synonymous with the public-individual implementation and social identity, where "you" is nothing else than the self-made public)[136].

It is evident that the realistic development of agency is a sequential treatment in which we have to deal with four overlapping processes: the individual realization exposed in private and public space (quadrant 1, 4) and the collective realization exposed in private and public space (quadrant 2 3). The first implementation of the Individual (quadrant 1) means ontic "solidification" of the agent as such, when in the course of internal conversation – reflexivity – stabilization of the subjective "I" takes place; when we deal with the formation of relatively permanent self (self-identification). The second implementation of the Individual (quadrant 4) is the appearance of an actor ("You"), which means a kind of a "clash" between the subjectively shaped self and a structured social world, where the self is "confronted" with the public individual agent exposure. In this system, the individual implementation of both private and public exposure is subject to additional two mechanisms: differentiation (the process of differentiation of individual self) and personification (the process where individual actors embody the social forces, political tensions or characteristics, properties, interests, power, etc. operating in a given socio-structural space). While the realization of the collective means socialization/objectification of individual subjective selves (quadrant 2) which by structural conditions must be identified against the background of the community as such, so they must find their position, location, role or status against others. It also means the appearance of the actor ("You"), which is the result and or the effect on a multifactorial interaction of the structural "subjective I".

Margaret S. Archer, creating a four-element sequence which forms agency, wanted to emphasize that in agent vs. structure relationship there is a significant number of "tensions" both inside the agent, as well as in the structural environment take, which in fact determine the shape and form of agency. Certainly, an attempt to separate private exposure from public exposure is to help in the study of multifactorial agent-structure merger. Through the analysis of four squares,

---

[136] M. S. Archer, *Being Human...*, pp. 260–282.

which are subject to mutual determination, the author tries to capture, and more analytically, to separate the complicated relationship between perpetration and social structure. Archerian conceptualization is a kind of morphogenetic synthesis, in which additionally we will find numerous threads of theoretical approaches (even threads relating to, inter al., Charles S. Peirce's pragmatism, Marurice Merleau-Ponty's phenomenology of perception), On top of that it reveals the desire to break the traditional dichotomy: part (methodological individualism) and entity (methodological holism). It cannot be forgotten that that morphogenetic strategy of defining and explaining agency is based on the ontological basis – reflective agent, which, as an active causal force is a key link to explanatory political praxis. At the same time Margaret S. Archer does not rule out the role and importance of the social structure, which generates emergence and contributes to the overall functioning of the reflective agency.

What is the political dimension of this kind of conceptualization then? It seems that morphogenetic perspective, similarly to the dialectic Marxist perspective, emphasizes the idea that political agency arises as a result of convergence and/or mutual determination of two independent spheres, i.e. the plane dominated by the perpetration of symptoms (subjective aspect) and the plane dependent directly on the socio-structural conditions (objective aspect). In such an arrangement, the political agency means:

1. The specified, gradated and time-variable characteristic of political agents, i.e. the individual and collective political actors, which is performed under certain structural conditions (the external environment).
2. Property, which, on the one hand, depends on the "subjective I" (immanent features of the agent; personal self, identical to the internal reflectivity and/or self-identification), on the other hand, is conditioned by many social interactions, including structural environment and/or structural effects.
3. Property, which expresses the driving force behind the agent, its capabilities and/or cognitive, decision making, imperious, structure-forming limitations. At the same time it is a property that depends on gradable way of objective-structural mechanisms of determination, which speaks about the real impact of the environment on human agency.
4. Property, which has no constructionist or discursive ground (negation of postmodern way of agency defined as such), but on the contrary –to which real political agents are entitled–these are the agents that hold real causal power, expressed by the parameter for specific actions and political decisions (no agency exists without ontologically defined and identified object – the agent as such).

5. Property that both objectively dependent on the politics (any economic activity is objectively embroiled in the political context. This means that regardless of the intent, knowledge and preferences of the agent their aspirations and actions or values that they profess are conditioned by the current socio-political environment. Therefore, all activities of agents are inextricably linked to the conflicts of interest within the political practice, which are *de facto* determinants of this activity. Besides. It is the sign of political self-awareness.

Summing up the previous discussion, it can be said that the morphogenetic perspective actually fits perfectly in multi-threaded theoretical and methodological discussion of dualism: subjective perpetration vs. social structure. Morphogenetic conceptualization by M. S. Archer is certainly a coherent epistemological stance, an attempt of which to evaluate for explanatory utility leads to several conclusions:

1. Morphogenetic perspective assumes holistic and realistic view of the agent vs. structure relationship, where the socio-political sphere involves real objects, structures and various types of causal forces, including personal agency.
2. Analysis of morphogenetic/static attempts to intellectually, theoretically and methodologically overcome existing points of view in the social sciences, especially those with conflationary thinking and/or one-dimensional theorizing, wherein on the one hand, a methodological deduction is made (or agent-based explanation – the individual or the structure – social entity), on the other hand, according to the proponents of morphogenesis, unauthorized – in the methodological sense – blurring the frontiers between the individual and structural agents is employed, i.e. between two separate, but mutually determining planes in the socio-political *praxis*.
3. Morphogenesis-oriented researchers are sceptical of the theory identified with central conflation, i.e. to epistemological approaches drifting, in their opinion, into the eclectic subjective-structural unity. In other words, the mechanism of blurring the boundaries between agent and structure results in the lack of precision and in the inability to find adequate explanations about the socio-political world. It should be noted that despite the escape of eclecticism, supporters of morphogenesis themselves get into some form of eclecticism, when attempting to connect conceptual dichotomies into one entity such as: individual – society; individualism – holism; causality – reflexivity; realistic mechanisticism – hermeneutics.
4. Agency in morphogenetic terms means rejection of the postmodern and constructivist demands for a realistic interpretation, where both the agent as such (individual and collective), as well as the social structure have a relative driving force or distinguishable emergent properties.

4. Understanding political leadership

4.1 The notion of political leadership

Scientific analysis of the phenomenon of political leadership is today the subject of many intellectual and theoretical controversies where basically it is difficult to reach definitional consensus with respect to the leader ↔ followers relationship[137]. This difficulty has its roots in the philosophy of history, when individual researchers of the social world tried to answer the fundamental question how leaders emerge in certain political circumstances. Does the emergence of leaders depend directly on outstanding and/or abilities distinguished from its surroundings, talents, psychophysical features of such leaders? Or just the opposite – it is a matter of objective conditions, treated as a resultant of various socio-structural references, in the extreme terms, which directly determine the emergence of leaders in the political space?

In other words, the two extremes of perception, describing, and explaining the meaning of leadership, where on the one hand we can talk about an idealized, almost omnipotent approach to the individual, with its unquestioned role and importance in the historical process; on the other hand, about the total subordination of the individual course of human history, when individuals become "a speck of dust in the wind" and/or statistically insignificant element in the process of scientific explanation of the social change. In this context, it includes the question of theoretical and empirical conflict concerning the definition of the phenomenon of leadership that oscillates between prominent individuals-leaders and the temporal and social environment. One may say that a constant tension in the case of explaining leadership is formed and that just boils down to two opposing types of justifications:

---

137 Current social researchers define the notion of power in numerous ways. For example: 1. (A) *has power* over (B) to the extent that (A) *can* get (B) to do something that (B) would not do otherwise (R. Dahl); 2. Power (*Macht*) is the probability that one actor within a social relationship will be in a position to carry out his own will, despite resistance, regardless of the basis on which this probability rests (M. Weber); 3. Power is the ability to establish control over another (E. C. Banfield). More in: R. Dahl, *The Concept of Power*, "Behavioral Science" no. 3, 1957, pp. 201–215; M. Weber, *The Theory of Social and Economic Organization*, The Free Press, New York, 1947, p. 152; E. C. Banfield, *Political Influence*, The Free Press, New York 1962, p. 348. More in: M. Haugaard, *Power: A Reader*, Manchester University Press, Manchester & New York 2002.

1. The arguments in favour of a real leader, where the emergence of a political leader result always (and only) from its subjective-personal features (e.g. charisma, authority, congenital and/or acquired qualities, qualities, competencies, organizational effectiveness, the impact on the environment; subjective alienation, knowledge tools and persuasive social engineering, managerial, governing, organizational predispositions, etc.).
2. Reason relating to the contextual or socio-structural factors, where the emergence of a leader is "outside" the individual, or rather is a consequence of an objective situation and/or unexpected confluence of circumstances (e.g. fortune, the case – in line with the thesis "no one else wanted", "the bench was too short "), where the leader appears as a result supraindividual calculation, the action plan, strategy, etc.; where the emergence of a leader is not a subjective ability and talent, but the coincidence of objective-subjective factors; where creative leader can be a sign of, for example, practical puppetry, in which the leader is not even aware that he or she was the exponent of one's will, interests, goals, plans, scheming, etc., it is a governing instrument or externally driven carrier in the hands of others.

Modern political science of has developed many approaches and methods of research on the phenomenon of leadership. Generally, it can be said that the political leadership – treated as strictly defined object of study – is subject to constant theoretical and empirical disputes. This involves formulating new empirical theories regarding the emergence of political leaders and the acquisition and maintenance of support for such a leader in certain political conditions. This means that research situation in the category of political leadership becomes the central point of reference for the various types of nomological analyses including such aspects of political reality as the problem of legitimacy and accreditation in the public space; the formation of formal and/or informal power relations between rulers and the governed (the phenomenon of asymmetry, submission, domination, etc. in the political practice); issue identification, the identification and determination of spheres of influence or impact of the operators, social groups, institutions, organizations, parties in relation to other agents, institutions or parties; the level of determination and/or dependence of a political leader on the inherent characteristics of the psychological personality or on the external structured environment.

In order to present a definitional variety relating to the political leadership in a fair and complete way we must start with the question of power. In modern political science we can, in principle, distinguish between the two basic ways of defining power:

1. Power as a feature and/or property – the notion of power occurs in the context of the characterization of an agent that has "ruling characteristics" and/or "domineering personality". In this sense, power is explained through the subjective-subjective perspective of characteristics, where the agent (the ruling agent) has a significant – often gradable impact, influence, causative power in relation to other agents (in other words, this is individualistic definition of power, where the practice of political power is identified with the "power to do something", i.e. the potency of doing something, achieving certain results, effects and implementation of specific plans, strategies, objectives, etc.). An example of such an interpretation of power is the definition proposed by Bertrand Russell:

> Power may be defined as the production of intended effects. It is thus a quantitative concept: given two men with similar desires, if one achieves all the desires that the other achieves, and also others, he has more power than the other. (…) Nevertheless, it is easy to say, roughly, that A has more power than B, if A achieves many intended effects and B only few[138].

2. Power as a relationship – power is seen as a kind of relation between two actors – between the imperious agent and the object – i.e. the individual (group of people) subordinate to imperious agent (relational definitions of power, where the practice of political power is identified with the "power over" when the relationship between analytically separate entities is asymmetric, which is related to the fact that one party has a greater impact on the other). An example of such perception of power can be found even in the definition proposed by Harold D. Lasswell, for whom power is an interpersonal situation according to the formula:

> *Power* is participation in the making of decisions: G has power over H with respect to the values k if G participates in the making of decisions affecting the k policies of H. The *arena* of power is the situation comprised by those who demand power or who are within the domain of power. The *political man* (*homo politicus*) is one who demands the maximization of his power in relation to all his values, who expects power to determine power, and who identifies with others as a means enhancing power position and potential[139].

The defining distinction given above refers to the intellectual attempt to create a universal formula describing and explaining the phenomenon of power and particularly – to the fundamentals of power as well as to the features that constitute the relationship at the intersection of the rulers –the ruled in political

---

138 B. Russell, *Power. A New Social Analysis*, Routledge, London & New York 2004, p. 23.
139 H. D. Lasswell, *Power and Personality*, Transaction Publishers, New Brunswick, New Jersey 2009, p. 223. Also in: L. Porębski, *Behawioralny model władzy*, Universitas, Kraków 1996, pp. 50–56.

practice. In the case of issues for the authority we can adopt a formal definition of power, proposed by John French, in which the foundation of any kind of authority include always (and only):

> Social influences [...] coordinated to force fields induced by person A on person B, and the strength of these forces is assumed to vary with the power of A over B. (...) The power of A over B (with respect to a given opinion) is equal to maximum force which A can induce on B minus the maximum resisting force which B can mobilize in the opposite direction[140].

Thus we may distinguish between the two types of power:

1. Position power – this kind of power includes: legitimate power (associated with having status or formal job authority); reward power (derived from having the capacity to provide rewards to others); coercive power (derived from having the capacity to penalize or punish others).
2. Personal power – this kind of power includes: expert power (based on followers' perception of the leader's competence); referent power (based on followers' identification and liking for the leader)[141].

Among the features that constitute the relationship the ruled – the rulers authority and coercion deserve special attention. Both attributes relate to the relationship between A and B agents, provided, however, that the relation of power built on authority is quite different from being created on coercion. As Jan Baszkiewicz noted, the authority:

> Has no means of coercion, is not able to impose our obedience by force (...) Our obedience to authority is therefore voluntary, but not disinterested. We are in fact convinced that the authority knows what they are doing; that they want and are able to provide us undeniable profits, success, satisfaction[142].

In turn, the relationship of authority arising on institutionalized and legal compulsion leads to obligatory obedience of the ruled, when under threat of sanctions, penalties, the use of violence and social isolation, gradable subordination to specific formal legal solutions and partly to the authority occurs (here the ruling agent becomes the personification of the rule of law where citizens are guided by the principle of trust in law, and thus trust in the public authority

---

140 J. R. P. French Jr., *A Formal Theory of Social Power*, [w:] J. Scott (ed.), *Power: Critical Concepts*, Routledge, New York 1994, pp. 310–326.
141 P. G. Northouse, *Leadership. Theory and Practice*, Sage Publications Ltd., London 2013, pp. 9–11.
142 J. Baszkiewicz, *Władza*, Wydawnictwo Ossolineum, Wrocław-Warszawa-Kraków, 1999, pp. 5–6.

which *a priori* guards the rule of law, peace and social order, which authorizes the authority to use coercion). In this perspective, there is no legal arbitrariness, but there is strict adherence to and acceptance of established standards, codes, laws, etc. by the ruled, which is associated with "legal forcing" of certain attitudes, behaviors or actions. In this perspective, leadership is synonymous with the phenomenon of power that actually fits perfectly into the question of asymmetry between the leader and the followers when you can say that:

> Typically, each individual with authority in the group is, at the same time, at least, the leader (in the sense that he or she determines decisions about members of the group), but not every leader is equipped with power (normatively guaranteed advantage of agency allowing the leader to make decisions about someone, possibly for someone, in the name of someone without them). Thus, the leader can only to a decisive or significant extent affect what happens in the group, what actions will be taken in it. However, leaders do not necessarily have to and often they do not even have the ability to make a certain decision themselves »in the name of the group« and »about the group«[143].

At the same time it should be noted that leadership is both a form and manifestation of power. In this respect, we can extract different conceptualizations about the nature of leadership, which are gradably associated with the notion of power. Among the many coincidental theoretical proposals we can distinguish those that interpret leadership as:

1. Personal authority – leadership is subjected to the mechanism of impersonation, which refers to the subjective aspect of power, which becomes the main characteristics of leadership as such. Being so interpreted, power can be both real (entire power/ leadership in the hands of one person), as well as the façade (power/leadership leadership is ostensible, i.e. It is determined by extrapersonal factors, e.g. environmental group, socio-economic conditions, opportunities for coalition, etc. and does not depend directly on the leader).
2. Specific role in the social system of power – leadership is interpreted as a specific result of the division of labour, tasks, competencies, responsibilities, etc., where the leader is "above" the rank and file members of the organization, institutions, parties or socio-civic movement. This position "above" means an increased concentration of power in the hands of leaders which simultaneously is synonymous with more governing, managerial, personal, decision-making opportunities in relation to subordinate agents and/or social groups.

---

143 K. Pałecki, *Przywództwo jako kategoria teoretyczna i przedmiot społecznych oczekiwań*, [in:] L. Rubisz, K. Zuba (eds.), *Przywództwo polityczne. Teorie i rzeczywistość*, Toruń 2005, p. 32.

3. Above-average concentration and strength of power – strength of leadership is the domain where weak leadership means the lack of leadership. In addition, the leader is nothing more than a person who, in socio-political practice, is referred to as a kind of distributor of impact and power. The consequence of such an above-average concentration of power by the leader is actual creation and initiation of structural and processual changes.
4. Informal authority and/or formal authority in formally ligitimised – leadership is explained through the perspective of microtheoretical paradigm in which structural task orientation and leadership integration are crucial and are understood as duality of key roles and functions of leadership (in this case we can talk about the leader of a social group, in which the leader – who holds the role of leadership – is oriented, on the one hand to achieve the objectives, tasks and implementation of the strategy, on the other hand, acts, formally or informally, as an integrating factor for all the group members).
5. A special way of governance – leadership is considered as a separate qualitative and quantitative relationship at the intersection leader-supporters. Here, leadership is a particular way of exercising power over subordinates, since the latter are, in extreme cases, even devout followers of a particular leader[144].

Explanation of leadership as the embodiment, forms or manifestations of power, in addition to multidimensionality of this phenomenon, also fosters the presentation of different ways of defining the political leadership. In fact, reducing the political leadership to one definition, one discriminant factor, or a plane of analysis is doomed not only to fail – this is an undeniable fact – but it is also a manifestation of the scientific naïvety, when researchers are trying by all means to simplify the surrounding of political reality in order to improve their own well-being or to generate seemingly scientific reliability. In the case of the concepts of leadership naïvety, according to Gayle Avery, results from several reasons:

1. *Leadership is not concrete entity*, but is more appropriately regarded as a social construction that occurs in a historical and cultural context, and within the minds of the people involved. So, to understand how concepts of leadership emerge, it is important to identify how people think about leadership and the mental models they employ.
2. *Ideas about leadership are affected by concepts of leadership held within a particular culture* or other context in which people find themselves

---

144 B. Kaczmarek, *Przywództwo polityczne a przywództwo organizacyjne*, [in:] T. Bodio (ed.), *Przywódzwo polityczne*, „Studia Politologiczne" vol. 5, Warszawa 2001, pp. 58–68.

3. *The study of leadership is replete with myths* bearing little relationship to reality.
4. The idea of the *heroic leader* abounds. Intellectually, it is evident that the lone heroic leader cannot continue to exist in today's complex, dynamic world (…) Rather, leadership is a distributed phenomenon[145].

Bearing in mind the above, it can be stated that in scientific practice, there are two basic explanatory paths of political leadership:

1. Subjective and personal definition of leadership, where the phenomenon of political leadership is considered in the context of the detailed characteristics and description of the leader against the background of the environment and/or followers, especially psychophysical features; qualities and personality characteristics; capabilities/interpersonal limitations; developed leadership styles and strategies; managerial skills; charisma and achieved accreditation, obedience, authority, trust, etc.
2. Processual definition of leadership, where leadership is analysed for a variety of interactions occurring at the interface of the leader ↔ followers; where leadership is interpreted as a continuous process of exchange between the ruling agent and the ruled, i.e. it is synonymous with a particular sequence of events, facts, states of affairs, or cause and effect sequences, leading to the occurrence of leadership under certain conditions (diagram 12).

Diagram 12: Two paths for defining leadership

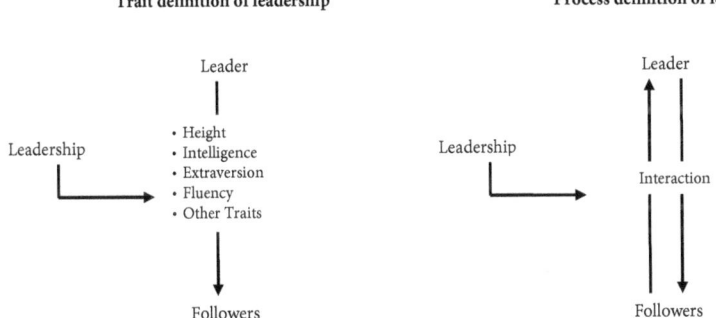

Source: *own work based on A. G. Jago*[146]

---

145   G. C. Avery, *Understanding Leadership. Paradigms and Cases*, Sage Publication, London 2004, p. 8.
146   A. G. Jago, *Leadership: Perspectives in Theory and Research*, "Management Science" 28 (3), 1982, pp. 315–336.

Diagram 12 shows that detailed research on the phenomenon of political leadership must take into account a variety of factors, both individual psychological as well as situational, structural and social, which affect the quality and quantity of interaction between the leader and the followers; which directly determine the position, status, role and functions of both leaders, as well as followers. Therefore, the analysis of political leadership should take into account, inter al., such parameters as:

1. Personality and origin of the leader – here leadership is analysed in terms of qualities and properties of the leader, the political beliefs, style, action, motivation to engage in the public sphere, origins and the course of the political career, or in terms of how the leader responds to emergency situations; the pressure of circumstances, political competition, etc.
2. Characteristics of groups and supporters led by the leader – leadership is considered as a "transaction" in which the leader receives a mandate to rule (lead) over a bunch of followers. Therefore, research on leadership should be based on analyses of target groups the leaders, i.e. individuals or groups that legitimize the activities of the leader (analysis of expectations, motivations, preferences, supporters of the leader).
3. Nature of the bonds linking the leader with those who follow the leader – here leadership becomes the result of interaction between the leader and the followers, where the leader primarily cares about building a proper relationship with supporters. Such techniques may include inter al. expanding organizational network in order to attract more members – supporters; arousing enthusiasm among supporters through various marketing, persuasive, rhetorical, social engineering activities, etc.; the formation and maintenance of the desired image of the leader in the external environment, including the public, the media, cyberspace; development of information policies and activities in the field of media relations.
4. Social context in which leadership is performed – the phenomenon of leadership in terms of the environment in which the leader operates is analysed here. It applies to the socio-political contexts, which affect directly the position, role and functions of leaders. Such conditions may include inter al.: presence and nature of formalized rules for making decisions about the community; place and time of the ruling activity of the leader; objective capabilities and/or organizational, economic formal and legal limitations with which the leader has to struggle; responsibilities of the leader appointed formally or informally; measures, mechanisms and resources available to the leader in given socio-structural conditions.

5. Effects of specific cases of the interaction between the leader and the subordinate –here leadership is examined through the analysis of cases when individual researchers link to the real practices of leadership[147].

Having taken into account the parameters and more holist perspective of leadership, the close interdependence of subjective (dependent on the leader) and objective factors (depending on the social circumstances) come to the fore. Of course, such a coincidence naturally translates into the political science, where we can define at least a few consistent explanatory patterns of leadership:

1. As a real impact on the environment and/or inequality of influence between the leader and the members of a specific community.
2. As a special type of activity in which the scope of authority and competence of political leaders is crucial.
3. As a bilateral and/or multilateral social bond.
4. As the relationship between the leader and the followers based on authority.
5. As a privileged and /or above-average position, the role and function of the leaders in the social structure.

In the first case, the political leadership is synonymous with the real impact or influence of the leaders of the external environment, specifically on individuals or social groups belonging to the community. Here the political leader is defined as:

> The one who to a greater degree than the other influences decisions made by a particular community (…) leadership is always determined realistically and not normatively by intentional influence. In this respect, it approaches the problem of manipulation and especially it is the political leadership that des so[148].

In fact, this is equivalent to the thesis that the leader is:

> Someone who influences a group whether or not he or she happens to be formally at the head of that group. Thus, not only are there leaders in informal bodies, but the real leader of a constituted organization may well be someone who does not occupy a formal position in the group[149].

---

147 M. G. Hermann, *Ingredients of Leadership*, [in:] M. G. Hermann (ed.), *Political Psychology. Contemporary Problems and Issues*, Josey-Bass, San Francisco-London 1992, pp.167–192.
148 K. Pałecki, *Wokół przywództwa politycznego – ramy dyskursu*, [in:] A. Kasińska-Metryka (ed.), *Studia nad przywództwem. Ustalenia metodologiczne i praktyka*, Wydawnictwo Adam Marszałek, Toruń 2011, pp. 14–15.
149 J. Blondel, *Political Leadership. Towards a General Leadership*, Sage Publications, London 1987, p. 13.

In turn, leadership explained by the specific activity of political leaders is nothing else than full compliance with the thesis regarding the decisions taken by the political leaders, which have a much higher rank than other types of decisions. In other words, political leaders:

> [..] have an impact on the life of certain communities in the state and of the society in general, and even on international relations. Therefore, the scope of power of the political leaders is much higher compared to the non-political leaders. (…) Political leader may therefore have a greater and more diversified resource of influence than people leading people in other areas of life[150].

Emphasizing the role and significance of the scope of authority resulting from the activities of the political leaders is related to the so-called competent leadership, where the powers of individual leaders prevail, especially their interpretive, creative and conciliatory skills, which translates into the quality of leadership. Hence the close link between a specific activity, including the decisions of political leaders and their political competence, which is defined as:

> The totality of characteristics that constitute a politician and demonstrated at the level set bystandards, as a basis for political action and taking responsibility for their perpetration. A collection of these features creates the capacity for action, including: knowledge; intellectual and emotional skills; behaviour; adaptation to changing conditions; individual system of values; external system of formal entitlements[151].

In the third proposal political leadership is defined as:

> Bilateral and multilateral social (communicative) bond formed in the course of and as a result of a complex social process. […] This means that someone is not so much of a leader but becomes one, remains one, or is no longer one – depending on the will of the collective system of forces and their effectiveness in efforts to solve social problems, implementation of group (community) interests. The intensity of personal aspirations, strength of ambition is an important factor here, but it is only one of the conditions necessary, but insufficient to acquire and maintain leadership[152].

In this sense, the terms of the existence of political leadership include:

1. Representativeness of candidate's views and plans for a certain part of society.

---

150 U. Jakubiak, *Przywództwo polityczne*, [in:] K. Skarżyńska, *Podstawy psychologii politycznej*, Zysk i S-ka Wydawnictwo, Poznań 2002, p. 85.
151 E. M. Marciniak, *Kompetencje przywódcy politycznego*, [in:] T. Bodio (red.), *Przywództwo polityczne*, „Studia Politologiczne" vol. 5, Warszawa 2001, p. 97–112.
152 M. Karwat, *O karykaturze polityki*, Warszawskie Wydawnictwo Literackie MUZA, Warszawa 2012, p. 75.

2. Social anointment and/or authorization to act as a leader, integrator, coordinator, decision maker, etc. (usually such authorization is directly connected with the commitment to the implementation of the rules, objectives or performance of specific tasks, strategies or action plans).
3. Having a clear and coherent program interpreted as a condition for recognition of the representativeness and legitimacy of action – is a necessary condition of obedience, appreciation and/or consent for a potential leader.
4. Bilateral (multilateral) communication within the community, i.e. between the supporters, and their co-followers and their empowered representative, which is associated with effective agitation against the external environment in which the candidate for a leader functions. In other words, the ability to expand the circle of trust by potential leader, i.e. both the supporters and people maintaining neutrality, which means agreement on the actions promoted by the leader[153].

In a similar interactive perspective, the definition of political leadership is constructed, and is understood as a relationship between the one who leads (the leader), and those who trust them, legitimise their actions and finally voluntarily surrender because of the leader's authority. So understood a political leadership:

> [...] differs from political power in a basic way. The leader may exercise power, but it is not the power that defines him or her as a leader but voluntary support given to him or her by supporters. Governing relationship is based on coercion and authority, leadership – only on the authority[154].

Actually, in this interpretation, the source of authority of a particular leader is – in the Weberian spirit – its unusual property, i. e. charisma. For Max Weber:

> The term »charisma« will be applied to a certain quality of an individual personality by virtue of which he is considered extraordinary and treated as endowed with supernatural, superhuman or at least specifically exceptional powers or qualities. These are not accessible to the ordinary person, but are regarded as of divine origin or as exemplary, and on the basis of them the individual concerned is treated as a »leader«. In primitive circumstances this peculiar kind of quality is thought of as resting on magical powers, whether of prophets persons with a reputation for therapeutic or legal wisdom, leaders in the hunt, or heroes in war. How the quality in question would be

---

153 M. Karwat, *O karykaturze...*, p. 76–77.
154 J. J. Wiatr, *Przywództwo polityczne. Studium politologiczne*, Wydawnictwo Wyższej Szkoły Humanistyczno-Ekonomicznej, Łódź 2008, p. 23. Exercising leadership equals generating authority among the supporters where the authority explains legitimisation of a given leader and vice versa.

ultimately judged from ant ethical, aesthetic, or other such point of view is naturally entirely indifferent for purposes of definition. What is alone important is how the individual is actually regarded by those subject to charismatic authority, by his »followers« or »disciples«[155].

Therefore, a leader, or rather above-average and/or "radiant" personality of such a leader, is treated by a particular community – most followers – as the leader holding a charismatic style of rule (leadership), which boils down to:

1. Generating the atmosphere of uniqueness – being surrounded by leaders and participation in initiatives with his or her participation and / or under leadership fosters extraordinary atmosphere, where the leader is perceived by its supporters not only as the initiator, but even as the demiurge – creator.
2. Transgressive thinking and action of the leader –the ability of heuristic departure from established patterns of thinking, standards of conduct and the limits of imagination, etc. of the leader, when the leader "infects" his or her own supporters or the wider audience with a different way of thinking, perception and action. In this sense, the leader also kidnaps and propitiates people, often inspires them to new ideas, concepts, or even creates an atmosphere of creative self-improvement[156].

While the political leadership is defined as a privileged position, the role or function of a particular leader in the social structure means that we look for the engagement between the leader and the external environment in leadership in which the leader operates (this may be either a group environment, as well as local or international environment). In this system, the key to the explanation of leadership is not so much the behavior of leaders as its objective location/structuration in the socio-political space. Leadership becomes the three-element system in the leader-supporters relationship (community) to perform the causative functions; to accept responsibility for structuring behaviour; manage decisions aimed at attaining the pursued objective[157].

---

155 M. Weber, *Economy and Society. An Outline of Interpretive Sociology*, University of California Press, Berkley 1978, pp. 241–242.
156 Charismatic leadership style based on the charismatic attributes, which can include, among others, such phenomena as a special gift of leadership seen as a "divine spark"; extraordinary powers; a sense of mission; suggestive faith in each other; halo of mysticism; the ability of self-creation and self-promotion. More in: M. Karwat, *Charyzma i pseudocharyzma*, [in:] T. Bodio (red.), *Przywództwo...*, pp. 126–175.
157 C. Ridgeway, *The Dynamics of Small Groups*, St. Martin's Press, New York 1983, pp. 205–206.

On the basis of the definitions presented above it can be concluded that the ambiguous concept of political leadership fits very well in the agent perpetration vs. social structure relationship, where the issue of political leader existence, its validation in a given environment and – more importantly – induction, maintenance and consolidation of accreditation among potential as well as current supporters can generally be considered from the two points of view:

1. On the agent's part (endogenous factors) – a phenomenon where political leadership is identified directly with the leader, and more specifically, with the observable and repeatable set of individual characteristics, qualities, attributes of a person who aspires to become a leader or is a leader (among the most frequently mentioned features: high level of intelligence, assertiveness, striving for dominance, extroversion, managerial abilities, consistency and perseverance, communication skills, willingness to take on challenges and take responsibility; precisely defined objectives, tasks, activities, etc.). In this sense, the scientific analysis of the political leadership focused on the ruling agent and/or leaders as such (personal power), who with their own abilities, personality traits and character and finally the causal strength (alienation of individual agents – see. scheme 3) is able to inspire and maintain certain social confidence. Of course, such interpreted leadership emerges primarily as a consequence of subjective qualities of a leader in the social demand for this type of leader.
2. On the structural part (exogenous factors) – where leadership is considered in the context of leaders' functioning in a particular external environment, where inter al.: aggregated patterns of behaviour; collective rules, norms, values and resources of formulating the political space play key roles; various relationships. In this perspective, political science research on leadership comes down to the location of multithreaded analysis (research position, status, role, functions, etc.) of the governing agent/or leaders in given socio-structural conditions (position power). At the same time, the centre of gravity (significance) for the explication of leadership is transferred from agent-personality justifications onto the process and interaction, where the emergence of leader does not depend directly on the leader, but is determined by the dynamics of the environment, the current socio-political and objective regularities, i.e. independent of the leaders, states of affairs, situations, events, etc. (in extreme cases, the emergence of leader is only accidental and/or a stochastic process).

4.2 Political leadership paradigms and attributes of political leadership

All the explanatory schemes, except for distinguishable attempts at describing and explaining the relationship between the leader and the followers at the same time related to different levels of analysis. On the one hand, we had to deal with defining leadership at micro theoretical level (society/individual-oriented explanation, where the explanatory mechanism was oriented towards leaders as such and/or agent-related reasons), on the other hand, with processing leadership at macro theoretical level (explanation focusing on the social entity and/or social conditions, where individual explanatory tools were limited to statements about the political space). In addition, the multiplicity of explanatory schemes with respect to the political leadership showed the actual complexity of relationships at the leader ↔ supporters intersection, which is subject to different leadership performance, both formal as well as informal determinants; where the process of the emergence of leader in a particular time-space environment cannot be reduced to a single factor (variable), because it is usually a multifactorial tangle of events, the core of which include accreditation attempts of the candidate for the leader; where modern scientific research on leadership even looks away from indicating the main determinants for this relationship[158]. In other words, we can say that in political science multiparadigmaticity applies. According to Gayle Avery, at least four paradigms of leadership can be distinguished, which are sets of ideas – points of view – situated on a different continuum, and which basically show the complexity of leadership in the best way:

1. Classical – leadership is explained through the perspective of the dominant leader, i.e. by an outstanding individual and/or an elite group of people who have the authority to issue a command and control over a particular group of subordinates. Hence the source of the legitimacy of leaders lies in the fear or respect and the desire by individual members of the community to gain reward or avoid punishment. The social recognition of the leader (leaders) stems from the belief that the chosen leader has the right to impose their views in respect of: birth; divine appointment; economic, military or political position; a particular system of beliefs (e.g. the cult of

---

158 Presented approaches and research schools of leadership and they listed such contemporary leadership theories as: cognitive; biological-genetic; situational, psychoanalytical; open system; interactive and social education. More in: B. M. Bass, R. Bass, *The Bass Handbook of Leadership: Theory, Research, and Managerial Applications*, Free Press, New York 2008, pp. 47–70.

the leader); cultural norms (e.g. the tribal chiefs, heads of families). In this paradigm, there is no need for any vision of leaders in order to secure obedience among followers.
2. Transactional – defining leadership, firstly, underlines the value of the other side of the relationship, i.e. supporters of the leader, and second, based on a procedural meaning, where individual leader deliberately affects a specific community-followers to "direct, organize and support activities and relationships within a group or organization." In this sense it refers to a specific transaction between the leader and/or the leaders and the followers, when it comes to understanding and agreement between the parties. Of course, in this variant interpersonal skills, knowledge and competence of the leaders are crucial, who in this way creates a good climate for leadership (management of subordinates). The process, however, has the impact on both parties, i.e. consultative decision-making style dominates and the leader takes into consideration the opinion of their supporters, which he or she manages to increase their commitment. At the same time the leadership is not only formal (*ex officio*, nomination, appointments, etc.), but may also be of an informal nature and involve the competence and knowledge of the leader. In this case, the vision of leaders can never be articulated to ensure obedience among a specific group of supporters.
3. Visionary – explication of leadership is based on the visionaries, i.e. such persons in the institution, organization, nation, country, a group who with their personality and character traits, more specifically, with presented vision, objectives, strategy, extraordinary erudition, intelligence and ideas become visionaries and creators of the future (the bases of leadership include emotions, where the leader inspires followers to perform a wider action). In this variant, the leader must have such features as: credibility, fairness and honesty; charisma, optimism, decisiveness, intelligence; pursuit of perfection; the ability to inspire, sense of encouragement and motivation; confidence; foresight. Equally important feature, if not the most important, is the vision of the leaders by which a leader can effectively exercise leadership, provided, however, that the followers can contribute to the shape and content of this vision.
4. Organic – leadership is examined in the context of progressive networking of our planet, which essentially translates into shape, quality and methods of formulating the leaders in both the organizational and political community. In this sense, the development of info-communicative tools and progressive complexity of the subjective interactions in the global scale generates a need

for completely new leaders, i.e. the leaders who rather act as coordinators for supporting communication and collaboration between dispersed individuals, employees or supporters. Hence, leadership becomes a process in which the leader is supposed to continuously analyse and revise objectives, goals, strategies and plans. On the other hand, the formal division into leaders and members of the organization, institution or state disappears (in this variant, the organic leader operates within a bilateral interaction where power, position or hierarchy does not stem directly from leader's position, but is conditioned by the trust and respect of the environment that constantly changes under clear influence of global circumstances[159]). Of course, in this approach, leadership is based on self-control and self-organization, where the leader and followers have both a sense of superiority of the common objective as well as a certain degree of autonomy[160].

It should be noted that the modern research on political leadership is also based on various theoretical models which, in addition to being subjected to empirical verification, are primarily a great confirmation and/or proof of the complexity and many aspects of this social phenomenon. Among the many theoretical proposals, a special attention deserve the following:

1. Models based on traits and characteristics of the leader – conceptualizations revolving around the study of personality traits, usually congenital and less vulnerable to any changes, of the certain leader, where he or she is subjected to a detailed analysis of the possibility of leader (intelligence, alertness, negotiating skills); personal achievements (education, knowledge); responsibility (reliability, initiative, perseverance, assertiveness); status (socioeconomic status); situational aspects (mental condition, needs, social expectations). Examples

---

159 Example is the concept of covert leadership which resembles "quiet management" of people. Similarly, the conductor of the orchestra: leader – conductor produces certain behaviours among musicians – the community, without simultaneous imposition and/or creation of any hierarchy of subordination. "Quiet management is about thoughtfulness rooted in experience. Wisdom, trust, dedication, and judgment are the qualities that apply here. Leadership works because it is legitimate, meaning that it is an integral part of the organization and so has the respect of everyone there. Tomorrow is appreciated because yesterday is honoured", which means that the future position and status of the leader result from respect and trust garnered in the past. More in: R. Bolden, B. Hawkins, J. Gosling, S. Taylor, *Exploring Leadership. Individual, Organizational & Societal Perspectives*, Oxford University Press, Oxford 2011, p. 33.
160 G. C. Avery, *Understanding Leadership. Paradigms and Cases*, Sage Publication, London 2004, pp. 17–36.

of this approach include leadership works of the following authors: R. M. Stogdill, S. J. Zaccaro, C. Kemp, P. Bader[161].
2. Behavioral models of leadership – models are directly related to the abilities, qualifications and skills of leaders who can develop, enhance, or undergo corrective actions to increase the efficiency of action, coordination and management. Among the behavioral models we can distinguish inter al. skill-based model of leadership, which has five components (competencies, individual attributes, leadership outcomes, career experiences, environment influences)[162].
3. Model of interdependence – this conceptualization is a multifactorial and/or a layered approach to the analysis of leadership. In this sense, leadership is formed as a phenomenon of interdependence between the leader and the followers (the environment), provided, however, that the leader is able to: properly identify and diagnose basic situational factors, including the feelings, needs, aspirations, goals of subordinates; adapt to specific external circumstances; combine well their behavior and personality traits with the requirements of the situation (the environment). Hence the correlation models are based on the general statement that: „effective leaders are those who can recognize what employees need and then adapt their own style to meet those needs". Among the numerous models based on the above thesis we can distinguish inter al.: the SLII model developed by Paul Hersey and Ken Blanchard. This dynamics of situational leadership model (SLII) is divided into two parts: leadership style and development level of subordinates. Thus we can, in turn, define four leadership styles: supporting – high supportive and low directive behavior; coaching – high directive and high supportive behavior; delegating – low supportive and low directive behavior; directing – high directive and low supportive behavior[163].

---

161 R. M. Stogdill, *Handbook of Leadership: A survey of theory and research*, Free Press, New York 1974; R. M. Stogdill, S. J. Zaccaro, C. Kemp, P. Bader, *Leader traits and attributes* [in:], J. Antonakis, A. T. Cianciolo, R. J. Sternberg (ed.), *The Nature of Leadership*, Sage, Thousand Oaks 2004, pp. 101–124.
162 M. D. Mumford, S. J. Zaccaro, F. D. Harding, T. O. Jacobs, E. A. Fleishman, *Leadership Skills for a Changing World: Solving Complex Social Problems*, "Leadership Quarterly" II (I), 2000, p. 23.
163 K. Blanchard, P. Zigarmi, D. Zigarmi, *Leadership and the One Minute Manager: Increasing Effectiveness Through Situational Leadership*, Harper Collins Publishers, New York 1985, pp. 54–61. In a similar vein Peter G. Northouse commented on the theoretical pluralism in the area of research on leadership, as evidenced by such theories of leadership as: contingency theory; path-goal theory; leader-member exchange theory; psychodynamic approach; transformational leadership. More in: P. G. Northouse, *Leadership: Theory and Practice*, Sage Publications, London 2010.

5. The problem of the scope in political leadership

5.1 Multi-level political leadership

Repeatedly stressing that leadership in temporal political conditions often leads to different ways of defining, describing and explaining the relationship at the leader ↔ followers intersection is intended to indicate the fact that political leadership can be studied on the basis of two analytically separate perspectives, i.e. from the agent as such (endogenous factors) and from the social structure (exogenous factors). Such overall, partly laconic premise, authorizes us to discuss the phenomenon of political leadership against the micro-macro dichotomy, which in its essence is a sign of intellectual and theoretical disputes between methodological individualists and holists. The essence of this speculative controversy boils down to determine the theoretical and practical priority, validity, significance, role of an individual (the social part) or the society (social entity) in the creation of adequate nomological explanations relating to political reality.

In order to move the issue of the scope of theorizing and explaining the political reality onto the category of political leadership, we must start from the premise discussed in the previous chapter. Multiparadigmaticity of leadership includes both theories with a micro theoretical scope (agent-oriented explanation of leadership), macro theoretical scope (explanation focused on the external environment – the social environment), as well as the concepts trying to go beyond the micro-macro dichotomy. We can say that modern theoretical and methodological procedures for the political leadership are not only trying to foster antagonism between the micro and macroanalysis, but also to connect and interweave different techniques and research tools in order to provide a more detailed insight into the phenomenon of leadership. In this perspective, some researchers abandon the traditional micro-macro antagonism for the benefit of dialectical reasoning, which is used to synthesize various contents, levels of analysis, areas of expertise and points of view. An example of this type of treatment may be hybrid theories of leadership, where various levels of analysis and/or research perspectives are consciously consolidated[164].

---

164 For instance, Stephen J. Zaccaro in his works describes the phenomenon of leadership and integrates such theoretical perspectives as cognitive, behavioural, strategic and

It should be noted that the contemporary theoretical and practical diversity relating to the political leadership is reflected in the taxonomy of this concept, where many instances of research clearly emphasize the need for analytical separation (distinction) of the characteristic levels of research. Table 1 provides an illustration of this type of reasoning and summarizes different levels of analysis for categories of political leadership with the subject of study and assigned sample theories.

Table 1: Research multi-level character of political leadership

Level of analysis	Subject of analysis	Examples of Leadership Theory/Theorists
Micro	Leadership qualities; personality and leadership skills; leadership styles; psychological profiles of leaders; competence, behavior, emotional intelligence of a leader; relationships at the leader ↔ followers intersection in dyadic dimension (one to one) and group (one to many)	The Great Man Theory by Thomas Carlyle; Theory of Classical Styles of Leadership by Kurt Lewin; Contingency Model of Leadership by Fred E. Fiedler
Macro	Multi-level character and complexity of leadership; social, organizational, environmental context, in which the leader operates; analysis of the relationship at the leader ↔ followers intersection in dynamic and multifactorial dimension; substitutive character of leadership, including the phenomenon of self-leadership; distributed leadership, networking, etc.	Complexity Leadership Theory (CLT) by Mary Uhl-Bien and Russ Marion; generative leadership theory by Gita Surie and James K. Hazy

Source: own work

It should be noted that an analysis of the micro and macro level applied in Table 1 does not separate the intermediate level, i.e. mesostructures that occur in the social sciences. Such simplification is not due to ignorance of the author, but is dictated by scientific practice of theories in the political leadership, where in the research process we often have to deal with the lack of precise separation on meso theoretical level. This results in extension of the micro-level onto supraindividual research, including group, intergroup, situational research, etc., referring to the specific party, organization or labour self-government. An example would be Leader-Member Exchange Theory (LMX), which comprises both

---

visionary. More in: S. J. Zaccaro, *The Nature of Executive Leadership: A Conceptual and Empirical Analysis of Success*, Washington 2001.

personal-psychological components as well as it breaks into the macro theoretical area in order to analyse complex intersubjective interactions in the external environment[165].

5.2 Micro-level political leadership theories

In the case of microtheoretical level we can talk about group theory and/or research methods, in which the explanation of political leadership is based on the mechanism of methodological reduction, where the phenomenon of leadership applies only to individual decisions, i.e., for analysis, research, putting forward empirical assertions towards the leader. In other words, it is a complex research process, in which the individualistic paradigm is the key based on the directives of methodological individualism. As pointed out by Raymond Boudon, individualistic paradigm used in the political science can be characterized on the basis of the established canon claims. In Boudon's interpretation, we can talk about the following course of individualistic reasoning

> To summarize, suppose M is the phenomenon to be explained. In the individualistic paradigm, to explain M means making it the outcome of a set of actions m. In mathematical symbols, M=M(m); in words, M is a function of the actions m. Then the actions m are made understandable, in the Weberian sense, by relating them to the social environment, the situation S, of the actors: m=m(S). Finally, the situation itself has to be explained as the outcome of some macrosociological variables, or at least of variables located at a level higher than S. Let us call these higher-level variables P, so that S=S(P). On the whole, M=M {m[S(P)]}. In words, M is the outcome of action, which are the outcome of the social environment of the actors, the latter being the outcome of macrosociological variables[166].

Applying foundations of individualistic paradigm to political analyses of leadership we can say that the centre of gravity in the complex leader ↔ followers relations (social environment) is moved to one side, i.e. all scientific conclusions focus on the leaders and the interactions that take place in specific socio-structural condition with leader's participation. The consequence of such micro-explanatory

---

165 LMX is a clear attempt at combining transactional and transformational theory of leadership with the typology of exchange at the intersection leader-followers. More in: D.V. Day, J. Antonakis (eds.), *The Nature of Leadership*, Sage Publications, London 2012, pp. 13–14.
166 R. Boudon, *The Individualistic Tradition in Sociology*, [in:] J. C. Alexander, B. Giesen, R. Münch, N. J. Smelser (eds.), *The Micro-Macro Link*, University of California Press, Berkeley & Los Angeles 1987, p. 46.

attitude is to study the phenomenon of political leadership in terms of, inter al., such parameters as:

1. Features of leadership (qualities, distinguishing features of character and personality of the leader).
2. Leadership style (behaviours, skills and competences).
3. Situational and social requirements for the emergence of leadership (analysis of the situational context in the micro- and meso-structural dimension).

In the case of political leadership analyses against the background of specific traits in leaders as such, the starting point is the assumption that "you have to be a born leader." In this research current we can find many theories that attribute specific qualities to the leader. This enables a particular leader to effectively and efficiently complete the assigned role, function or leadership task. In many research works, on the basis of broadly defined social sciences scholars elaborated on countless attributive features that are conducive to effective leadership, to name just a few: intelligence, responsibility, motivation, initiative, self-confidence, sociability, cooperativeness, influence, etc. It should be noted that empirical research on effective political leader, or rather its essential personal characteristics, highlighted several trends and tendencies of research, which were dominated by multithreaded individual-personal analysis. This type of conceptualisations creating patterns and/or psychological profiles of individual leaders on the basis of previous empirical practice usually revolve around:

1. Building scientific models of personality – attempts at systematizing various empirical researches on the characteristics of leadership in a sensible and coherent theoretical model. An example would be the Five – Factor Model of Personality analysed by T. A. Judge, D. M. Heller and K. Mount, in which the five universal and immutable characteristics and/or mutually intertwining dimensions of personality leaders can be defined and separated, i.e.: surgency; adjustment, conscientiousness, openness to experience; agreeableness[167].
2. Enumeration and identification of the different characteristics of leadership – attempts to identify the specific characterological distinguishing features of the leader (such characteristics can include, inter al., striving for achievement,

---

[167] T. A. Judge, D. Heller, M. K. Mount, *Five-Factor Model of Personality and Job Satisfaction: Meta-Analysis*, "Journal of Applied Psychology", vol. 87, no. 3, 2002, pp. 530–541.

sensitivity to others, high energy, stability, confidence, sense of control, emotional intelligence[168], flexibility).
3. Creating motivation profiles of leaders – to find the causes and/or type of needs for the creation of an effective leader in the socio-political space. The most frequent reasons to become a leader include, inter al., the need for power (desire to influence others; gradable willingness to subordinate their own environmental goals, aspirations, preferences); the need for affiliation (striving for good relations with the environment) or the need for achievement (desire for self-improvement)[169].

It is clear that the analysis of leadership based on the characteristics of leaders highlights the role and importance of personal characteristics, which in this system is the leading determinant of explaining the phenomenon of political leadership. From a psychological point of view, it involves creating different personality patterns which are designed to diagnose and determine the psychological profiles of political leaders. An example of such analytical procedures in the field of psychodiagnostics includes MIDC (Millon Inventory of Diagnostic Criteria) created by Theodore Millon, whose primary function is to diagnose psychological profiles of political leaders and its pathological variants[170].

---

168 Contemporary leadership studies also refer to the emotional intelligence of leader which means the emergence of resonant leadership. In this case, the leader: „was attuned to people's feelings and moved them in a positive emotional direction. Speaking authentically from his own values and resonating with the emotions of those around him, he hit just the right chords with his messager, leaving people feeling uplifted and inspired even in a difficult moment (…) One sign of resonant leadership is a group of followers who vibrate with the leader's upbeat and enthusiastic energy". Więcej w: D. Goleman, R. Boyatzis, A. McKee, *Primal Leadership. Realizing The Power of Emotional Intelligence*, Harvard Buisness School Press, 2002, p. 54.
169 R. N. Lussier, Ch. F. Achua, *Leadership. Theory, Application, & Skill Development*, South-Western Cengage Learning, Mason 2010, pp. 32–47.
170 It should be noted that: "Millon's model encompasses eight attribute domains, namely expressive behavior, interpersonal conduct, cognitive style, mood/temperament, self-image, regulatory mechanisms, object representations, and morphologic organization. In short, political personality assessment grounded in Millon's system is multidimensional, which affords the distinct advantage of accounting for »the patterning of [personality] variables cross the en tire matrix of the person«". More in: A. Immelman, *The Political Personality of U. S. President George W. Bush*, [in:] L. O. Valenty, O. Feldman (ed.), *Political Leadership for The New Century. Personality and Behavior Among American Leaders*, Praeger Publishers, Westport 2002, pp. 81–103;

At the same time, it should be noted that the scientific analyses of the political leadership with indications, identification and enumeration of specific leadership traits are in their assumptions limited both in theoretical-methodological and cognitive-practical terms. The opinions that the research on leadership cannot be reduced to the parameters and/or indicators and/or strictly symptoms, but should expand each prospect because of the multiplicity of conditions of daily practice of leadership prevail among the many voices criticizing the personality tests. This view is accompanied by the opinions, among which the inability to create a universal, and thus quantifiable canon of leadership is demonstrated, which means that the phenomenon of modern political leadership does not lie within the homogeneous classification of and/or schematization. This state of affairs is mainly due to the diversity of political practice, which is inter al. conditioned by:

1. Type of political regime – political regime determines the governing agent in the social structure, including the position, role and status of the leader.
2. Applicable political culture – where the political culture – interpreted as a comprehensive system of meanings, symbols, their values, etc. – is an integral creative part within the community, which directly or indirectly affects the definition and perception of leaders.

The summary of the scientific criticism of the personal analysis of political leadership seems to be encapsulated properly by Fred Greenstein, for whom the study of leadership in political practice is pointless because:

1. Personality characteristics tend to be randomly distributed in institutional roles (any immanent features of political leaders become secondary with regard to social functions, roles, resources, institutions, structures, expectation, situations – emphasis F. P.). Personality, therefore, »cancels out« and can be ignored in political analysis.
2. Personality characteristics are less import ant than social characteristics in influencing behavior.
3. Personality is irrelevant, because individual actors are severely limited in the impact they can have on events.
4. Personality is not an important determinant of behavior, because individuals with varying personal characteristics tend to behave similarly when placed in common situations[171].

    T. Millon, *Disordes of Personality: DSM-IV and Beyond*, John Wiley & Sons, Inc., New York 1996.

171 F. I. Greenstein, *Personality and Politics: Problem of Evidence, Inference, and Conceptualization*, Markham, Chicago 1969, p. 34. Also in: S. Strack (ed.), *Handbook*

In contrast, the studies of political leadership based on the styles of political leadership, understood as a combination of qualities, skills and behaviours of a particular leader used in interactions with followers were initiated in the late 1930s by Kurt Lewin[172]. Today, based on the work of this American researcher, there are three basic styles of leadership:

1. Autocratic – the leader of the group himself or herself defines the objectives, assignsor defines the powers and responsibilities, enforces the execution of tasks. Leader opts for penalties rather than prizes; the leader wants maximum control over all areas of institutional activity, which is associated with reduction of autonomy in the public sphere.
2. Democratic –is characterised by partner relationship between the leader and followers, where the objectives, targets and business strategies are set jointly on the principles of equal deliberation of all sides. Here there is the lack of leadership that arbitrarily imposes controls or enforces obedience to the leader. Instead, leadership enters into the mechanism of objective political pluralism, where the political leader, wanting to stay in power has to reconcile conflicting interests, needs, visions and preferences according to the argument that the overriding objective of leaders in conditions of democracy it is to integrate society and the means of implementation include negotiation and/or search for compromise.
3. Liberal (laissez-faire) – is a denial of the phenomenon of leadership. In this perspective, leadership, interpreted as influencing pre-defined governing agent, is getting blurred in favour of the social environment, in which the leader operates. Here it is not the leader who plays the dominant role in taking

---

of Personology and Psychopathology, John Wiley & Sons, Inc., New Jersey 2005, pp. 211–212.

172 In the 30s of the 20th century, before behavioral approach became popular in the social sciences, Kurt Lewin and colleagues from the University of Iowa in the United States of America on the basis of empirical analysis had separated the two basic styles of leadership, i.e. autocratic and democratic, which were antagonistic poles on the leadership continuum. More in: K. Lewin, R. Lippitt, R. White, *Patterns of Aggressive Behavior in Experimentally Created »Social Climates«*, "Journal of Social Psychology", vol. 10, 1939, pp. 271–299; R. Bolden, B. Hawkins, J. Gosling, S. Taylor, *Exploring Leadership. Individual, Organizational, and Societal Perspective*, Oxford University Press, New York 2011, p. 27.

action, decision or determination of the strategy but the followers, i.e. the social group, which does include the leader[173].

Lewinian typology became in fact the inspiration for other researchers who in the style of leadership saw the essence of leadership. Theoretical examples worth mentioning for the study of contemporary political leaders include at least the research works by M.G. Hermann, J.T. Preston and J. Kaarbo, where the authors noted that the style of leadership in politics, or repeated courses of action including broadly understood creation of relationships with the environment, is made up of five basic elements: the range of interests of political leaders, which depends on the understanding of the leadership being exercised; tolerance of conflicts within their own environment; dominant type of motivation in leadership activities; strategy to collect different types of information; ways to resolve conflicts[174]. Another Lewinian-inspired example can be the analysis of the phenomenon of leadership in the organization led by Viktor Vromma and Arthur Jago, who on the basis of the theory of situational decision created a time-driven leadership model based on the juxtaposition of two planes of analysis, i.e. they joined five leadership styles with seven situational factors, which generated a matrix with different combinations intended to reflect the complexity and temporality phenomenon of leadership. From the point of view of the distinct leadership styles the authors listed:

1. "Decide" Style –*the leader makes the decision alone and either announces or sells it to the team.* The leader uses personal expertise and collects information from the team or others who can help solve the problem. The role of employees is clearly one of providing specific information that is requested, rather generating or evaluating solutions.
2. "Consult individually" style – *the leader presents the problem to team members individually, getting their ideas and suggestions and then makes the decision without bringing them together as a group.* This decision may not reflect their influence.
3. "Consult team" style – *the leader presents the problem to team members in a meeting, gets their suggestions, and then makes the decision. It may or may not reflect their influence.*
4. "Facilitate" style – *the leader presents the problem to the team in a meeting acts as a facilitator, defines the problem to be solved, and sets the boundaries within which*

---

173 D. Katz, *Patterns of Leadership*, [in:] J. N. Knutson (ed.), *Handbook of political psychology*, Jossey-Bass, London 1973, pp. 203–233.
174 M. G. Hermann, J. T. Preston, *Presidents, advisers, and foreign policy: The effects of leadership style on executive arrangements*, "Political Psychology" vol. 15, 1994, pp. 75–96; J. Kaarbo, *Prime minister leadership styles in foreign policy decision-making: A Framework for research*, "Political Psychology", vol. 3, 1997, pp. 553–582.

the decision must be made. (...) The leader's role is much like that of chairperson, coordinating the discussion, keeping it focused on the problem, and being sure that essential issues are discussed. The leader doesn't try to influence the team to adopt her or his solution.

5. "Delegate" style –*the leader permits the team to make the decision within prescribed limits*. The team undertakes the identification and diagnosis of the problem, developing alternative procedures for solving it and deciding on one or more alternative solutions. The leader doesn't enter into the team's deliberations unless explicitly asked, but plays an important role by providing needed resources and encouragement[175].

It should be added that research on leadership based on distinguishable styles of leadership has a broader formula than the very study of leadership. An essential and important part here is broadening the subject of research, where besides personal distinguishing features, researchers are also interested in the skills[176]competences and behaviours of leaders in the context of their function in the situational, social or organizational environment. Hence, empirical studies have been conducted on the leaders, where attempts have been made to diagnose and describe different styles of leadership. In this regard, scholarly analyses of management deserve special attention, where by explaining the different types of combinations of styles of leadership, an attempt was made to point out a different nature of the skills and behaviors of leaders (managers), which by definition would affect the quality and efficiency of management. Examples of such analyses can be found in Robert R. Blake and Jane S. Mouton works, who developed The Managerial Grid, which is a fairly easy method to evaluate the involvement of individual managers in the teamwork. The authors appointed two dimensions of management by the leader, i.e. concern for result and concern for people. In the first case we are dealing with manager attitude to, among others, issues such as quality of decisions concerning the adoption and implementation of policies, procedures and processes in the company; creativity in research activities; the quality of services provided; productivity or output. In the second case,

---

175 D. Hellriegel, J. W. Slocum, *Organizational Behavior*, South-Western, Mason 2007, pp. 308–310.

176 Inreference literature we can come across an opinion that leadership skill seems to be a compound of at least four major ingredients: 1. The ability to use power effectively and in responsible manner; 2. The ability to comprehend that human beings have differing motivation forces at different times and in different situations; 3. The ability to inspire; 4. The ability to act in a manner that will develop a climate conducive to responding to and arousing motivations. More in: B. Bjerke, *Buisness Leadership and Culture. National Management Styles in The Global Economy*, Edward Elgar Publishing, Inc., Northampton 1999, p. 61.

the manager refers to issues such as: maintaining self-esteem among workers; transfer of responsibility on the basis of trust; the provision of adequate working conditions and care for satisfying relationships between employees. On the basis of these two dimensions, authors recognize four extremes of leadership styles, which in leadership practice are subject to numerous configurations:

1. Impoverished manager – exhibit little concern for other people or result and have minimum involvement in their jobs.
2. Team leaders – display the highest possible dedication both to people and the results in their action. They are able to mesh the production needs of the enterprise with the needs of individuals.
3. Country club manager – managers have little or no concern for results but are interested only in people. They promote an environment where everyone is relaxed, friendly and happy but no one is concerned about putting forth a coordinated effort to accomplish goals.
4. Autocratic task managers – are concerned only with developing an efficient operation, who have little or no concern for people and who are quite autocratic in their style of leadership[177].

In addition, scientific analyses of the styles of leadership are part of the theoretical stream describing numerous interdependencies at the leader ↔ followers intersection, where there is no way to delimit style of leadership from the complex environment in which the leader operates (both at the micro and mesostructural level). On this basis, the so-called situational leadership model developed, where attempts were made to go beyond the plane of individuality in favour of psychological analyzes taking into account the social context. To put it simply, it can be said that the approach to the phenomenon of situational leadership refers to a detailed analysis of three factors, i.e. a leader as such, his or her supporters and a situation in which there is a complex interaction between them. An example of this type of research may be theoretical research carried out by Fred E. Fiedler, who was one the first researchers in the social sciences who took up the topic of contingency leadership[178]. The author identified three key elements of direct relevance to the rise of the phenomenon of leadership in a particular environment and social structure:

---

177 B. Bjerke, *Buisness Leadership and Culture. National Management Styles in The Global Economy*, Edward Elgar Publishing, Inc., Northampton 1999, p. 60.
178 Contingency Theory of Leader Effectiveness was developed by Fred E. Fiedler in 1951 r. It was one of the first theoretical leadership conceptualisations which linked personality features with particular behaviours and separate situations emerging at the leader ↔ followers intersection.

1. The atmosphere in the group – a mood which prevails in relation ↔ leader of the group members according to the statement that where there is a good / friendly atmosphere, where the leader enjoys the trust, sympathy and loyalty of their supporters (group). On the other hand, where there is bad / unfriendly atmosphere, the leader must use additional forms of pressure, influence or manipulation to gain accreditation, obedience, respect and enforce certain obligations, tasks, goals.
2. Structure of the task – in a given organizational structure of the task may be determined or may lack such systematization. In this approach, attention is paid to the simple relationship: It is where the group has clearly and precisely articulated a list of tasks, objectives, priorities, etc. (manual task, strategy for achieving those objectives, an exhaustive list of priorities) that the management and leadership of the group become easier. At the same time, this also works the other way, i.e. where there is lack of task systematization and precision, we can talk about various leadership difficulties, which means i.e.: gradable level of organisational chaos; exclusive activity of individual members of the group (organization); lack of coherence in achieving the intended objectives or results.
3. Scope of leader's authority – in leadership practice the correlation – leadership position and/or the status of leader in a particular social environment depends on the scope of the ruling force expressed in terms of number of instruments and resources thanks to which the leader can have a real impact on the group. Hence, those leaders who have been awarded many prizes, as well as have sanctions have a significant impact on the group. In turn, the position of leaders is poor when they have little expertise or less impact on the members of the group[179].

On the basis of experimental and analytically separate elements Fiedler came to the conclusion that leadership behaviours are either task-oriented (emphasis put by the leader on the job done by activities such as: distribution of tasks, organization of work, strict enforcement and control of various stages of the work) or people-oriented (the leader is open and friendly to the members of the group, the leader cares about the needs of members). Fiedler's model also points to the fact that leadership style is mainly conditioned by the temporality of environment, and – more specifically – is to adjust the leaders himself or herself to a specific socio-structural situation, where the methods of operation, methods of

---

179 R. Brown, *Group Processes. Dynamic within and between group*, Blackwell Publishing Ltd., Oxford 2000, pp. 99–112.

determining and implementing the objectives, targets and strategies for leaders directly depend on external conditions. In other words, the model emphasizes that the dynamics of social practice even enforces "adaptation" of the leader to the exigencies of the situation, which automatically undermines the stability and integrity of specific styles of leadership (negation of uniquely defined traits or parameters of a particular style of leadership). Thus, in Fiedler's analyses include three types of leadership situations, which are characterized by high, medium or low level of control of the leader in relation to the social environment[180].

It should be noted that Fiedler, explaining the relationship between a specific situational leader and the followers, developed the research instrument in order to get a chance for an empirical measurement of the level of control of a situational leader, i.e. the least preferred co-worker scale (LPC), where, based on the definition of the hierarchy of motivation of individual leaders, two types of leaders were distinguished, i.e. low-LPC leaders –the basic and only motivation for such leaders is to perform a specific task, whereas interpersonal relationships with supporters are secondary; high-LPC leaders – basic and only motivation for such leaders is to build a proper relationship with supporters, whereas the realization of individual tasks is secondary. In addition, a complex Fiedler's model is equipped with a variable – situational favourability – which examined the scope of the leaders in the social environment. Situational favourability included three components: leader ↔ member relations (is the most powerful of the three sub-elements in determining overall situation favorability. It involves the extent to which relationships between the leader and followers are generally cooperative and friendly or antagonistic and difficult. Leaders who rate leader ↔ member relations as high would fell they had the support of their followers); task structure (here the leader would objectively determine task structure by assessing whether there were detailed descriptions of work products, standard operating procedures, or objective indicators of how well the task is being accomplished); position power(is the weakest of the three elements of situational favorability. Leaders who have titles of authority or rank, the authority to administer rewards and punishments, and the legitimacy to conduct follower performance appraisals have greater position power than leaders who lack them)[181].

---

180   A. J. DuBrin, *Leadership: Research, Findings, Practice, and Skills*, South-Western Cengage Learning, Mason 2007, p. 145.
181   The above-mentioned factors create the scale of situational enforcement of the leader where the minimum level is marked with eight octans and maximum level with one octan. The leader with high level of situational enforcement has a high leadership position which is structured with by the task grid and enjoys a rapport with sup-

Comprehensive illustration of situational leadership model by Fred E. Fiedler is presented in diagram 13 which shows the correlation between analytically designated agents and/or determinants of the Fiedlerian theory.

Diagram 13: Three-element relationship in the situatonal theory of leadership

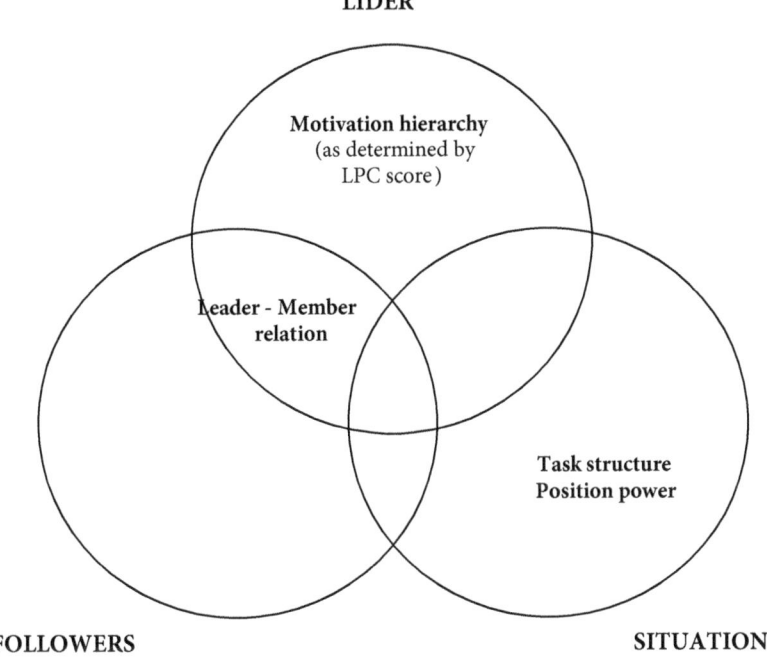

Own work after R. L Hughes, R. C. Ginett i G. J. Curphy[182]

Concluding the research in macrotheoretical scale on the political leadership, we can generally say that there are two types of scientific explanations of relation leader ↔ followers. In this sense, we can distinguish between such schemes and/or track explanatory as:

1. Direct leader– the scientific explanations are mainly based on the personal-psychological justifications related to the leader and/or ruling agent, where

---

porters. More in: R. L. Hughes, R. C. Ginett, G. J. Curphy, *Contingency Theories of Leadership*, [in:] G. R. Hickman (ed.), *Leading Organizations: Perspectives for New Era*, Sage Publications, Inc., London 2010, pp. 101–121.

182   R. L. Hughes, R. C. Ginett, G. J. Curphy, *Contingency...*, p. 112.

explanatory elements are precisely defined skills and competencies of leaders; exhaustive list of personality traits of a leader; exemplary behaviour or styles of leadership.
2. Focused on the temporal relationship between leader and followers – scientific explanations relate primarily to the time-varying dyadic or group dimension, which significantly and noticeably translate into political leadership. Therefore, situational social contextbecomes crucial, where the explanatory elements are: the atmosphere in the group; the governing range of the leader depending on various circumstances; gradable level of control of the leader in relation to supporters.

5.3 Macro-level political leadership theories

A different point of view and/or explanatory scheme occurs in macrosociology, where multi-level analysis of research is applied, which in addition to the individual plane recognizes and underlines its value at the supraindividual macrostructural level. In other words, it means a situation in which the fundamental axiom for various scientific studies on the basis of political science is to adopt a realistic and holistic research perspective. In this system, the analysis of political reality – both in the ontological, epistemological as well as methodological terms – is based on macroscopic justifications, where the key to descriptions, understanding and explanation of the world of politics lies mainly in an integrative entity; where there is consent and full understanding of the concept of emergence, including variously defined emergents, which can be inter al.: qualities, characteristics, patterns and social structures (*cf.* Chapter 1 of this book); where political practice is not only the result of a specific activity or interactions of individual political actors, but it is a complex structural space and more specifically the social entity which is subject to permanent structuring, which boils down to the innumerable multitude of intersubjective interactions – individual, group or collective agreements.

In the macrotheoretical variant, political reality is considered through the perspective of critical realism, where the relationships, properties and processes of supraindividual nature are brought to the fore. At the same time it is the reality understood as a complex and temporal socio-structural space (reality defined as "interconnected hierarchies of levels"; reality where action and structure are co-determined), in which:

(1) social structure, unlike natural structure, do not exist independently of the activities they govern;

(2) social structures, unlike natural structures, do not exist independently of the agents' conceptions of what they are doing in their activity;
(3) social structures, unlike natural structures, may be only relatively enduring, so that the tendencies they ground may not be universal in the sense of space-time invariance[183].

In such conditions, competent researchers of political phenomena speak about the application of scientific analysis of conceptual macro-structural schemes, in which a social structure is defined by an appropriate combination of the so-called. structural parameter, expressing the complexity of the whole society. Such parameters include:

1. *Heterogeneity* – is the extent of differentiation of the members of a collectivity into nominal groups. Society's division of labor illustrates heterogeneity; so does a community's linguistic diversity. (...) The criterion of heterogeneity is the chance expectation that two randomly chosen persons belong to different groups.
2. *Inequality* – is the extent of differentiation of a population in terms of resources or ranked status. The concentration of wealth is a form of inequality; so is the extent of differences in education. The criterion of a society's or community's inequality in a given dimension is the mean absolute difference in status or resources between any two persons proportionate to the mean status or resources for all persons.
3. *Intersecting* – if differences in social positions along various lines are strongly correlated, they consolidate group boundaries and class distinctions and strengthen the barriers between ingroup and outgroup or between persons who differ in hierarchical status. Illustrations are the typically close connections among racial background, education, occupation, income, and power[184].

Applying the macro theoretical approach to the category of political leadership it must be stated that such a research perspective is in fact a methodological procedure of crossing rigid, *a priori* assumptions of micro theoretical analysis, where the study based on personal-psychological characteristics is questioned to some extent, particularly reducing the phenomenon of leadership to an exhaustive list of leadership qualities of individual leaders or preferred styles of leadership. In this sense, macroanalysis is a broader and comprehensive perspective on the process of political leadership, in which two sides of leadership relations

---

183 K. M. Kontopoulos, *The Logics of Social Structure*, Cambridge University Press, Cambridge 1993, p. 221. Here political reality is understood as: "the combination of complex and compounded externalities, corporate and collective actors and many-person systems leads to what may be colled »entangled interdependent system« or »metastructure« (a complex combination of simple structures of interaction) or »a structure of structures«. Ibid., p. 147 and subsequent.

184 P. M. Blau, *Contrasting Theoretical Perspectives*, [in:] J. C. Alexander, B. Giesen, R. Münch, N. J. Smelser (ed.), *The Micro-Macro...*, pp. 76–78.

are crucial, i.e. both the political leader, as well as his or her supporters, including the socio-political environment, situational institutional or systemic requirements. Generally, it can be said that this point of view bringing leadership into the political praxis does not belong so much to the subject-personality component, but the view oscillates around the processual perspective (see. diagram 12). Therefore macroanalyses of leadership overcome the borderline of microresearch in favour of multi-level or complex research, in which, on the one hand, temporality, on the other hand, complexity of progressive politics are emphasized.

Currently, in the social sciences, macro theoretical research on leadership takes many forms and characters. Particularly popular are inter al.: system approach or institutional approach. In the first case leadership as such is a feature of the entire system, resulting in the current interaction process between the elements of the whole society. In other words, the political leadership is a process resulting from multiple interactions between the elements (intrasystemic conversion) belonging to the pre-defined political system; This feature, which is created on the basis and as a result of intrasubjective interaction, and it is not only the consequence of individual features of a single leader. As Gayle C Avery put it:

> Leadership arises when people work together in reciprocal relationship – a distributed process shared by many ordinary people, rather than the result of a single extraordinary person. This notion, consistent with the Organic leadership paradigm, goes well beyond the idea that leadership is a personal trait or set of behaviours vested in special people. It goes beyond the idea that anyone can be a leader, and beyond the idea that leadership can and should be shared between leader and followers. Instead, what leaders do is not independent of, but is interdependent with follower's actions and organizational processes. Leadership is thus related to a complex system that contains various subsystems, including: members' personalities; intergroup processes; tasks; work processes and practices; accountability systems; policies and administrative structures[185].

As a result, the phenomenon of leadership dispersion, or rather its re-orientation from the individual as such (features and psychophysical predispositions) to a specific social entity (organization, a large social group, society, state, nation, ethnic group, etc.) enables researchers to perceive and appreciate the scientific analyses of such phenomena as:

---

[185] In this understanding, the process of leadership is directly linked to the functioning of the general social system where there i san exchange of subsystems within the system. The subsystems include: personality of members, inergroup processes, tasks, principles, structures, clearance systems, etc. More in: G. C. Avery, *Understanding Leadership. Paradigms and Cases*, Sage Publication, London 2004, pp. 114–115.

1. Substitutes for leaders – where various elements of the social system take over the function of leadership as such. In this perspective, the subsystems of the political system provide the necessary leadership in the whole society. The substitutes for leadership, inter al., include: working out consistent teams of experts and / or highly skilled workers; working out and generate detailed operating instructions, guidelines, policies or procedures; developing knowledge management system and expert systems.
2. Self-leading – a mechanism in which individual members of the organization (the social entity) are trying to become leaders for themselves, so the entity as such (organization) functions better and more efficiently. In this system, the key is to develop the appropriate organizational culture, through which it will be possible to develop mechanisms of self-leadership (culture determines the quality of leadership, where shared values, standards and developed habits, styles of thought, as well as the atmosphere are conducive to building relationships at the leader ↔ followers intersection, and often modify this relationship in order to eliminate any relationship to the overall leadership (organizational) cooperation between positive self-creating leaders)[186].

The second approach attempts to link the category of leadership to the institutional environment, where the process of leadership and the formal institutionalization, including fulfilling the role and function of leadership is determined by the sphere of institutions functioning in given political conditions. In this arrangement, the practice of political leadership is directly related to factors such as:

1. Type of political regime – leadership process, including the role, status, the scope of the impact and the importance of certain political leaders is directly dependent on the current political regime. Therefore, leadership will take a completely different shape in totalitarian conditions(agent is synonymous with the dictator based on his or her own worship, where there is a dysfunction in the leader ↔ followers relationship involving, among others: lack of freedom in the formation of leadership, lack of participation of followers in the process of leadership; commonly used terror of "indelible" political leader) than in authoritarian conditions (similar dysfunction in leadership practice) or democratic conditions (leadership formed in conditions of political pluralism, which boils down to the equivalent deliberation between the freely elected leader and the supporters).

---

186   Ibid, pp. 115–118.

2. The nature and form of the political system – political leadership depends on the political system in force in a given country. Hence, the leadership process will take a completely different form in formal and legal as well as institutional terms in the parliamentary, presidential or semi-presidential political system. In this variant, the key is the division of powers, the number of prerogatives or systemic status of a political leader (individual and collective political agent) in relation to the other participants of collective life[187].

We should not forget that various macroanalyses on the political leadership are *a priori* included in the set of research techniques and methods based on methodological holism, where the political reality is interpreted in a holist and/or multi-level manner. This means, on the one hand, acceptance as the basis of all analytical and theoretical studies of extracted specific levels of analysis (the level of individual, group, large social groups and the entity of a higher order, i.e. the additive complexity), on the other hand, the use of empirical research techniques which do not adopt some form of reductionism, but include and take into account supraindividual events or phenomena. In addition, macroperspective regarding the scientific study of leadership sees empirical confirm ability and the importance of phenomena such as emergence, nonlinearity, blurred chaotic matter of politics. In this arrangement, the political space becomes a dynamic and complex social structure, which is constituted by such distinguishing features as: structural emergent self-organization; endogenous agents/actors (individual and collective political actors), and heterogeneous relativeness; causal uncertainty and/or causal fuzziness or diffusing the structural system. At the same time, such a comprehensive and/or multi-level look at the political practice resulted in theoretical and methodological reconceptualization on the traditional description or explanation of the relationship of leadership. Empirical observation and record of the phenomenon of multiform uncertainty in the social space became the turning point, which essentially denied the linear, mechanistic explanation of the social world. The moment when the principle of strict causality of phenomena was undermined changed the traditional understanding of leadership (the leader, interpreted as a person occupying an official position of authority in the structural hierarchy had a quantifiable impact on supporters, which resulted in predictable facts, states of affairs, activities, etc. in the process

---

187 J. J. Linz, *Totalitarian and Authoritarian Regimes*, Lynne Rienner Publisher, London 2000; N. Ezrow, E. Franz, *Dictators and Dictatorship. Understanding Authoritarian Regimes and Their Leaders*, Continuum International Publishing Group, New York 2011.

of leadership) and proposed a dynamic analysis of relations leader ↔ followers taking into account instead the progressive and unpredictable complexity of the world policies or emergent nature of the social change. Complex Systems Leadership Theory (CSLT) is an example of research on the political leadership in the dynamic and emergent view, in which the relation to the leader ↔ followers is examined through the prism of temporal complexity-dedicated socio-structural entity. In other words, it is a set of theories, in which explanation of political leadership takes place in the broader context of research (multi-level analysis), which involves the integration of various research techniques. In short, it can be stated that the application of CSLT to the phenomenon of leadership means:

1. Expanding the locus of leadership from isolated, role-based actions of individuals to the innovative, contextual interactions that occur across an entire social system.
2. Extending current theory and practice by focusing on micro-strategic leadership actions across all organizational levels and across organizational boundaries.
3. Increasing the relevance and accuracy of leadership theory by exploring how leadership outcomes are based on complex interactions, rather than "independent" variables.
4. Highlighting the relational foundations of change in emerging organizational fields, through the idea that leadership occurs in the "spaces between" agents.
5. Providing a new and rich foundation for explaining the constructive process of collective action as well as the influential "behaviors" of collective actors.
6. Connecting to innovative methodologies that can enrich our understanding how leadership gets enacted and received in complex environments[188].

It should be emphasized that a holist explanatory scheme in the case of scientific research on leadership cannot be reduced only to accept a particular method of analysis of reality or the implementation of specific directives of research consistent methodological presuppositions of CSLT, but also praise pluralism theory, due to which scientific explication of leadership is often based on different points of view or theoretical schools (table 2).

---

188 P. L. Jennings, K. J. Dooley, *An Emerging Complex Paradigm in Leadership Research*, [in:] J. K. Hazy, J. A. Goldstein, B. B. Lichtenstein (ed.), *Complex Systems Leadership Theory. New Perspectives from Complexity Science on Social and Organizational Effectiveness*, ISCE Publishing, Mansfield 2007, pp. 18–29.

Table 2: Sample theories of collective leadership

Leadership Theory/ Theorists	Complexity View of Leadership	Focus	Key Concepts
Leadership as Metacapability/ J. K Hazy	Process focus	Macro / organizational	Leadership as resource & information processing mechanisms: • Leadership distributes organizational resources towards exploitation or exploration • Defines convergent, generative, and unifying leadership mechanisms that perform different functions
Complexity Leadership/ R. Marion, M. Uhl-Bien	Leaders as objective observers shape interactions	Organizational and team level	Leadership as the interplay of three forms enabled by formal leader: • Leaders play various roles: managerial, adaptive and enabling leadership • Formal leaders use tensions to induce adaptive change • The formal leader is balancing managerial and enabling leadership roles • Team members emerge as adaptive leaders if enabled by the formal leader
Complex Responsive Processes R. D. Stacey	Leadership as a relating process of agents' communicative acts	No distinction between micro and macro	Leadership as acts of agents' communication: • Agents jointly act to transform their environments through acts of communications • Interactions are reflective of agents' freedom, however repetitive forms of interactions curtail freedom

Own work based on C. Panzar, J. K. Hazy, B. McKelvey, D. R. Schwandt[189]

---

[189] C. Panzar, J. K. Hazy, B. McKelvey, D. R. Schwandt, *The Paradox of Complex Organizations: Leadership as Integrative Influence*, [in:] J. K. Hazy, J. A. Goldstein, B. B. Lichtenstein (eds.), *Complex...*, p. 312.

Therefore, consideration of leadership in the paradigm of complexity is, on the one hand, based on synthesizing certain levels of analysis, i.e. the micro-level (individual person and personal interactions), meso-level (groups or collectives, formal organizations, social movements and some aspects of institutions) and macro-level (social structure and societies overall)[190], and on the emphasis of their mutual conditions and determination within the complex adaptive system (micro-macro co-evolving interactions[191]), on the other hand, on the elaboration of specific axioms of theoretical research. Such irrefutable statements included in the complexity paradigm relating to the scientific study of leadership, particularly the leadership of the organization, can include, inter al., such theses as:

1. Assumption of non-linearity – interactions between the participants in the social entity are usually non-linear, which in the case of leadership means the inability to predict the effects of the leader's own actions and/or measure the real impact and the actual impact in a specific socio-structural environment (among the supporters). This state of affairs is a consequence of largely incalculable number of interactions between the participants of public life whose nature is unpredictable. The prominence of nonlinear interactions in organizations creates the following leadership dilemma: *"Leaders are often responsible for bringing about change in organizations yet non-linear interactions can amplify small adaptations outside the control or knowledge of the leader, unleashing changes never intended by the organization's leader, and perhaps counter to leader's intentions"*.

2. Assumption of far-from-equilibrium conditions – a departure from the balance in favour of instability, where in the case the organization it is synonymous with many tensions and conflicts within the organizational structure. This causes another leadership dilemma: *"Leaders are responsible for reducing*

---

190 N. J. Smelers, *Problematics of Sociology: The Georg Simmel Lectures*, University of California Press, Berkley 1995. For example, for a neofunctionalist Jeffrey Alexander, the analysis of changes in social perspective is connected with coupling micro and macro research. It results from the fact that social reality is "multidimensional: there are norms and interests, individual negotiation and collective force. A theorist may ignore significant parts of this complex reality, but he can not [sic] make them go away". More in: A. van den Berg, *Is sociological theory too grand for social mechanisms?*, [in:] P. Hedström, R. Swedberg (eds.), *Social Mechanisms. An Analytical Approach to Social Theory*, Cambridge University Press, Cambridge 1998, p. 229.

191 D. R. Schwandt, *Individual and Collective Coevolution: Leadership as Emergent Social Structuring*, [in:] M. Uhl-Bien, R. Marion (ed.), *Complexity Leadership. Part I: Conceptual Foundations*, Information Age Publishing, Inc., Charlotte 2008, pp. 101–127.

conflict and creating order in organizations, yet disequilibrium is the source of most novelty and innovation in organizations".

3. Assumption of emergent self-organization – "turning point" of the theory of complexity where the phenomenon of emergence is treated as a new phenomenon, consistent and observable at a higher level of complexity of the organization. If the organization by their progressive complexity and permanent structural complication is able to produce emergent properties, it generates another leadership dilemma: "*Leaders are responsible for creating organizational structure that bring about desired outcomes, yet people and groups in organizations will self-organize in spite of organizational blueprints*"[192].

It is clear that these theories of complex leadership (table 2) represent complex (multi-level) approach to scientific analysis of various phenomena of leadership. An element common to these theoretical proposals – provided that such element can be specified – certainly includes the thesis which says that the process of leadership is "distributed" in a given socio-structural environment, which means that it is not only and exclusively related to a specific, single agent leadership (isolated political leader), but mainly results from the dynamic interaction between participants/agents of a particular political space, organization or environment. Therefore, we can talk here about at least four observations (basic assumptions), which accompany the comprehensive theory of leadership, and more importantly, can provide an important platform for integration of frequently differing justifications of leadership, including political leadership, at macrotheoretical level:

1. Leadership is a dynamic process – the process of interaction occurring between agents and/or entities in a particular environment (the designated social, structural, organizational, political area, etc.). The environment is understood as a complex system of communication, in which leadership takes various forms (e.g. formal, emergent, communitive, etc.). Here, the political space is interpreted as a multi-level interaction and/or communication between agents, e.g. individual/collective, explicit /classified participants in political life.
2. Leadership is not only synonymous with the formal division of tasks/resources – leadership in a complex and dynamic socio-structural environment may also emerge as a response to various tensions or conflicts. In this perspective, leaders use the relative impact by contributing to the resources of the

---

192 D. A. Plowman, D. Duchon, *Emergent Leadership: Getting Beyond Heroes and Scapegoats*, [in:] J. K. Hazy, J. A. Goldstein, B. B. Lichtenstein (eds.), *Complex...*, pp. 109–127.

environment with a set of agents. But their leadership is based primarily on: reputation (referent power); skills and knowledge (expert power).
3. Leadership is the agents' co-evolution – is an interdependent evolution of agents/entities in a dynamic interactive space. At the same time, such an environment creates a specific context – morphological field in which agents co-evolve between one another and in relation to the changing environment[193].

We can conclude that the macro theoretical analyses of leadership go beyond the personal-psychological justification of leadership relations in favour of the contextual and/or multi-level perspective. Structural parameters by which researchers are able to explain the complexity and dynamics of the practices of leadership play the key role. In addition, many contemporary scholars of leadership phenomena, who have been using complexity paradigm, fully accept the thesis of emergent self-organization of the environmental leadership. This means a situation in which the emergence of the formal leader, its real impact and influence on followers is shaken (undermined), favouring such phenomena as: self-leadership, multi-level distributed leadership, spatial leadership, etc.

---

193 C. Panzar, J. K. Hazy, B. McKelvey, D. R. Schwandt, *The Paradox...*, pp. 318–325.

6. Morphogenetic characteristics of political leadership

6.1 Determinants of political agency in leadership

Previous discussion of the study of the phenomenon of leadership indicated that the in modern political science we have to deal with the actual theoretical and methodological pluralism. In addition, a summary of the problem of micro-macro link with the dualism human agency vs. social structure suggests some preliminary conclusions:

1. Political leadership is a reflection of a particular relation between the ruling leader and the followers. At the same time, it is a relationship built primarily on authority, respect and obedience from voluntary supporters in relation to the leader rather than coercion or violence, which is directly linked to obtaining accreditation by the socio-political leadership among their potential, as well as real followers.
2. Leadership relationship is synonymous with temporal distribution of influences between two extreme forces, i.e. between the political leader and a group of followers. The vectors of these forces provide the quality and form of political leadership. For example, the dominance of the subjective factor over supporters means the leadership in totalitarian conditions, where the leader wants to obtain absolute power based on: the cult of personality; sacralisation of the leader; the image of "clean" leader, i.e. the one that in the opinion of the general public does not have any bad intentions, perfectly directs the nation, the state, the organization of the party. In turn, the dominance of the socio-structural conditions, for example, can mean "a blur" of leadership, which in turn can lead, among others, to self-leadership, where various elements of the social environment take on the role and function of the agent of leadership.
3. In political practice, leadership is nothing but the distribution of power be tween the leader (agent of leadership) and supporters (social structure), which determines on the one hand, the form and the quality of political leadership, on the other, authorizes the use of micro-macro scale towards theoretical and methodological implications for the individual practices of leadership. Therefore, in the political science the two main trends of research are reflected: a) the methods using personal-subjective justifications where explication of leadership is focused on microanalysis; b) methods based on systemic and

comprehensive justifications where explication of leadership is performed with macroanalyses.
4. If the essence of political leadership boils down to mutual determination and the continuum between the leader as such a separate structural environment, the scientific explanation for this phenomenon must take into account both the endogenous factors (subjective), as well as exogenous (structural), and most importantly – dialectic of these variables. In the research of political science, this means a situation in which the analysis of the practice of leadership should hover around the dialectical subjective-objective relationships.

6.1.1 Endogenous factors

Considering the endogenous factors in the context of explaining the political leadership appreciation of one side of leadership relationship is clear – the leader. In this system, the role and importance of political leader becomes doubly important. Firstly, the leader is recognized not as an object – unimportant, secondary, reified element in the process of leadership – but as a key actor in ruling relation. Secondly, it is a real leader, and more importantly, the primary creative-causal component in the leader ↔ followers relationship that is changeable in time. Therefore, explaining the political leadership with subjective determinants highlights the importance of such explanatory parameters as:

1. The power of causal and/or measurable perpetration of a particular political leader – is an empirically observable phenomenon of alienation of the leader in given social conditions where there is a manifestation of the inherent strength (energy) of the leader. From the activist point of view, it supposed to mobilize leaders, or specific actions or decisions that have a direct (indirect) influence on the form and quality of political leadership. In other words, the leadership strength of causal individual or collective entity activity becomes the essence of the relationship at the leader ↔ followers intersection. It is thanks to the personal alienation that the leader is able not only to seek support and recognition among the supporters, but also consciously stimulates and shapes the relationship of leadership, including the attitudes, opinions, views, decision-making, etc. in a broader social perception.
2. Agent-leader control of socio-structural environment – it is a gradable influence of leaders on the external environment, where the leader has a sense of efficiency and the effectiveness of his agency. In the sense of cause-and-effect relationship, that control performed by the leader in relation to the social environment can have the following character:

a) Predictability of cause and effect – political leader totally "reigns" over a given political matter, including the followers. Unhindered externally, the leader implements plans, goals, strategies, intentions etc. and the domineering relationship which he or she co-creates, which in most cases takes the authoritarian or totalitarian form;
b) Unpredictability of the causes and consequences – political leadership has the characteristics of randomness, chaotic, situational and organizational unpredictability. In this variant of the process of emergence of the leader, his or her social accreditation, leadership or disappearance are unexplained and characterized by spontaneous, uncontrolled enthusiasm, approval/disapproval of the broad masses of society. Leadership, its authority and influence are unquantifiable and it is very difficult to determine its real value and meaning. This type of the so-called political career of leaders "from nowhere" –the political leaders, whose phenomenon is hardly explicable from the point of view of typical political careers;
c) Predictability of the causes and consequences of unpredictability – the leader in a limited way to control the environment. Its influence in relation to the supporters focuses on eliciting stimulation of specific facts, operations, events, processes. In this way, the leader becomes the initiator of new ideas, puts forward far-reaching plans, strategies or visions, but is not able to predict their future implementation (consequences) in the socio-structural environment. The leader is fully aware of his or her position, including the previously obtained legitimacy and accreditation of society, but its current status is somewhat unpredictable, i.e. he is not able to determine their own future on the basis of actions or decisions taken ad hoc;
d) Unpredictability of the causes and consequences of predictability – here we can talk about the reverse situation, when there is lack of a clearly defined basis and/or specific reasons for the emergence of a specific political leader. This is a situation in which the leader himself/herself has difficulty in defining precisely their impact and/or impact on the social environment, and more importantly supporters, from whom he/she acquired accreditation or legitimacy for further political activity. In this variant, it is difficult to clearly define the conditions for the emergence of leadership. Actually, is not known whether the high level of support for the leader results from the leader himself/herself, his or her qualities, political style, level of expertise, or just the opposite – the actual facilities, moods and demands of society, the economic situation, historical moment, rhetorical activities or manipulation, and perhaps it is a bit of everything. This results is "intuitive and consistent"

leadership activity, which means the performance of previous commitments, declarations, program assumptions, election promises etc. according to the thesis: "If all this guaranteed my leadership, then you should just stick to it."

Explication of political leadership based on the subjective conditions drives most studies in political science towards introspection, where the key role is played by explanatory micro-scale. In this sense we are dealing with the scientific analysis, in which the essential elements explaining the leadership qualities include inter al.: personal leadership styles, knowledge, skills, emotional intelligence and situational dimension. It should be noted that dependence on factors directly from the agent of leadership means that the political theorist accepts and recognizes the legitimacy of two explanatory mechanisms for political leadership:

1. Impersonation – identifying politics with the symbolic and/or perceptual sphere, where a political leader embodies the political struggle, power, specific political decision, ideas, reform, etc.
2. Personalization – in political practice is nothing more than a mechanism for the maximum concentration of a given political leader, where any political activity, party or election is based only (and always) on a particular leader. In other words, this constant "investment in leadership" (in his/her image, position, influence, prestige, popularity) has to be a guarantee of promotion and success of the leadership process[194].

In addition, the mechanism of personalization of politics – understood as the tendency of research involving the reduction of political practice to the leader – refers to the personalized interpretation of politics, where:

1. Politics is increasingly associated with the leaders, which indicates that the role and status of the leaders in the world of politics are gaining importance. Such regularity results from the increasing awareness of the main actors of the political scene. This is a consequence of the requirements set both by the mass media, public opinion, as well as the part of the electoral law (a tendency for detailed speaking and writing about the leaders, even waiting for news from the life of a specific politician).
2. Political practice increasingly depends on electronic media. On the one hand, the media focus attention on the life and image of individual political leaders, on the other, it is the formation of the personality of leaders by the media

---

194 M. Karwat, *Metody i metamorfozy walki wyborczej*, [in:], D. Waniek (ed.), *Partie polityczne w wyborach 2005*, ALMAMER Wyższa Szkoła Ekonomiczna „DrukTur", Warszawa 2006, pp. 65–66.

hierarchy of topics and mobilization of voters (two processes that accompany the mediatization of politics: political agenda setting and priming)[195].

6.1.2 Exogenous factors

In the case of exogenous determinants, the process of scientific explanation of the agent in leadership ↔ followers relationship is extended from the study of agents (microanalysis) to the structural perspective (macroanalysis). In this sense, leadership is no longer exclusively the domain of the leaders. On the contrary, explication of leadership takes place through a holist-structural reasons. In other words, it is an emphasis of the complexity and multi-dimensionality of the phenomenon of leadership, personal and psychological factors are set aside, and the method, diagram and directive of methodological holism are prioritised. Location of leadership in a broader, multi-level analytical context means that political science research practice of leadership can take the following character:

1. Structural and spatial character – orientation of the research studies on the issue of superiority or inferiority occurring in the given community, where the key role is played by the structural hierarchy of elements included in a separate social entity. Therefore, the phenomenon of leadership is considered in the context of structural relationships, where both the leader (agent), as well as supporters of (the external environment) become elements/structural parts of the specific environment where their objective position or location resulting from external interactions and influences directly affects the shape and quality of political leadership.
2. Functional and spatial character – orientation of the research studies on the functional side and/or the relationship existing between the analytically separate elements of a particular social entity. In this sense, political leadership is interpreted through the prism of functions that satisfy both the leader, as well as the supporters in the socio-structural surrounding. At the same time, emphasizing the functional aspects of leadership means that the leader along with his or her followers, performs a specific function and/or multiple functions in a structured environment. Those functions may be also performed by the "impersonal" structure, which may result from the previously approved procedures, laws, standards, axiology or cultural codes.

---

195 I. McAllister, *The Personalization of Politics*, [in:] R. J. Dalton, H. D. Klingemann (eds.), *The Oxford Handbook of Political Behavior*, Oxford University Press, Oxford 2009, pp. 571–589.

3. **Multi-level and spatial character** – the use of multi-level analysis with regard to the explanation of descriptions and specific practices of leadership. In this variant, the starting point is the division of the temporal and the complex reality of political analytically separate research plane, between which there is a continuous exchange and interaction. Scientific objective of such fragmentation is to delimit the precise determination of the distribution of influence and power within the limits of the researched social entity. For political science in the research on leadership, this means focusing on the dynamic interactions between leader and followers in the socio-structural context. For example, to make the explanation of the complex relationships at the intersection of the leader ↔ supporters four levels of theoretical analysis have been separated, which make up a holistic research perspective:

   a) level of individual variables – test parameters, e.g.: leadership skills; contact with the followers of the leaders; identity of supporters; engagement of the leader;
   b) level of group interaction – test parameters, e.g.: trust; group cohesiveness; correlation in the group; the relationship between exchange among the members of the group;
   c) level of the organizational impact – test parameters, e.g.: organizational hierarchy; the complexity of the organizational environment; degree of professionalism; the degree of organizational culture;
   d) level of environmental impact – test parameters, e.g.: cultural environment; the social level of interference and conflicts; institutional exchange[196].

In addition, it should be noted that the explication of political leadership on the basis of the structural determinants emphasizes the weight and importance of the socio-structural independence, in which there is a complex process of leadership, more precisely – multiple interactions between a particular leader and his or her followers. In this way, by the fact that the appreciation of the external environment towards the leader, an attempt is made to depersonalise (to create a theoretical and intellectual counterweight to the reduction mechanism of the agent), but not to reify (objectify the agent) the political practice of leadership for the objectively existing multilevel matter of politics, which produces a

---

[196] M. D. Mumford, S. T. Hunter, T. L. Friedrich, J. J. Caughron, *Charismatic, Ideological, and Pragmatic Leadership: An Examination of Multi-Level Influence on Emergence and Perfomence*, [in:] F. J. Yammarino, F. Dansereau (eds.), *Multi-level Issues in Organizational Behavior and Leadership*, Emerald Group Publishing, Bingley 2009, pp. 79–116.

distinct and independent agency in the case of facts, properties, states of affairs, structures, events and processes. Here, the relation of leadership does not depend directly on the leader's personality traits, skills or competence, but depends inter al. on factors such as the balance of intersubjective power occurring in the political regime; socio-economic conditions; normative order. Additionally, holistic and structured look at the political leadership is a fully justified observation of the nature of contemporary political practice, where this perspective is exposed to such distinguishing features as:

1. Progressive-emergent diversity – synonymous with the complexity of the matter of politics, which in addition to being subject to constant changes (structural reconfiguration), creates quantitative and qualitative changes, which are the actual confirmation of the progressive complexity, or more precisely, of the additive nature. The consequences of such structuring movements within the political space are far-reaching, and include both stabilizing and/or consolidating specific practices and they form the basis of unpredictability, non-deducible internal self-organization. In the second scenario, we deal with the phenomenon of emergence, where the primary emergent of political practice is the structure that makes changes relating to all participants of political reality, including the political leaders.
2. Causal pluralism – emphasizes that political practice in the whole of its traits and properties is not simply the result of assumptions of causal monism, where clearly defined cause always leads to a particular (and only) effect. In the case of complex matter of politics it refers rather to the objective multiplicity of causes and effects, which authorizes the use of invariant thinking in scientific analysis. Breaking the strict causal rules releases scientific indeterminist thinking, which in practical terms means acceptance of such phenomena in the world of politics, as the randomness of events; unplanned and spontaneous self-organizational leadership and unpredictability of the leader ↔ followers relationship.

6.1.3 Dialectic of conditions

The previous considerations show that the leadership in modern political science can be explained on the basis of two different explanatory diagrams:

1. Analyses based on subjective-psychological factors (research microperspective) – the subject of the research is a political leader, interpreted as the agent of leadership, with a continuum of ruling and/or causal force, through which

he is able to realistically affect the structural and social environment, including gradable influence on supporters.
2. Analyses based on structural and overall justifications (research macroperspective) – the subject of the research is a dynamic social structure and objective position and/or location of the leaders of the structural political environment. Here the separated social entity undergoes analysis in which the leader (part) occupies a specific place and fully specified function in the whole structure (whole). In the systemic interpretation it is the research of intraconversion and relationships at the system-environment interface in which the leader is a part of the system. Talking about holistic view of the leader, which is explained, inter al., through the variables such as status and political position; capabilities/limitations of leadership; context of political action; objectivity of relations and intrasubjective antagonisms occurring in the system.

Equally important research strategy is the dialectical combination of the above explanatory diagrams, where, on the one hand a univariate (single-stage) studies on the relationship between the leadership are set aside – in return offering a wide spectrum of problem-analysis. On the other hand, in the objective entanglement of the agent from the existing socio-structural conditions and the other way roundlies both the essence as well as the starting point of any theoretical activities in the realm of politics[197]. For the category of political leadership the transfer of dialectical reception onto endogenous and exogenous determinants means the following:

1. Synthesizing thinking – leadership is considered in the holistic fusion of different points of view, ontological-epistemological arguments or inference diagrams. Leadership vs. social structure duality (followers) combines exclusive orders of scientific reflection – situational, personal-psychological, systemic and structural, organizational arguments, etc..in order to create measurable and heuristic scientific value.
2. Multivariate coincidental analyses – the use of dialectical method allows us to show multiple links in temporal relation at the interface political leader ↔ followers, which has a decisive influence on the nature of the analysis of political science, i.e. their multi-level (realistic approach to political reality where the world of politics is analytically separated into multi-level space activity

---

[197] It must be added that the dialectic method involves moving from exclusive concepts, categories, theories, laws to a higher level of scientific reflection (synthesizing metareflection).

of the various players involved, i.e the micro, meso and macro space interpreted as a structural social unit consisting of tangible/intangible elements) and multivariate elements (explication of policy must necessarily take into account various factors, i.e social, economic, cultural, religious, etc.).

6.2 Morphogenesis of political leadership

In order to clearly examine the agent-structure duality, expressed in constant tension between the two independent, but directly determined energies, i.e. the force of individual agents (perpetration) and the structural force (structural activity), in the context of the emergence of the phenomenon of political leadership one can use the morphogenetic interpretation. It seems that the Archerian approach is ideally suited to the analysis of political science, in which we can explore the potential, as well as the real entanglement of conditions in agent-structure process of emergence and functioning of political leader. In this respect, a realistic research perspective expressed by the concept of analytical dualism seems to be very good, and more importantly, useful research instrument in explanatory terms.

The starting point of morphogenetic study of political leaders is the assumption that political space is a dual reality in which there is a "continuous clash of" two analytically separate spheres, i.e. the agent-reflective and socio-structural plane. In other words, it is the thesis that political reality must be explained through the two autonomous but mutually determining areas – the subjective world belonging to the various agents; the objective world associated with the structural circumstances. Moreover, such an argument against the political matter has several epistemological and methodological consequences, which are reflected in the following propositions:

1. Political practice is just a peculiar structural configuration consisting of reciprocal agents (individual and collective). The overall political order results in objective properties subject to the social entity and subjective factor based on causal activity and interaction. In morphogenetic approach it is a multi-level subjective-objective coincidence, where the first component is synonymous with subjective reflexivity of the agent, while the second element with objective cultural and structural properties.
2. To explain the political space means to analyse a specific part of reality that will keep the proportion and balance of micro-macro scale; where one-dimensional theorizing is replaced by precise two-dimensional integrative explications.

3. Any changes in the realm of politics with respect to shape, form, structure, division of tasks, the emergence of new phenomena, values, states of affairs, leadership, etc. are referred to as morphogenesis, i.e. process or processes directly connected with order and structure transformations.

It is worth noting that the application procedure for the analysis of assumptions morphogenetic practice of political leadership can be done on the subject-realistic test plane[198] where political leadership is considered through subjective-objective determination with gradable impact on the functioning of the agent's leadership. It includes an explanatory diagram based on a matrix of subjectivity, in which Margaret S. Archer defined four autonomous but combined levels of analysis: selves / "Subjective I"; primary agents / "objective I"; collective agents / "We"; actors / "You" (diagram 11). However, the realistic picture of subjectivity as targets research tool in this work must undergo some correction. This is due to the need to adapt both the same conceptual apparatus as well as the explanatory diagram into the category of political leadership. A matrix of leadership agency is therefore proposed, which would serve as a theoretical explanatory model to deal with specific cases. In this arrangement, a matrix of agency becomes a theoretical conceptualization through which it is possible to capture multiple practical relationships or the determination at the intersection leader ↔ followers (diagram 14). This Archerian diagram prototype consists of four separate components of analysis (quadrants) reflecting the agent (the equivalent of "subjective I"); party leadership (the equivalent of "I am concerned"); political leader (the equivalent of "We");structured agent (the equivalent of "you").

---

198 Morphogenetic approach proposed by M. S. Archer was subject to some conceptual changes. Such a tendency is clearly visible in various publications regarding the duality of agent vs structure. In 1995 in the first compact monograph on the morphogenetic scene the author presented a research tool in the form of a series of morphogenetic cycle (*Realist Social Theory: The Morphogenetic Approach*, Cambridge University Press, 1995). However, in subsequent publications the same subjective-structural relationship the author tried to explain on the basis of the reflectivity of the subject (*Being Human. The Problem of Agency*, Cambridge University Press, 2000; *The Reflexive Imperative in Late Modernity*, Cambridge University Press, 2011).

Diagram 14: Morphogenetic matrix of Political Leadership

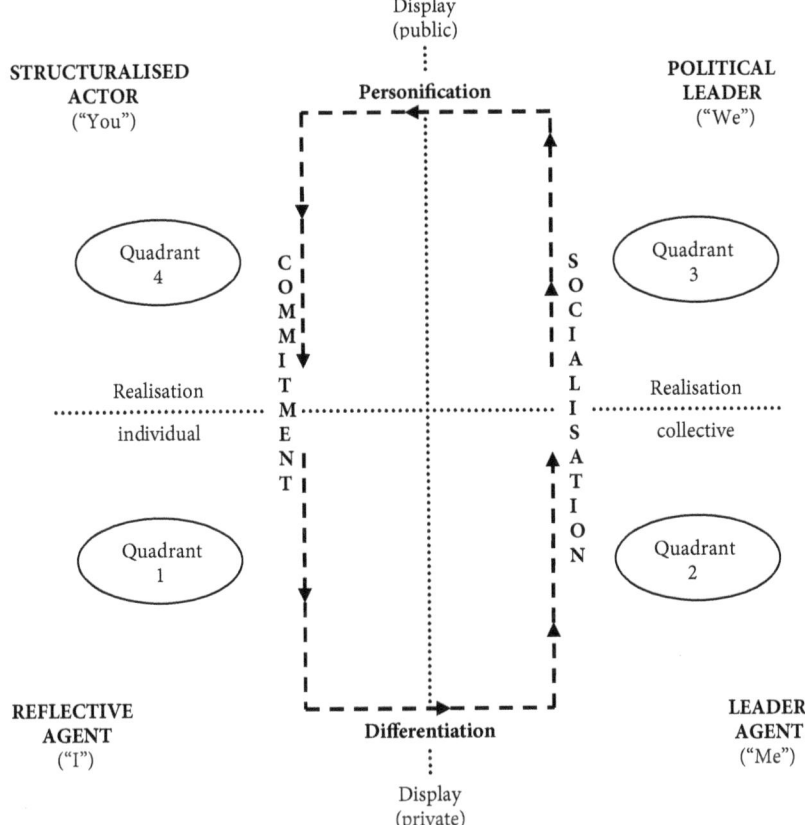

Source: own work

In this morphogenetic understanding, the subjective matrix of leadership keeps the division into private/public exposure and individual/collective realization, which in fact means that the phenomenon of political leadership directly depends on the individual and social reality and/or agent and structure reality. However, each quadrant in this matrix can be characterized in the following way:

1. Reflective agent (quadrant 1) – is a synonym of a conscious political agent (individual and collective). In the case of leadership phenomenon, quadrant 1 expresses self-identification of the leader, their self-control (control of the surrounding), which results in reflectivity based on volitional and intentional

processes. Such self-consciousness is also a foundation for the emergence of agency (person, social group, employee's self-government, etc. becoming a conscious participant of the group life. At the same time the participants realize their own political agency. In other words, it is an agent who fully understands that he or she is made objectively political and/or is is involved in various ways in the political matter and that their broadly understood activity is directly or indirectly based on political matter *par excellence*; that their activity in the political sphere might be and very often is dependent n or convergent to many various interests, pressure groups, decision centres, lobbyists, flow networks, etc.[199]) Reflectivity mechanism means at the same time that a given political agent notices that some personal traits, inclinations or properties may indicate a gradual leadership potential. It concerns not only individual personal features thanks to which the agent may show the power of leadership but also the awareness of the agent concerning intentional, situational, institutional and strategic possibilities thanks to which the leadership will be performed by the leader. It should be added that reflexivity of the agent towards own possibilities for leadership, potential political intentionality of leadership in particular, may prove that there are at least a few types of the agent's abilities, i.e. potential for structure creation (ability to create changes in the social surrounding); skilfulness to maintain status quo (ability to maintain social and political conditions); regressive skill (ability to recover the expected states of affairs and/ or structural circumstances).

2. Leader agent (quadrant 2) – means the stage of immersion of the reflective agent who exhibits a gradual leadership potential into the structural and political space where the agent is located in its specific real structural configuration (localization of the political agent in the structural hierarchy). But this location is directly connected with accepting the role, function, position or working out the status of leader in a given social surrounding. In this variant quadrant 2 is a synonym of socialising, adapting and adjusting and structuring processes where the reflective agent who so far has been focused solely on immanent self-identification moves on to the structural-public sphere. It means that the leadership potential is made available to the public by self-conscious agent, so far a 'private property'. Moving from the reflective agent to the leadership agent means also placing the agent in the social distribution and allocation of resources including social understanding and perception

---

[199] M. Karwat, *Człowiek polityczny. Próba interpretacji marksistowskiej*, Państwowe Wydawnictwo Naukowe, Warszawa 1989, pp. 5–103.

or definition of leadership. In such a situation the leader becomes the carrier of the individual and social identity, which actually means, inter al. constant confrontation of personal image of leadership with social expectations towards the leader; comparison of agent possibilities with structural constraints and the other way round; juxtaposition of psychological conditions and social-cultural requirements. We can see here a leadership agent who in gradual way starts building his position in the collective social space and therefore he tries to replace self-conscious leadership potential with specific leadership practice.

3. Political leader (quadrant 3) – means real political leadership in given structural conditions. This approach determines the area in quadrant 3 and means real leadership in politics in given structural conditions and what is more, he effectively performs leadership in the public and political space. Here the leader has been aware of his strengths/weaknesses and opportunities/limitations resulting from accepting a specific role, function, style, behaviour, conduct, etc. towards his/her followers. One might say that the leader becomes a full-blooded leader who is at the same time auto-reflective and society-sensitive to supporters. In other words, it is a leader who is highly self-controllable with full awareness with which accreditation and legitimisation activities one gains and maintains political leadership. Therefore, quadrant 3 refers to personifying mechanisms in public-collective display where the leader personifies a given vision, authority, ideology or style of doing politics including solving conflicts, leading negotiations, waging wars, holding talks in coalition, thanks to which he is able to get support and voluntary consent from supporters to perform leadership. At the same time, the stage in which one becomes the political leader is interpreted as the emergence of a real power which creates structure, where the political leader is an evocative agent and modifies a given political space (it is a synonym to the causative force where causality of the leader becomes an essential element in various general social processes, inter al. accumulation, transformation, exchange or revolution).

4. Structured actor (quadrant 4) – is a synonym for the multi-lateral influence of the social and structural surrounding on the leader – in particular, on the level of self-consciousness of the leader. In this system, through the location of reflective agent in structural conditions and his actual activity and leadership in specific political conditions a multi-channel influence is exerted, in particular – from other participants of the collective life (e.g. political supporters or opponents) or structural forces (e.g. social processes, impersonal indexes, unpredictable catastrophes, scandals, military conflicts, etc.), on the

political leader giving feedbacks. Thus quadrant 4 means exiting from individual-private display through public-private display and public-collective to get back to public-individual display. In other words, structured agent is a reflective agent changed by external and objective factors who emerges as a result of involvement in the political and public sphere. Thus we can see a new established consciousness, i. e. leader throughout actual performance of political leadership may undergo gradual transformation thanks to which his leadership potential, consciousness or political activity may but does not have to undergo some corrections and/ or radical change.

In the following part of the work methodological usefulness of the morphogenetic matrix of leadership agency will be presented. For this purpose, Leszek Miller, the prime minister of the Polish government in the years 2001–2004 will be subject to analysis.

6.2.1 Leszek Miller's case – on the intensification of structured agent

The starting point for morphogenetic approach to a detailed analysis of the practice of leadership by Leszek Miller – understood as a single agent of leadership interacting with the socio-structural surrounding – is to determine the time limits. In the case of the creation of morphogenetic matrix of subjective leadership we are interested in 926 days, i.e. two years and six months, when Miller was the president of the Council of Ministers of the Republic of Poland (the period from 19 October 2001 to 2 May 2004). In other words, it is a period of great success, which he achieved as a politician known as the "Iron Chancellor" – after the elections in 2001 (parliamentary elections of 23 September brought a historic victory for a coalition of the Democratic Left Alliance and the Labour Union, which obtained 216 deputy seats 75 senator seats), until his resignation in the shadow of the so-called "Rywingate".

Political leadership of Leszek Miller will be examined on the basis of morphogenetic matrix of subjective leadership, which means a four-fold explanatory plane, thanks to which it is possible to precisely diagnose the dialectical relationship between the agent of leadership and the structural environment. In this sense the activity of Miller's leadership will be examined in view of the dynamic changes taking place in the agent's leadership, his immediate environment (political party, colleagues, subordinate ministers etc.), as well as further social environment including the followers of the socio-economic situation. Hence morphogenetic matrix of subjective leadership is based on the analytical separation of the four areas of analysis (the reflexive agent, the subject of leadership, political leader; structured agent) which, in addition, to being mutually independent, aims to pinpoint and explicate the dialectical structural dependence in the dimension of the practice of leadership. In the case of Prime Minister Miller the matrix has the form illustrated in diagram 15.

Diagram 15: The Morphogenetic matrix of Leszek Miller

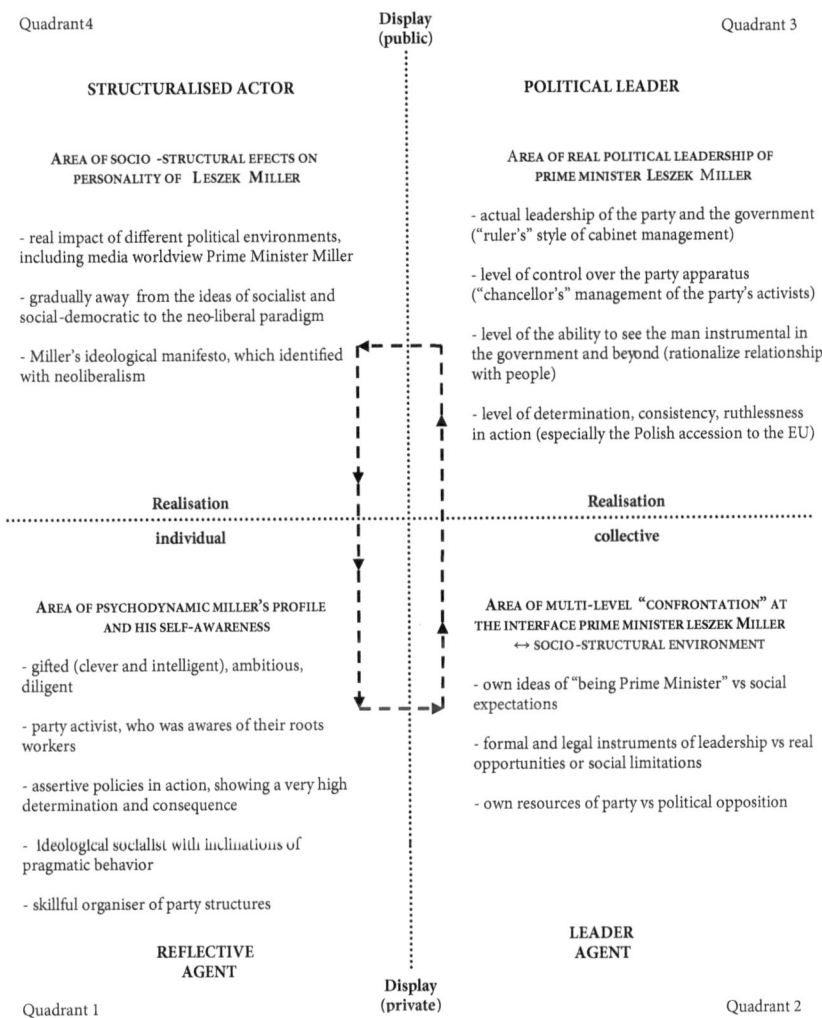

Source: own work

Diagram 15 shows the close interaction and exchange between the various fields of activity in leadership of Prime Minister Miller, where the two scales overlap, i.e. private ↔ public exposure and individual ↔ collective implementation. Here the individual squares of the matrix should be discussed in detail.

Quadrant 1 is the area of activity of the reflective agent (resultant exposure of private and individual realization) where the characteristics of individuality-personality of political leader and its subjective self-awareness are analysed, which means: awareness of one's origin (occupied place in social stratification or class affiliation, etc.) or subjective understanding and self-reflection to their own capabilities/limitations of the intellect, formal education, organizational skills, decision making skills and temperament. In the case of subjective reflexivity of Leszek Miller, this step means inter al.: full acceptance of his working class origin; the need for employment at the age of 17 in the factory in Żyrardów; fully aware of his career with the left; assertive and ambitious activity in the party structures (starting from the Polish United Workers' Party (Polska Zjednoczona Partia Robotnicza), to the Social Democracy of the Republic of Polish (Socjaldemokracja Rzeczpospolitej Polskiej), to the Democratic Left Alliance (Sojusz Lewicy Demokratycznej), which provides large predispositions and leadership potential for the future prime minister.

Confirmation of the individual personal characteristics of Miller and his real aptitude for leadership can be found in numerous memories of both her friends and acquaintances from his youth, the former colleagues, as well as political opponents. As noted by Jerzy Morawski, one of the authors of the biography of the future prime minister, Leszek Miller was an example of real "cunning apparatchik", who since the very beginning in the party was extremely active and ambitious activist ("apparatchik"). Quoting the statements of people who came into contact with Miller during his many years of public activity, opinions about his leadership inclinations and predispositions and organizational leadership widely dominated ("Miller had the skill of self-education"; "He was an orthodox activist of the extreme left"; "He entered the life of the party, in a very profound and non-superficial manner"; "He was damn ambitious"; "He was hard and consistently defended its line "; "He knew his value and place"; "He was regarded as a specialist in contact with young people"; "The last in the party to believe in the ideas of socialism"; "Extremely busy, always carefully prepared for speeches"). Besides, Miller himself said that "the boy was immediately on the left side", which was the aftermath of family roots and authentic faith in the socialist state ("I am the heir to the Communist Party")[200].

---

200 J. Morawski, *Portrety w podczerwieni*, Niezależna Oficyna Wydawnicza Nowa, Warszawa 1994, pp. 50–64.

Aleksander Kwaśniewski spoke in a similar vein, who in this way remembered the founding fathers of a new political formation of the Social Democracy of the Republic of Poland:

> I was looking for people who would not miss the old times, who would unreservedly accept the democratic and sovereign character of the state, who would understand the need for deep political and economic reforms, but also they remain loyal to pro-social, leftist orientation. The famous "sixty" were not any "Kwasniewski people" who were only to "grind" the party hard liners and provide controllability of the whole system. I must admit that the aim was among other things, to break the old internal systems and prevent them from being reborn in SDRP. (…) They were also active people before in the structures of the party who made reformist attitude and action on democracy authentic and changed the face of the party. (…) I cannot of course ignore the role of Leszek Miller (he was Secretary General of the newly established party, which appeared in 1990 on the political scene as the heir to the Polish United Workers' Party – emphasis added, F. P.), with a significant share of which it was possible to create efficient structures throughout the country[201].

The organizational efficiency, pragmatism and "political intuition" of Leszek Miller can also be confirmed by his comments on the Round Table talks of 1989 when as a member of the government (Secretary and member of the Political Bureau of the Central Committee of the Polish United Workers' Party) he took part in negotiations with the political opposition:

> It was the time of great tension and reflection. When in February I went to the inaugural meeting of the Round Table, I was aware of its meaning, but I could not really imagine what would appear at the end of the road which we entered. Over the famous piece of furniture there was a lot of fog, edges much obliterated. (…) The country's economy was in the stalemate. It was evident that the socialist system of central control and planning ultimately loses the competition with the market (…) In those days, the ideology was only an ornament. Pragmatism pushed by Rakowski's team mattered. We wanted to communicate with the opposition and involve them in the responsibility for the state, but not to transfer them the power. Round Table agreements clearly indicate that we meant a slow, evolutionary change[202].

For analytical purposes, the quoted selective comments show, on the one hand, the right, and more importantly, Leszek Miller's necessary personality traits which were appreciated by the left-wing environment. On the other hand, they confirm the self-awareness of leadership of the future prime minister – assertive pursuit

---

201 J. Machejek, J. Olczyk, A. Machejek, *Kwaśniewski: „nie lubię tracić czasu!". Wywiad-rzeka z liderem SLD*, HamalBooks, Łódź 1995, pp. 62–63.
202 J. Sadecki, *Trzynastu. Premierzy wolnej Polski*, Universitas, Kraków 2009, pp. 219–245.

of goals, clear formulation of political aspirations, persistence and consequences in politics, understanding the strengths/ weaknesses of their character and self-reflection – as well as the managerial and organizational skills of the leader of the Polish left. This state of affairs had a direct impact on the practice of governance, because this politician, before he became prime minister in 2001, served numerous functions and took important positions in the governments of the left and in the party structures (President of SDRP, chairman of the DLA, the minister of labour and social policy in the governments of Waldemar Pawlak and Józef Oleksy, head of the Office of the Council of Ministers in the government of Włodzimierz Cimoszewicz, Minister of interior affairs and administration), which undoubtedly affected his future premiership.

Quadrant 2 is the area of activity of the agent's leadership (the resultant exposure of private and collective implementation), where the reflective agent is located in the socio-structural configuration of politics. In the case of Miller it was October 19, 2001 r., when after winning the elections by a coalition of the DLA-LU (Labour's Union) he was appointed chairman of the Council of Ministers. In other words, the moment when with the previous baggage of experience of political and measurable potential leadership expressed by personality features he takes on the function/role of the prime minister. This is the stage in which Miller-the politician becomes Miller-the prime minister, which involves multiplanar "confrontation" at the crossroads of psychological vs. socio-structural predispositions. For Miller, the moment was connected directly with the adoption of a particular position of leadership – the constitutional and actual head of the executive power in the Polish democratic system. Thus, in this area there are at least two planes "roughing up" reflective subject of leadership and practice of governance on a national scale, i.e. morphogenetic dependency at the interface of leader ↔ external environment contact:

1. Own ideas about "being Prime Minister" vs social expectations.
2. Formal legal instruments of leadership vs opportunities/structural constraints.

In the case of the first plane relating to the personal ideas of "being Prime Minister" vs. social expectations of the future head of government we are dealing with two mechanisms of formation of the subjective leadership. On the one hand, it is an active work of Miller as the most important politician of the post-communist environment (at the time he was the chairman of the DLA, as well as the chairman of the parliamentary club). Miller certainly began building the myth of a "strong chancellor" as head of the Prime Minister's office, Włodzimierz Cimoszewicz in 1996. He recalls:

Some even claimed that this position is more important than the Prime Minister's. The Head of the Prime Minister's Office, if he wanted to, could decide what Prime Minister has to do[203].

In another interview he said:

> Polician counts until he occupies a formal position. If he no longer has a formal position, his influence declines (...) There is no political party without a leader[204].

The focus of future prime minister on a strong, effective and efficient leadership resulted not only from his personality, which is undisputed, but also was associated with the climate prevailing on the left in the allocation of key positions or the creation of party leaders. It is a phenomenon of routinism, the bureaucratization of the party apparatus, which was associated with the exercise of power, and more importantly – the tightness of the political elite[205]. Józef Oleksy accurately described the state of affairs:

> The natural process of selecting new leaders, promoting young talents was halted. The party elite has become co-optative – the older freely choose the young without the need for competition and validation in action[206].

An equally important element was the efficiency and effectiveness of the organization in the field of politics at the time when DLA was in opposition (3rd term of office of the Sejm). It is thanks to Miller that the top-down managed consolidated and the political party was created which later became a strong party with complex structures, reaching the electoral victory and success in the exercise of power[207].

All these factors more or less significantly influenced the perception and imagination of Leszek Miller as an ideal of effective leaders of modern social democracy. Confirmation of such a reflexive understanding of political leadership can be found in the election campaign in 2001when Miller – as the leader of the left – embodied courage, strength, efficiency, and social sensitivity, socialist roots

---

203 J. Sadecki, *Trzynastu...*, pp. 219–245.
204 *Upadek ojca marnotrawnego. Z Leszkiem Millerem rozmawiał Piotr Najsztub*, „Przekrój" nr 31 (3136), 28.07.2005, pp. 12–15.
205 T. Godlewski, *Polski system polityczny. Instytucje – procedury – obywatele*, Wydawnictwo Adam Marszałek, Toruń 2007, p. 154.
206 *Atrakcyjni dla większości. Z Józefem Oleksym, przewodniczącym Klubu SLD, rozmawiała Eliza Olczyk*, „Rzeczpospolita" 30 grudnia 2002, A 4.
207 D. Waniek, *Uwarunkowania społeczne, polityczne i ekonomiczne wyborów parlamentarnych 2005*, [in:] D. Waniek (ed.), *Partie polityczne w wyborach 2005*, ALMAMER Wyższa Szkoła Ekonomiczna „DrukTur" Warszawa 2006, pp. 7–29.

or "leftist empathy and conscience." It seems that he just wanted to be seen in this way because he understood his role in the public space. Hence, the election campaign in 2001 was characterized by a high degree of individualization of electoral media (media focus on Leszek Miller). The aim of such marketing efforts was the "possibility of creating self-government, and fight for each voter required the use of emotional arguments." This trend became apparent, inter al., in a paid TV spot titled "Appeal of the Leader"

> "... Poles need a strong, uniform and efficient government,
> Such a government is at hand.
> Whether this chance will come true depends on your votes
> Every vote will matter. The voice of the future is being decided now ...."[208]

At the same time the future prime minister during commercials was portrayed with a little girl. In this way the election team wanted to create a left-wing leader as a "typical father"[209]. This image and their own idea of Miller for a modern social democratic leader perfectly fitted in a very bad public mood. It is worth noting that 2001 Polish society was going through a hard period when among others, general social problems culminated: the impact of four reforms pushed through by Prime Minister Jerzy Buzek; strategy of "cooling the economy" proposed by Leszek Balcerowicz, involving the suppression of domestic, investment and consumer demand; deterioration of the economic situation of the European economy including rising oil prices; decline in GDP from 7% to 1%, which resulted in increasing poverty and the spread of poverty[210]. In principle, these problems, sombermood of the public in response to the governments of the coalition Solidarity Electoral Action- Lierty Union (Akcja Wyborcza Solidarność – Unia Wolności; AWS-UW) and the syndrome of "punishing defeat" of the ruling party[211] was reflected in the huge electoral success of Leszek Miller, who as the "face of the left" perfectly sensed the mood of public opinion, which was articulated in

---

208 W. Peszyński, „Liderzy jako symbole partii politycznych". Analiza reklam telewizyjnych z polskich kampanii parlamentarnych 2001–2007, [in:] J. Golinowski, F. Pierzchalski (eds.), Symboliczność przestrzeni polityki. Między teorią a praktyką, Wydawnictwo Uniwersytetu Kazimierza Wielkiego, Bydgoszcz 2011, pp. 179–196.
209 Ibid.
210 D. Waniek, Uwarunkowania..., Warszawa 2006, pp. 7–29.
211 The "punishing defeat" syndrome of the ruling party is an outcome of an increasing infidelity of voters towards previously elected political parties or party leaders. It results in inevitable single term in office of the next governments. This happened also in 2001 when "the core electorate was shrinking gradually and no longer supported post-Solidarity or post-PRP (People's Republic of Poland, PRL) parties

the electoral coalition of the DLA-LU. In this document we find inter al., demands such as: profound repair of public finances; repair of four reforms introduced by the right; introduction of modern education and the computerization of the country; need to increase budget revenues and rationalization of public expenditure; completion of negotiations with the European Union. The strategic objective of the future left-wing government was:

> To equal opportunities and eliminate educational, social, environmental and economic barriers. Equal access to education, support for vulnerable groups and help in enforcing their equal rights as citizens – is a great reserve of civilizational development[212].

The second plane of confrontation refers to the formal and legal instruments of leadership vs real possibilities and/or structural restrictions. We talk about the statutory prerogatives of the head of the party and the formal and legal position of the Prime Minister, his real leadership in relation to their subordinates or wider socio-structural environment. Certainly, the position of Prime Minister Leszek Miller in the public-political space depended both on internal factors (functioning of the cabinet, constitutional and statutory regulations regarding the responsibilities of ministers, decision-making style of government, powers of the Prime Minister), as well as external factors (legislation defining the powers of government to the parliament; presidential powers to the government, provisions on the appointment of civil servants; characteristics of the party system, structure of social interests)[213]. At the same time, a number of initiatives to reform the administrative apparatus of the government, and more specifically, the institutional and procedural apparatus in force in the process of government decision-making process were taken. An example would be the formation of government decision-making mechanisms during the term of Leszek Miller, when in 2002 the government adopted a resolution on the introduction of the Rules of the work of the Council of Ministers and Order No. 77 of the President of the Council of Ministers of 27 June 2002 on the standing committee of the Council of Ministers as the sole advisory and assistant body in matters within the scope

---

and candidates. More in: M. Gulczyński, *Charakterystyka głównych sił politycznych uczestniczących w wyborach 2005*, [in:] D. Waniek (ed.), *Partie...*, pp. 31–58.
212 http://sld.org.pl/public/ckfinder/userfiles/files/Program_Wyborczy_SLDiUP_2001.txt (27.08.2012).
213 A. Jabłoński, *Rząd i administracja publiczna*, [in:] A. Antoszewski, R. Herbut (ed.), *Polityka w Polsce w latach 90. Wybrane problemy*, Wydawnictwo Uniwersytetu Wrocławskiego, Wrocław 1999, p. 141.

of the Council of Ministers or the Prime Minister[214]. In contrast, referring to the real possibilities and/or limitations of the process of political leadership by Miller under the structural circumstances we can distinguish between at least two groups of factors:

1. Factors resulting from the political coalition game – attempts to form a government under fragmented political scene and numerous coalition frictions. In the case of Miller's government it meant the situation in which he had to contend with external coalition partner – the Polish Peasants Party (Polskie Stronnictwo Ludowe), which occurred to a number of discrepancies in the participation in the coalition government decisions. At the same time these are problems resulting from the participation of other left-wing entities in the process of management (entities that formed the background support of the left-wing party, e.g. trade unions and associations striving for the realization of special interests)[215].
2. Factors arising from the socio-economic situation in Poland and the future of Europe – the main challenges for the Miller's cabinet were real social inequalities, including a sharp increase in unemployment, the impoverishment of different social groups, intensifying social exclusion affecting the general social climate and the current political situation[216]. Undoubtedly, one of the biggest challenges for Miller's office was among problems such as the growing oligarchic capitalism – corruption (intensifying since the early 90s a tendency to corruption, nepotism and clientelism in the public-political sphere); reducing the state budget deficit; the prospect of Polish accession to the European Union.

Quadrant 3 is an area of active political leader (the resultant public exposure and the collective implementation), which refers to the actual work of government with Miller at the helm. Undoubtedly, the left-wing government from the years 2001–2005 can be classified as very active in terms of legislative (Miller's cabinet proposed 598 bills to the Sejm; generated 652 regulations; made 819 framework, analytical and information documents[217]). At the same time it was a very sensitive period for Poland when the fate of Polish accession to the European Union

---

214 G. Rydlewski, *Lewica w rządach i rządzeniu w III RP*, [in:] D. Waniek (ed.), *Lewica w praktyce rządzenia. Problemy wybrane*, Wydawnictwo Adam Marszałek, Toruń 2010, pp. 54–75.
215 G. Rydlewski, *Lewica…*, pp. 54–75.
216 D. Waniek, *Uwarunkowania…*, Warszawa 2006, pp. 7–29.
217 G. Rydlewski, *Lewica…*, pp. 54–75.

was weighing. In fact, negotiations with the EU were, in addition to reducing the budget deficit and deal with the ever increasing unemployment and poverty – the priority of the government. When Miller was asked what was the primary importance for his cabinet, he said:

> The issue number one was the completion of accession negotiations and the introduction of Poland to the European Union. The situation was difficult: among the candidate countries to the EU, Poland was last in the amount of closed negotiation chapters. Buzek's team left the hardest things unsettled[218].

Among the colleagues the prime minister was regarded as a hard negotiator, who built a relationship with subordinates on the leadership basis. His leadership was characterized by very high determination in achieving goals. In an interview, Jerzy Hausner, a minister in the Miller's government, described him in the following way:

> The party barons believed that they should be the ministers and those like me – vice-ministers. Because it was they who won the election and assured him the power. And they will guarantee him control over the authority so they deserve positions. Miller pacified them then and very firmly opposed (…). Miller's government generally was not a poorly constructed government. There were the people to whom Miller had confidence in, but – it was obvious – that he wanted also to their competence. It was supposed to be a good team. (…) But Miller's feature is that he knows how to discover the instrumental value of the person, he can rationalize his relationships with people[219].

In a different place he describes the leader role of the prime minister:

> He did not have a designated destination of vision. There was no vision of Poland in 10, 15 years. The only hard point that – indeed justifies, in my view, positive assessment of the Miller's government – was the European Union and bringing us to it. Here his determination, consistency, his absolute ruthlessness served the purpose. And since he had Cimoszewicz, Hübner and Pietras, all this was completed[220].

Quadrant 4 is the area of activity of the structured agent (resultant public exposure and the realization of the individual), when the actual impact of the socio-structural environment on a particular political leader takes place. In the case of Miller we can talk about intensified and/or strong and unilateral socio-political impact on the prime minister. It was so suggestive that it led to the leader of the Left to an ideological break with social democracy in favour of neo-liberal paradigm. The origins of this apparent change occurred in 2003, when at the

---

218 J. Sadecki, *Trzynastu…*, pp. 219–245.
219 J. Hausner, *Z „Kuźnicy", z rządu i spoza…*, Universitas, Kraków 2009, pp. 20–25.
220 Ibid., pp. 26–27.

meeting of the National Council of the SLD Miller announced the withdrawal of the party from the election promise of realizing social market economy. PM Miller spoke about the withdrawal from the election promise of the implementation of the party's postulates:

> The Left must finally say it openly – we can no longer divide poverty. (…) The economy is the key to the realization of the social-democratic vision of society. No vision can be achieved without money. With the words of social justice we will not feed the people, from these words we will not pay out annuities or pensions. I will repeat what I said on many occasions: to distribute you must first prepare. To give a chance for social democratic dreams, you first need to give a chance to the economy. (…) But this doesn't mean the end of social sensitivity of the left. It just should manifest itself differently. (…) There must be clarity between us – economic liberalism, but rigor in compliance with the law. (…) We must equally seriously treat the reform of public finances. This primarily means lower costs.. We spend a lot of money on the social sphere, yet unreasonably. This leads to a paradox – the more we spend, the more dissatisfied people we have around[221].

A radical change of orientation in Miller's outlook was expressed in "Miller's manifesto" in which he clearly emphasized that:

> The economy, which for one and a half century was the scene of the radical polarization, ceases to be a confrontation area for the left and right. Differences have slowly been blurring, because the dispute between liberalism and socialism has been resolved. The naked eye can see that the system is more efficient. You can also easily prove that we should not argue with the market, because in the end the market is always right[222].

Such claims were accompanied by neoliberal newspeak, where Miller found a recipe for poor economic performance of his government. Economic development became the key word (media trademark). Miller repeated the primary aim of the government like mantra – to foster economic development. Thus, in the manifesto he included the following thoughts:

> If we think of the modern left, which wants to achieve a sustainable and high economic growth and equitably share its fruits, it is needless to say that the traditional values of the left should be carried out of the market and through the mechanisms which do not collide with the market mechanism. This means separation of the economic policy from the social policy and admitting that production of national income and its share are largely

---

221 *Koniec świata. Z premierem Leszkiem Millerem rozmowę poprowadził Marek Barański*, „Trybuna" 22.09. 2003, [after:] „Polityka społeczna" No 10, październik 2003, pp. 23–24.
222 L. Miller, *Manifest Millera*, „Wprost" No 30, 31.07.2005, pp. 38–39.

separate areas, which are governed by different rules. First are determined by hard and objective laws of economics, the second –by the principles of social justice[223].

It should be added that the external impact on Leszek Miller was gradable and multi-layered. The main socio-structural determinants that changed the outlook of the left prime minister interpreted as a single agent leadership include:

1. European left-wing party leaders – i.e. Gerhard Schröder (advocate of the policy of the "new centre") and Tony Blair (advocate of the "third way") and their common conception of the so-called new "third way". In other words, it was the announcement of the introduction of free market mechanisms, including the liberalization of certain sectors of the economy, deregulation of financial markets and "dismantling" the welfare state into the programs of left-wing political parties. The origins of these fundamental changes to the European left can be found, inter al., in a radical revision of the programme of the Labour Party implemented by Blair. It was a political strategy which, besides the fact that this politician brought unquestionable leadership on the left, meant "linking the two great currents of thought in the centre-left – democratic socialism and liberalism," which was to promote the implementation of the major political objective, i.e. an "open, equitable welfare society"[224]. It must be stressed that Leszek Miller was, on the one hand, clearly influenced by such particular ideological policies, on the other hand, fascinated by the effectiveness of leadership based on the principles and philosophy of economic liberalism. He expressed it in his manifesto, where he repeated the words of Blair and Schröder: "We don't go to the right, we go forward"[225]. Of course, this attitude was reflected in the practice of leadership, which in the case of the government meant inter al.: the reduction of corporate income tax from 27% to 19%; the introduction of 19% tax for self-employed persons; adoption of the law on freedom of economic activity or an intention to introduce a flat tax.
2. Internal pragmatism – refers to the current and temporary practice governing Democratic Left Alliance, which directly translates into real leadership by Leszek Miller. In this perspective, in terms of the actual impact of the

---

223 L. Miller, *Manifest...*, pp. 38–39.
224 T. Kowalik, *Trzecią drogą do centrum. Wzloty i upadki socjaldemokracji europejskiej i polskiej*, [in:] P. Żuk (ed.), *W poszukiwaniu innych światów. Europa, lewica, socjaldemokracja wobec zmian globalnych*, Wydawnictwo Naukowe SCHOLAR, Warszawa 2003, pp. 163–196.
225 L. Miller, *Manifest...*, pp. 38–39.

environment on the political activity of Miller's leadership, when the leadership of the Democratic Left Alliance and prominent left-wing activists focused primarily on staying in power pragmatically. This meant a situation in which the DLA completely forgot about the implementation of leftist social project, where, as Krzysztof Teodor Toeplitz put it:

> Temporariness of activities unstructured with any keynote and the fascination with the pragmatics of governance, led consequently to mismatch with the fundamental values associated traditionally with the concept of the Left (…).Pragmatism was considered as a value in itself, and not as an instrument to achieve the ideological objectives[226].

Such environmental and/or group thinking also accompanied Miller, who prioritised the fascination with ideological neoliberalism higher than the implementation of election promises (an example of such a diagram of conduct was the adoption of "Entrepreneurship – work – development" programme by Miller's government in early 2002).

In addition, objective changes on the Left and the European internal party climate were conducive to the emergence of the phenomenon of inconsistency in ideological programme within the DLA, and especially for Leszek Miller. This dissonance between the declared leader's attachment to the socialist-leftist roots and simultaneous "turn" towards neoliberal solutions was symptomatic of the Polish social-democratic circles. From the point of view of the agent, more precisely Miller's leadership, we can talk about confidence and unjustified optimism of the political leader not only towards globalization or European integration, but mostly towards the market economy. The consequences of such an attitude of leadership seem to be far-reaching and represent "top-down" ideological erosion that has taken place in the DLA. Miller's concession for "axiom market", more precisely, for the thesis that he was fond of: "there is no point in arguing with the market, because in the end the market is always right", essentially affected the condition of the worldview of individual DLA members. Confirmation of the crisis on the ideological left are reflected in empirical research results made during the meetings with voivodeship delegates of DLA in April and May 2008. When even an astonishing similarity of views between political DLA activists and liberally oriented Civic Platform was visible (Platforma Obywatelska). We can talk here about significant differences between the views of the delegates and the

---

226 K. T. Toeplitz, *Pragmatyzm i przywództwo*, [in:] P. Żuk (ed.), *W poszukiwaniu…*, pp. 27–38.

DLA programme line where the latter is in conflict with what the individual members of the party really think[227].

In conclusion, the detailed analysis of the matrix of subjective leadership of Leszek Miller in morphogenetic perspective leads to the following conclusions:

1. Leadership practice of Prime Minister Leszek Miller is a reflection of the dialectical agent-structure dependencees, where there is a mutual dependence between the individual-personal features, adopting the role/function of the leadership and the socio-structural environment. The matrix showed that dialectical subjective-structured conditions could be isolated in accordance with the principle of analytical dualism making it easier to understand and explain the specific sequence (steps) in the creation of a political leader in a given socio-political environment.
2. Agency of Miller's leadership is the result of both individual characteristics and suitability of policy, as well as various objective requirements which were external to Miller, i. e. situational conditions, organization, party, etc.
3. Morphogenetic matrix of agency showed a real change and the evolution of attitudes and beliefs of Leszek Miller – from ideological socialist to pragmatic liberal – where the real impact of structural factors on the reflective leader was indicated.
4. The case of Prime Minister Miller also points to a very strong, even intensified impact of the external environment of structural political self-awareness of this politician, where, as the undisputed leader of the left, he underwent internal "ideological metamorphosis." The result is a heightened structured agent – left-wing leader pushing and introducing liberal political solutions, who, paradoxically, contributed to the so-called programme and ideological crisis of DLA.

---

227 This is evidenced by, inter al., the following data: 25% of activists definitely support the idea that the state should generally not interfere in the economy; 11.1% support the introduction of a flat tax in Poland; 26.4% oppose that unions should have a greater impact on economic and social issues. More in: M. Leroy, *Między neoliberalizmem a „trzecią drogą": poglądy społeczno-ekonomiczne w PO i SLD*, [in:] A. Pacześniak, J. M. De Waele (eds.), *Ludzie partii. Idealiści czy pragmatycy? Kadry partyjne w świetle badań empirycznych*, Wydawnictwo Naukowe SCHOLAR, Warszawa 2011, pp. 46–65.

Conclusion

Archerian morphogenetic theory, which by definition relates to the analysis of the impact of the distribution (determination) and multi-level fusion formed at the interface between the active agent / agents ↔ active structural environment, can be – and often is – coherent and relatively easy-to-use research tool, which provides:

1. Accurate demarcation of the realm/domain of subjective activity (perpetration of a particular political agent, which is directly related to the alienation of the subject, its real impact on the environment, the so-called subjective driving force that can take on a processual character) and the spheres/domains of structural activity (growth and changes resulting from the environment itself, which is irreducible to the activity of certain agents; it is the structural and causal force, which also creates the structure).
2. Quite a precise demonstration of separateness and autonomy of both analytical planes with a clear indication of their deep, multi-level dialectical relationship between the agent and structure, where both spheres of activity (conflationary thinking) are not eclectically blurred. In this arrangement the agent does not exist without structure, and vice versa, which for the Archerian model means dual ontology (real units and structures); dual perpetration (the actual activity and measurable impact of the agent and structure); dual emergence (emergent includes both intersubjective interaction, as well as structural interaction).
3. Continual reminder of realistic thesis, for which the public (social entity) is not always (and only) quantifiable sum of individuals, but is temporal and complex space of interactions and connections between different types of agents, where the pre-existence of social forms (structural entities) in relation to agents defines their relative autonomy, and the causal force formulates their reality. However, the causal force of these structural entities is closely associated with the personal perpetration.

At the same time the agent-structure dualism can be successfully used for various types of analyzes of practices of leadership, where the leadership process contains in the logic of the functioning of the two realms/domains: the personal, where the perpetration of symptoms is identified with a single entity or a collective leadership; structural environment where socio-structural surrounding is synonymous with broadly defined supporters. The structural domain can be explained in *sensu stricto* (specific supporters of the leader, the addressees of the procedures of accreditation) or *sensu largo* (a holist system of structural and spatial socio-political practices, in which there is a formal and/or informal distribution of both intersubjective forces as also the forces independent of the entities constituting the structural complexity, i.e. external, driving forces – impersonal procedures, rules, network interactions, etc.). No less important is the dialectic of these areas, where the practice of leadership is shown as temporary and complementary relationship at the intersection of a leader (agent of leadership) ↔ supporters (structural environment). This means the research situation in which leadership is explained in the following categories:

1. Multivariate process – breaking monocausality for real invariant character or unpredictable processes of leadership; highlighting the role and the importance of the scientific strategy of synthesizing, expressed, inter al., by coincidental subjective-objective analyzes; emphasizing the validity of often conflicting factors, the dependent and independent variables, non-reducible dependence etc. the different spheres of social life, affecting leadership indirectly or directly.
2. Multidimensional process – showing that the complex relation of leadership may be considered at micro, meso and macro theoretical level where leadership becomes nothing but a dialectical relationship between the leader and the pre-defined structural and political environment in which the leader operates.

In this respect, the morphogenetic perspective becomes an important and essential research tool for detailed analyses of political leadership, which by the very fact of the location of the complex relation of leadership in analytical dualism facilitates identification and isolation of completely new factors (variables) that have a real impact on the qualitative and quantitative changes, co-creating at the same time an overall picture of the various practices of leadership. Therefore, such a conceptual and methodological operations seem fully justified. It consists in the combination, and more precisely, in the reinterpretation of the morphogenetic assumptions with the category of political leadership.

In fact, we can talk about a number of important theoretical consequences for politics of such methodological procedures, which in this case means to:

1. Capture, diagnose, and analyse in detail the temporal and complex relationships in leadership, which in morphogenetic terms means distinguishable (autonomous), but at the same time, mutual determination occurring between the agent's leadership and structured environment.

2. Demonstrate the phenomenon of political leadership in a new conceptual and methodological light where through multi-layered synthesis of psycho-individual plane of socio-political structure the process of leadership becomes more understandable, especially in terms of different types of relationships, tension, determination, etc., randomness occurring in the political space.

References

Agger B., *The Discourse of Domination. From the Frankfurt School to Postmodernism*, Northwestern University Press, Evanston 1992

Ajdukiewicz K., *Pragmatic Logic*, D. Reidel Publishing Company, Dordrecht-Boston 1974

Alexander J. C., *The Antinomies of Classical Thought: Marx and Durkheim*, University of California Press, Berkeley 1982

Alexander J. C., *Action and Its Environments: Toward a New Synthesis*, Columbia University Press, New York, 1988

Alexander J. C., Giessen B., Munch R., Smelser N. (ed.), *The Mico-Macro Link*, University of California Press, Berkeley 1987

Althusser L., *For Marx (Radical Thinkers)*, Verso, London 2005

Althusser L., Balibar É., *Reading Capital*, Verso, London & New York 2009

Anderson P., *Arguments within English Marxism*, Verso, London 1980

Antonakis J., Cianciolo A. T., Sternberg R. J. (ed.), *The Nature of Leadership*, Sage, Thousand Oaks 2004

Antoszewski A., Herbut R. (ed.), *Polityka w Polsce w latach 90. Wybrane problemy*, Wydawnictwo Uniwersytetu Wrocławskiego, Wrocław 1999

Archer M. S., *Culture and Agency: The Place of Culture in Social Theory*, Cambridge University Press, New York, 1988

Archer M. S., *Realist Social Theory: The Morphogenetic Approach*, Cambridge University Press, Cambridge 1995

Archer M. S., *Being Human: the Problem of Agency*, Cambridge University Press, Cambridge 2000

Archer M. S., *Making our Way through the World: Human Reflexivity and Social Mobility*, Cambridge University Press, Cambridge 2007

Archer M. S., *The Reflexive Imperative in Late Modernity*, Cambridge University Press, Cambridge 2012

Archer M. S., Bhaskar R., Collier A., Lawson T., Norrie A. (ed.), *Critical Realism: Essential Readings*, Routledge, London 1998

Atrakcyjni dla większości. Z Józefem Oleksym, przewodniczącym Klubu SLD, rozmawiała Eliza Olczyk, „Rzeczpospolita" 30 grudnia 2002, A 4

Avery G. C., *Understanding Leadership. Paradigms and Cases*, Sage Publication, London 2004

Baert P., Carreira da Silva F., *Social Theory in the Twentieth Century and Beyond*, Polity Press, Cambridge 2010

Banfield E. C., *Political Influence*, The Free Press, New York 1962

Bass B. M., Bass R., *The Bass Handbook of Leadership: Theory, Research, and Managerial Applications*, Free Press, New York 2008

Baszkiewicz J., *Władza*, Wydawnictwo Ossolineum, Wrocław-Warszawa-Kraków 1999

Berger P. L., Luckmann T., *The Social Construction of Reality. A Treatise in the Sociology of Knowledge*, Penguin Books, New York 1966

Berrill N. J., Karp G., *Development*, McGraw-Hill, California 1976

Beyme K. von, *Die politischen Theorien der Gegenwart. Eine Einführung*, Sringer Fachmedien, Wiesbaden 2006

Bhaskar R., *The Possibility of Naturalism. A Philosophical Critique of the Contemporary Human Science*, Taylor & Francis, London 2005

Bhaskar R., *Dialectic: The Pulse of Freedom*, Routledge Taylor & Francis Group, London, New York 2008

Bjerke B., *Buisness Leadership and Culture. National Management Styles in The Global Economy*, Edward Elgar Publishing, Inc., Northampton 1999

Blake R. R., Mouton J. S., *The Managerial Grid. The Key to Leadership Excellence*, Gulf Publishing Co, Houston 1964

Blanchard K., Zigarmi P., Zigarmi D., *Leadership and the One Minute Manager: Increasing Effectiveness Through Situational Leadership*, Harper Collins Publishers, New York 1985

Blau P. M., *Exchange and Power in Social life*, Transaction Publishers, New Brunswick, New Jersey 1986

Blondel J., *Political Leadership. Towards a General Leadership*, Sage Publications, London 1987

Bodio T. (ed.), *Przywódzwo polityczne*, „Studia Politologiczne" vol. 5, Warszawa 2001

Bolden R., Hawkins B., Gosling J., Taylor S., *Exploring Leadership. Individual, Organizational& Societal Perspectives*, Oxford University Press, Oxford 2011

Bourdieu P., Wacquant L. J. D., *An Invitation to Reflexive Sociology*, Polity Press, Blackwell Publishers, Cambridge 1992

Brown A., Fleetwood S., Roberts J. M. (ed.), *Critical Realism and Marxism*, Routledge, London &New York 2002

Brown R., *Group Processes. Dynamic within and between group*, Blackwell Publishing Ltd., Oxford 2000

Buckley W., *Sociology and Modern Systems Theory*, Prentice Hall, New Jersey 1967

Bunge M., *Causality and Modern Science*, Transaction Publishers, New Brunswick, London 2009

Cackowski Z., *Człowiek jako podmiot działania praktycznego i poznawczego*, Wydawnictwo „Książkai Wiedza", Warszawa 1979

Callinicos A., *Making History. Agency, Structure, and Change in Social Theory*, Brill, Leiden-Boston 2004

Carchedi G., *Behind the Crisis. Marx's Dialectics of Value and Knowledge*, Koninklijke Brill NV, Leiden-Boston 2011

Carlyle T., *On Heroes, Hero-Worship, and The Heroic in History*, Longmans, Green, and Co., New York 1906

Cartwright D. (ed.), *Group Dynamics: Research and Theory*, Harper&Row, New York 1953

Cruickshank J. (ed.), *Critical Realism: The difference that it makes*, Routledge, New York 2003

Dahl R., *The Concept of Power*, "Behavioral Science" no. 3, 1957

Dalton R. J., Klingemann H. D. (ed.), *The Oxford Handbook of Political Behavior*, Oxford University Press, Oxford 2009

Danermark B., Ekström M., Jakobsen L., Karlsson J. Ch., *Explaining Society: Critical Realism in The Social Sciences*, Routledge, London &New York 2002

Day D. V., Antonakis J. (ed.), *The Nature of Leadership*, Sage Publications, London 2012

DuBrin A. J., *Leadership: Research, Findings, Practice, and Skills*, South-Western Cengage Learning, Mason 2007

Durkheim É., *The Rules of Sociological Method*, The Free Press, New York 1982

Elder-Vass D., *The Causal Power of Social Structures. Emergence, Structure and Agency*, Cambridge University Press, Cambridge 2010

Elias N., *The Society of Individuals*, The Continuum International Publishing Group Inc., New York 2001

Emmeche C., Køppe S., Stjernfelt F., *Explaining Emergence: Towards an Ontology of Levels*, "Journal for General Philosophy of Science", vol. 28, 1997

Engels F., *Collected Works*, vol. 25: *Anti-Dühring, Dialectics of Nature*, International Publishers, New York 1987

Eve R. A., Horsfall S., Lee M. E. (ed.), *Chaos, Complexity, and Sociology. Myths, Models, and Theories*, Sage Publications, London 1997

Ezrow N., Franz E., *Dictators and Dictatorship. Understanding Authoritarian Regimes and Their Leaders*, Continuum International Publishing Group, New York 2011

Feigl H., Sriven M. (ed.), *The Foundations of Science and the Concepts of Psychology and Psychoanalysis*, University of Minnesota Press, Minneapolis 1976

Giddens A., *The Constitution of Society. Outline of the Theory of Structuration*, Polity Press, Cambridge 1990

Godlewski T., *Polski system polityczny. Instytucje – procedury – obywatele*, Wydawnictwo Adam Marszałek, Toruń 2007

Goleman D., Boyatzis R., McKee A., *Primal Leadership. Realizing The Power of Emotional Intelligence*, Harvard Buisness School Press, 2002

Golinowski J., Pierzchalski F. (ed.), *Symboliczność przestrzeni polityki. Między teorią a praktyką*, Wydawnictwo Uniwersytetu Kazimierza Wielkiego, Bydgoszcz 2011

Greenstein F. I., *Personality and Politics: Problem of Evidence, Inference, and Conceptualization*, Markham, Chicago 1969

Guigon G., Rodriquez-Pereyra G. (ed.), *Nominalism about Properties*, Routledge, New York 2015

Hamilton P. (ed.), *Talcott Parsons. Critical Assessments*, vol. II, Routledge, New York 1992

Haugaard M., *Power: A Reader*, Manchester University Press, Menchester & New York 2002

Hazy J. K., Goldstein J. A., Lichtenstein B. B. (ed.), *Complex Systems Leadership Theory. New Perspectives from Complexity Science on Social and Organizational Effectiveness*, ISCE Publishing, Mansfield 2007

Hausner J., *Z „Kuźnicy", z rządu i spoza…*, Universitas, Kraków 2009

Hedström P., Swedberg R. (ed.), *Social Mechanisms. An Analytical Approach to Social Theory*, Cambridge University Press, Cambridge 1998

Held D., Thompson J. B. (ed.) *Social Theory in Modern Societies: Anthony Giddens and his Critics*, Cambridge University Press, Cambridge 1989

Hellriegel D., Slocum J. W., *Organizational Behavior*, South-Western, Mason 2007

Hermann M. G. (ed.), *Political Psychology. Contemporary Problems and Issues*, Josey-Bass, San Francisco-London 1992

Hermann M. G., Preston J. T., *Presidents, advisers, and foreign policy: The effects of leadership style on executive arrangements*, "Political Psychology" vol. 15, 1994

Hickman G. R. (ed.), *Leading Organizations: Perspectives for New Era*, Sage Publications, Inc., London 2010

Hollis M., Lukes S. (ed.) *Rationality and Relativism*, MIT Press, Cambridge 1982

House R. J., Hanges P. J., Javidan M., Dorfman P. W., Gupta V. (ed.), *Culture, Leadership and Organizations: The GLOBE Study of 62 Societies*, Sage Publications, Inc., Thousand Oaks 2004

Isajiw W. W., *Causation and Functionalism in Sociology*, Routledge, New York 2010

Jago A. G., *Leadership: Perspectives in Theory and Research*, "Management Science" 28 (3), 1982

Jarymowicz M., *Psychologiczne podstawy podmiotowości. Szkice teoretyczne, studia empiryczne*, Wydawnictwo Naukowe PWN, Warszawa 2008

Jessop B., *State Theory: Putting the Capitalist State in Its Place*, Polity Press, Cambridge 1990

Judge T. A., Heller D., Mount M. K., *Five-Factor Model of Personality and Job Satisfaction: Meta-Analysis*, "Journal of Applied Psychology", vol. 87, no. 3, 2002

Kaarbo J., *Prime minister leadership styles in foreign policy decision-making: A Framework for research*, „Political Psychology, vol. 3, 1997

Kaczmarek B. (red.) *Metafory polityki*, Dom Wydawniczy ELIPSA, Warszawa 2001

Karwat M., *Podmiotowość polityczna. Humanistyczna interpretacja polityki w marksizmie*, Państwowe Wydawnictwo Naukowe, Warszawa 1980

Karwat M., *Człowiek polityczny. Próba interpretacji marksistowskiej*, Państwowe Wydawnictwo Naukowe, Warszawa 1989

Karwat M., *Polityczność i upolitycznie. Metodologiczne ramy analizy*, „Studia Politologiczne", vol. 17, 2011

Karwat M., *O karykaturze polityki*, Warszawskie Wydawnictwo Literackie MUZA, Warszawa 2012

Kasińska-Metryka A. (red.), *Studia nad przywództwem. Ustalenia metodologiczne i praktyka*, Wydawnictwo Adam Marszałek, Toruń 2011

Kim J., *Making Sense of Emergence*, „Philosophical Studies", vol. 95, nr 1–2, 1999

Kmita J., *Problems in Historical Epistemology*, D. Reidel Publishing Company, Dordrecht 1988

Kmita J., *Essays on the Theory of Scientific Cognition*, Springer Science, Business Media B.V., Dordrecht 1991

Knorr Cetina K., *Epistemic Cultures. How the Sciences Make Knowledge*, Harvard University Press, Cambridge 1999

Knutson J. N. (ed.), *Handbook of political psychology*, Jossey-Bass, London 1973

Kofta M., Szustrowa T. (red.), *Złudzenia, które pozwalają żyć: szkice z psychologii społecznej*, Warszawa 1991

Koniec świata. Z premierem Leszkiem Millerem rozmowę poprowadził Marek Barański, „Trybuna" 22.09. 2003

Kontopoulos K. M., *The Logics of Social Structure*, Cambridge University Press, Cambridge 1993

Kotarbiński T., *Praxiology. An Introduction to the Sciences of Efficient Action*, Pergamon Press, Oxford 1965

Landesman Ch. (ed.), *The Problem of Universals*, Basic Books, London 1971

Lasswell H. D., *Power and Personality*, Transaction Publishers, New Brunswick, New Jersey 2009

Layder D., *Understanding Social Theory*, Sage Publications Ltd, London 2006

Lepin J. (ed.), *Scientific Realism*, University of California Press, London 1984

Lewin K., Lippitt R., White R., *Patterns of Aggressive Behavior in Experimentally Created »Social Climates«*, "Journal of Social Psychology", vol. 10, 1939

Linz J. J., *Totalitarian and Authoritarian Regimes*, Lynne Rienner Publisher, London 2000

Lipiec J., *Wolność i podmiotowość*, FALL, Kraków 1997

Luhmann N., *Social Systems*, Stanford University Press, Stanford 1995

Luhmann N., *Introduction to systems theory*, Polity Press, Cambridge 2013

Lussier R. N., Achua Ch. F., *Leadership. Theory, Application, & Skill Development*, South-Western Cengage Learning, Mason 2010

Machejek J., Olczyk J., Machejek A., *Kwaśniewski: „nie lubię tracić czasu!". Wywiad-rzeka z liderem SLD*, Hamal Books, Łódź 1995

Mainzer K., *Thinking in Complexity. The Computational Dynamics of Matter, Mind and Mankind*, Springer-Verlag, Berlin 2007

Marsh D., Stoker G. (ed.), *Theory and Methods in Political Science*, Palgrave Macmillan, New York 2002

Mayr E., *Understanding Human Agency*, Oxford University Press, New York 2011

Márai S., *Dziennik (fragmenty)*, Spółdzielnia Wydawnicza „Czytelnik", Warszawa 2008

Marx K., *Capital*, Volume I, International Publishers, New York 1967

Matravers D., Pike J. (ed.), *Debates in Contemporary Political Philosophy. An Anthology*, Routledge, London 2003

Merton R. K., *Social Theory and Social Structure*, The Free Press, New York 1968

Miller J. H., Page S. E., *Complex Adaptive Systems. An Introduction to Computational Models of Social Life*, Princeton University Press, Princeton 2007

Miller L., *Manifest Millera*, „Wprost" nr 30, 31.07.2005

Millon T., *Disordes of Personality: DSM-IV and Beyond*, John Wiley & Sons, Inc., New York 1996

Mingers J., *Systems Thinking, Critical Realism and Philosophy: A Confluence of Ideas*, Routledge, New York 2014

Morawski J., *Portrety w podczerwieni*, Niezależna Oficyna Wydawnicza Nowa, Warszawa 1994

Mumford M. D., Zaccaro S. J., Harding F. D., Jacobs T. O., Fleishman E. A., *Leadership Skills for a Changing World: Solving Complex Social Problems*, "Leadership Quarterly" II (I), 2000

Nagel E., *The Structure of Science: Problems in the Logic of Scientific Explanation*, Routledge & Kegan Paul, London 1961

Niiniluoto I., Sintonen M., Woleński J. (ed.), *Handbook of Epistemology*, Springer-Science, Business Media, B.V., Dordrecht 2004

Northhouse P. G., *Leadership: Theory and Practice*, Sage Publications, London 2012

Nowak L., *Property and Power: Towards a Non-Marxian Historical Materialism*, D. Reidel Publishing Company, Dordrecht 1983

Nowak L., *The Structure of Idealization: Towards a Systematic Interpretation of the Marxian Idea of Science*, D. Reidel Publishing Company, Dordrecht 2010

Nowak S., *Methodology of Sociological Research. General Problems*, D. Reidel Publishing Company, Dordrecht/Boston 1977

Pacześniak A., De Waele J. M. (ed.), *Ludzie partii. Idealiści czy pragmatycy? Kadry partyjne w świetle badań empirycznych*, Wydawnictwo Naukowe SCHOLAR, Warszawa 2011

Parsons T., *The Social System*, The Free Press, MacMillan, New York 1964

Parsons T., *Social Structure and Personality*, The Free Press, Collier-MacMillan Ltd. London 1970

Perelman Ch., *The New Rhetoric and The Humanities. Essays on Rhetoric and its Applications*, Reidel Publishing Company, Dordrecht 1979

Peirce Ch. S., *Philosophical Writings of Peirce*, Selected and Edited with an Introduction by Justus Buchler, Dover Publications, New York 2011

Poczobut R., *Między redukcją a emergencją. Spór o miejsce umysłu w świecie fizycznym*, Wydawnictwo Uniwersytetu Wrocławskiego, Wrocław 2009

Popper K. R., *Conjectures and Refutations. The Growth of Scientific Knowledge*, Routledge and Kegan Paul, London 1963

Porębski L., *Behawioralny model władzy*, Universitas, Kraków 1996

Ridgeway C., *The Dynamics of Small Groups*, St. Martin's Press, New York 1983

Richards D., *Political Complexity. Nonlinear Models of Politics*, The University of Michigan Press, Michigan 2000

Roberts B., *Micro Social Theory*, Palgrave Macmillan, New York 2006

Rodriquez-Pereyra G., *Resemble Nominalism. A Solution to the Problem of Universals*, Oxford University Press, Oxford 2002

Rubisz L., Zuba K. (red.), *Przywództwo polityczne. Teorie i rzeczywistość*, Wydawnictwo Adam Marszałek, Toruń 2005

Russell B., *Power. A New Social Analysis*, Routledge, London & New York 2004

Rybicki P., *Struktura społecznego świata, Studia z teorii społecznej*, Państwowe Wydawnictwo Naukowe, Warszawa 1979

Sadecki J., *Trzynastu. Premierzy wolnej Polski*, Universitas, Kraków 2009

Sawyer R. K., *Social Emergence. Societies As Complex Systems*, Cambridge University Press, Cambridge 2005

Sayer A., *Realism and Social Science*, Sage Publication Ltd., London 2000

Schütz A., *On Multiple Realities*, "Philosophy and Phenomenological Research", vol. 5, no. 4

Scott J. (ed.), *Power: Critical Concepts*, Routledge, New York 1994

Sewell W. H. Jr., *A Theory of Structure: Duality, Agency and Transformation*, "American Journal of Sociology" vol. 98, no. 1

Sibeon R. A., *Rethinking Social Theory*, Sage Publications Ltd, London 2004

Siegel H., *Relativism Refuted. A Critique of Contemporary Epistemological Relativism*, Springer Science+Business Media B.V., Dordrecht 1987

Skarżyńska K. (red.), *Podstawy psychologii politycznej*, Zysk i S-ka Wydawnictwo, Poznań 2002

Smelers N. J., *Problematics of Sociology: The Georg Simmel Lectures*, University of California Press, Berkley 1995.

Strack S. (ed.), *Handbook of Personology and Psychopathology*, John Wiley & Sons, Inc., New Jersey 2005

Stogdill R. M., *Handbook of Leadership: A survey of theory and research*, Free Press, New York 1974

Strawiński W., *Jedność nauki, redukcja, emergencja. Z metodologicznych i ontologicznych problemów integracji wiedzy*, Fundacja Aletheia, Warszawa 1997

Szmatka J., *O holizmie i indywidualizmie w naukach społecznych*, „Studia Filozoficzne", nr 7 (128), Warszawa 1976

Szmatka J., *Jednostka i społeczeństwo. O zależności zjawisk indywidualnych od społecznych*, Państwowe Wydawnictwo Naukowe, Warszawa 1980

Szmatka J., *Małe struktury społeczne. Wstęp do mikrosocjologii strukturalnej*, Wydawnictwo Naukowe PWN, Warszawa 2007

Szmatka J., Skvoretz J., Berger J. (ed.), *Status, Network, and Structure: Theory Development in Group Processes*, Stanford University Press, Stanford 1997

Sztompka P., *Sociological Dilemmas. Toward a Dialectic Paradigm*, Academic Press, New York 1979

Sztompka P., *Sociology of Social Change*, Blackwell, Oxford 1993

Sztompka P. (ed.), *Agency and Structure. Reorienting Social Theory*, Routledge, London & New York 2014

Thomson K. S., *Morphogenesis and Evolution*, Oxford University Press, Oxford 1988

Topolski J., *Methodology of History*, D. Reidel Publishing Company, Dordrecht 1976

Twyman R. M., *Instant Notes. Developmental Biology*, Taylor & Francis, Oxford 2000

Uhl-Bien M., R. Marion (ed.), *Complex Leadership. Part I: Conceptual Foundations*, Information Age Publishing, Inc., Charlotte 2008

Upadek ojca marnotrawnego. Z Leszkiem Millerem rozmawiał Piotr Najsztub, „Przekrój" nr 31 (3136), 28.07.2005

Waniek D. (ed.), *Partie polityczne w wyborach 2005*, ALMAMER Wyższa Szkoła Ekonomiczna „DrukTur", Warszawa 2006

Waniek D. (ed.), *Lewica w praktyce rządzenia. Problemy wybrane*, Wydawnictwo Adam Marszałek, Toruń 2010

Watkins J. W. N., *Historical Explanation in the Social Sciences*, "British Journal for the Philosophy of Science" 8 (2) 1957

Weber M., *The Theory of Social and Economic Organization*, The Free Press, New York, 1947

Weber M., *Economy and Society. An Outline of Interpretive Sociology*, University of California Press, Berkley 1978

Weingartner P., Dorn G. J. W. (ed.), *Studies on Mario Bunge's Treatise*, Rodopi B.V., Amsterdam-Atlanta 1990

Wiatr J. J. (ed.), *Polish Essays in the Methodology of the Social Sciences*, D. Reidel Publishing Company, Dordrecht 1979

Wiatr J. J., *Przywództwo polityczne. Studium politologiczne*, Wydawnictwo Wyższej Szkoły Humanistyczno-Ekonomicznej, Łódź 2008

Wittgenstein L., *Philosophical Investigations*, Basil Blackwell, Oxford 1973

Wittgenstein L., *Tractatus Logico-Philosophicus*, Routledge Classics, London & New York 2002

Wojtaszczyk K. A., Mirska A. (ed.), *Demokratyczna Polska w globalizującym się świecie*, Warszawa 2009

Valenty L. O., Feldman O. (ed.), *Political Leadership for The New Century. Personality and Behavior Among American Leaders*, Greenwood Publishing Group, Westport 2002

Yammarino F. J., Dansereau F. (ed.), *Multi-level Issues in Organizational Behavior and Leadership*, Emerald Group Publishing, Bingley 2009

Zaccaro S. J., *The Nature of Executive Leadership: A Conceptual and Empirical Analysis of Success*, American Psychological Association, Washington 2001

Zahle J., Collin F. (ed.), *Rethinking the Individualism-Holism Debate: Essays in the Philosophy of Social Science*, Springer International Publishing, London 2014

Żuk P. (ed.), *W poszukiwaniu innych światów. Europa, lewica, socjaldemokracja wobec zmian globalnych*, Wydawnictwo Naukowe SCHOLAR, Warszawa 2003

List of Figures

Diagram 1. Phenomenon of emergence in analitically distinguished societal structure (S)..................29

Diagram 2. Image of the political space in a dynamic emergent tangle of processes..................33

Diagram 3. Subjective approach to political reality..................48

Diagram 4. The Duality of Structure by Anthony Giddens..................61

Diagram 5. Bhaskar's three overlapping domains of reality..................71

Diagram 6. Bhaskar's model of the society/individual connection..................75

Schemat 7. Bhaskar's refined transformational model of structure and praxis (TMSA)..................76

Diagram 8. The limited time span of conflationary theories compared with the Archerian morphogenetic approach..................81

Diagram 9. Co-picturing Methodological Realism and the morphogenetic/static approach..................87

Diagram 10. The morphogenesis of structure..................89

Diagram 11. Realism's account of the development of the stratified human being..................96

Diagram 12. Two paths for defining leadership..................107

Diagram 13. Three-element relationship in the situatonal theory of leadership..................131

Diagram 14. Morphogenetic matrix of Political Leadership..................153

Diagram 15. The Morphogenetic matrix of Leszek Miller..................157

Table 1. Research multi-level character of political leadership..................120

Table 2. Sample theories of collective leadership..................138

Explanatory notes for key terms

Terminology of political science may seem confusing at places since it employs terms and notions from various disciplines. For example, for the purpose of this book the term "subject" is replaced with the term "agent" because it refers to an individual who is in charge of the leading process within an organisation and not to the syntactical term defining parts of sentence in grammar. In turn, subjectivity refers to agenthood and personal activity of an individual whereas objectivity stands for truth and neutrality. Respectively, "subjective" is an attribute of subjectivity and agenthood. Terminological choices were intentionally made in such a way in order to avoid terminological tension and potential confusion resulting from overlapping terminologies in various disciplines.

Studies in Politics, Security and Society

Edited by Stanisław Sulowski

Vol. 1 Robert Wiszniowski (ed.): Challenges to Representative Democracy. A European Perspective. 2015.

Vol. 2 Jarosław Szymanek: Theory of Political Representation. 2015.

Vol. 3 Alojzy Z. Nowak (ed.): Global Financial Turbulence in the Euro Area. Polish Perspective. 2015.

Vol. 4 Jolanta Itrich-Drabarek: The Civil Service in Poland. Theory and Experience. 2015.

Vol. 5 Agnieszka Rothert: Power of Imagination. Education, Innovations and Democracy. 2016.

Vol. 6 Zbysław Dobrowolski: Combating Corruption and Other Organizational Pathologies. 2017.

Vol. 7 Vito Breda: The Objectivity of Judicial Decisions. A Comparative Analysis of Nine Jurisdictions. 2017.

Vol. 8 Anna Sroka: Accountability and democracy in Poland and Spain. 2017.

Vol. 9 Anna Sroka / Fanny Castro-Rial Garrone / Rubén Darío Torres Kumbrián (eds.): Radicalism and Terrorism in the 21st Century. Implications for Security. 2017.

Vol. 10 Filip Pierzchalski: Political Leadership in Morphogenetic Perspective. 2017.

www.peterlang.com

www.ingramcontent.com/pod-product-compliance
Ingram Content Group UK Ltd.
Pitfield, Milton Keynes, MK11 3LW, UK
UKHW041902230426
12049UKWH00002B/11